INDEPENDENT SECTOR

INDEPENDENT SECTOR is a coalition of 650 corporations, foundations, and voluntary organizations with national interests in and impact on philanthropy, voluntary action, and other activities related to the educational, scientific, cultural, and religious life, as well as the health and welfare, of the nation.

INDEPENDENT SECTOR is a meeting ground where diverse elements in and related to the sector can come together and learn how to improve their performance and effectiveness.

INDEPENDENT SECTOR is serving the sector through

- education, to improve the public's understanding of the independent sector.
- research, to develop a comprehensive store of knowledge about the sector.
- government relations, to coordinate the multitude of inter-government relations between the sector and the various levels of government
- encouragement of effective sector leadership and management, to maximize service to individuals and society, by promoting educational programs for managers and practitioners
- communication within the sector to identify shared problems and opportunities

The impact of INDEPENDENT SECTOR's effort can be measured by the growth in support of the sector, as manifested by increased giving and volunteering.

For additional information, please contact

INDEPENDENT
SECTOR

1828 L Street, N.W.
Washington, DC 20036
(202) 223-8100

Faith and Philanthropy
in America

Robert Wuthnow
Virginia A. Hodgkinson
and Associates

Faith and Philanthropy
in America

Exploring the Role
of Religion
in America's Voluntary Sector

Jossey-Bass Publishers

San Francisco   •   Oxford   •   1990

FAITH AND PHILANTHROPY IN AMERICA
Exploring the Role of Religion in America's Voluntary Sector
by Robert Wuthnow, Virginia A. Hodgkinson, and Associates

Copyright © 1990 by: Jossey-Bass Inc., Publishers
350 Sansome Street
San Francisco, California 94104
&
Jossey-Bass Limited
Headington Hill Hall
Oxford OX3 0BW

Library of Congress Cataloging-in-Publication Data

Faith and philanthropy in America : exploring the role of religion in
America's voluntary sector / Robert Wuthnow, Virginia A. Hodgkinson,
and associates.
p.   cm. — (The Jossey-Bass nonprofit sector series)
ISBN 1-55542-252-7
1. Church charities — United States.   2. Jews — United States —
Charities.   3. Voluntarism — Religious aspects.   I. Wuthnow,
Robert.   II. Hodgkinson, Virginia A.   III. Series.
HV530.F35   1990
361.7'5'0973 — dc20   90-35069
                                                                        CIP

Manufactured in the United States of America

The paper in this book meets the guidelines for
permanence and durability of the Committee on
Production Guidelines for Book Longevity of the
Council on Library Resources.

JACKET DESIGN BY WILLI BAUM

FIRST EDITION

Code 9060

INDEPENDENT
SECTOR   A Publication of INDEPENDENT SECTOR

*The Jossey-Bass
Nonprofit Sector Series*

Contents

ix

Contents

Preface

The world's great religions speak with one voice about compassion. Believers are counseled to love their neighbors as themselves. Mercy and kindness are taught universally.

In our own society these teachings are much in evidence. We hear pulpit messages on the parable of the Good Samaritan, and public figures cite biblical arguments for showing compassion toward our enemies in moments of grief and for manifesting kindness and gentleness toward the needy in our midst. Millions of Americans regularly attend religious services, and a large proportion give of their time and money to charitable causes and voluntary organizations.

All this is perhaps obvious. And yet we remain in the dark about most of the connections between religion and giving in our society. Virtually every other aspect of American volunteerism has been explored more fully. We have countless studies of the governmental, economic, and organizational dimensions of volunteerism. By comparison, we know little of the ways in which religious institutions and philanthropic or charitable activities intersect.

The questions that need attention fall into three broad categories. First, we need to understand the larger connections between religion and volunteerism in our society, both historically and in the contemporary period. In other words, we need a conceptual map to help us locate each within the broader cultural terrain of our past and present. Second, we need to understand better how giving is patterned in each of America's major faith traditions. The fact of our pluralism in religion is clear; less clear is how this pluralism influences philanthropy and volunteerism. Finally, we need guidance, both for researchers and for practitioners, in thinking about the future of American religion and how that future will affect the voluntary sector.

Organization of the Book

Faith and Philanthropy in America seeks to increase our understanding in the three areas described above. Part One presents an overview of the links between religion and philanthropy. Chapter One surveys the cultural characteristics of American society that are the context in which both religion and the voluntary sector acquire their distinctive features. Chapters Two and Three provide historical background on the ways in which religion has influenced the development of the voluntary sector in general and charitable activities in particular. Chapter Four, the final chapter in this section, discusses the psychological connections between spirituality and philanthropy that were discovered in a major study of the wealthy.

Part Two examines the patterns of giving and caring in each of the major faith traditions in the United States. Although the chapters in this section cannot address all the rich questions that might be posed about specific denominations and religious subgroups, they provide a valuable overview of much of the evidence currently available on giving in the dominant religious traditions. We have included chapters that present results from several new empirical studies as well as discuss the distinctive assumptions about giving and caring in the various traditions, such as Roman Catholicism; Judaism; mainstream, evangelical, and black Protestantism; and Mormonism.

Part Three addresses questions about the future of philanthropy in and through religious institutions. The chapters in this section are intended not as efforts to foresee the future but as attempts to specify a range of relevant considerations for thinking about the future of philanthropy. Questions about larger societal changes, the implications of volunteering and giving for democracy, and the alternatives that religious institutions face within the nonprofit sector form the central concerns of these chapters. The last two chapters suggest a number of concrete topics in need of further research and a number of specific areas in which practical efforts to promote religion and philanthropy might usefully be concentrated.

What animates all the chapters in *Faith and Philanthropy in America* is a dual conviction: that religious institutions have been (and are) one of the significant ways in which our society has channeled money and time to those in need, and that many indications point to a weakening of the capacity of religious institutions to continue fulfilling this function. As scholars, we recognize that religious institutions have long been unable to care for the needy or to support educational and cultural activities by themselves: We recognize the importance of government and private nonsectarian efforts. We also recognize that a large part of the philanthropic funds raised under religious auspices goes toward the maintenance of religious institutions themselves. Nevertheless, we believe that the contours of religion's contribution to philanthropy need to be better understood, both to appreciate their strengths and to correct their weaknesses. These are our aims.

Audience for the Book

Faith and Philanthropy in America is intended primarily for three audiences. First, in attempting to present new evidence and to explore the historical and theoretical questions raised by religion and giving, we have tried to address concerns that will be of interest to a wide range of scholars and students in fields such as sociology, religious studies, American studies, political science, history, and psychology. Second, we believe the arguments and evidence in this volume, as well as the book's emphasis on the distinctive characteristics of religion and giving in particular faith traditions, will address the concerns of religious leaders, denominational officials, and clergy who are on the front lines of organizing, administering, supporting, and participating in the active work of promoting caring and giving. Finally, insofar as one of our aims is to demonstrate the vital role religion plays in the voluntary sector, we believe these essays should be of special interest to foundation officials, the heads of voluntary organizations, and leaders of all kinds in the voluntary sector.

June 1990   Robert Wuthnow
                                              Princeton, New Jersey

                                              Virginia A. Hodgkinson
                                              Washington, D.C.

The Authors

Emmett D. Carson is an assistant program officer in the Human Rights and Social Justice Program of the Ford Foundation. Prior to joining the foundation, Carson directed a three-year national study at the Joint Center for Political Studies on the charitable giving and volunteer behavior of blacks and whites. He is the author of two books and numerous articles on black philanthropic activity.

Timothy T. Clydesdale is pursuing his Ph.D. in sociology at Princeton University. He is concentrating on the sociology of religion, cultural analysis, and American religious history. His current research interests are the evangelical left and the gospel music industry.

Peter Dobkin Hall, an independent scholar and consultant, has taught at Wesleyan University and in Yale's School of Organization and Management. Long associated with Yale's Program on Non-Profit Organizations, he has also served as scholar-in-residence at the Rockefeller Archives Center. Hall is the author of *The Organization of American Culture, 1700–1900: Institutions, Elites, and the Origins of American Nationality* (1982) and *Inventing the Nonprofit Sector: Private Institutions in American Life, 1789–1989* (forthcoming).

Virginia A. Hodgkinson is vice president of research at INDEPENDENT SECTOR and executive director of the National Center for Charitable Statistics. Formerly, she was executive director of the National Institute of Independent Colleges and Universities. Her recent publications include *Dimensions of the Independent Sector* (with M. S. Weitzman, 1986), *Giving and Volunteering in the United States* (with M. S. Weitzman, 1988), *From Belief to Commitment: The Activities and Finances of Religious Congregations in the United States* (with M. S. Weitzman and A. D. Kirsch, 1988), and *Motivations for Giving and Volunteering* (1990).

Arthur D. Kirsch is professor of statistics and psychology at George Washington University. He has also held appointments at Warwick University, University College London, The Datatrol Corporation, the National Security Agency, and Gallup & Robinson.

William E. McManus, a native Chicagoan, is a former resident bishop of the Roman Catholic diocese of Fort Wayne–South Bend, Indiana, which includes the University of Notre Dame. A veteran Catholic educator, he spent eleven years in the church's national school office in Washington, D.C., where he vigorously advocated federal aid for nonpublic schools and their students. Thereafter, he became superintendent of the Chicago archdiocesan school system of 490 schools, which enrolled 350,000 students. Raising funds for Catholic schools has been his constant activity. Reverend Andrew Greeley, a noted sociologist, and Bishop McManus coauthored *Catholic Contributions: Sociology and Policy* (1987), a brief treatise on the unsatisfactory conditions of Roman Catholic church finances and ways to ameliorate the situation.

Dean L. May is associate professor of history at the University of Utah, Salt Lake City. May's main research activities have been in American social history. He was a contributor to the *FDR Encyclopedia* and *The Harvard Encyclopedia of American Ethnic Groups* and has published extensively on the social history of the American West. His books include *Building the City of God: Community and Cooperation Among the Mormons* (with L. J. Arrington and F. Y. Fox, 1976), *From New Deal to New Economics: The American*

Liberal Response to the Recession of 1937 (1980), and *Utah: A People's History* (1987).

Mordechai Rimor is a research associate at the Cohen Center for Modern Jewish Studies at Brandeis University and an instructor and visiting fellow at the Center for Jewish Studies at Harvard University. Rimor has published reports and books on his research on achievements, attitudes, and behaviors of subpopulations. Forthcoming articles include "The Relationship Between Jewish Identity and Philanthropy" (with G. A. Tobin) and "Trends in Intermarriage." Currently, Rimor is involved with research on Jewish motivations for giving.

Paul G. Schervish is associate professor of sociology and director of the Social Welfare Research Institute at Boston College. He directed the recently completed Study on Wealth and Philanthropy, a three-year study based on intensive interviews with 130 millionaires, sponsored by the Thomas B. Murphy Foundation. Schervish is currently preparing two monographs based on this study: *The Modern Medicis: The Worldly Power and Spiritual Secret of Money* and *Charity and Strategy: The Meaning of Philanthropy and Its Practice Among the Wealthy*. Most recently he established the Center on Culture and Economy at Boston College to pursue interdisciplinary research on the cultural content of economic life.

Max L. Stackhouse is the Herbert Gezork Professor of Christian Social Ethics and chair of the Department of Religion and Society at Andover Newton Theological School. He presently also serves as president of the Joint Graduate Program of Boston College and Andover Newton. DePauw University named him an "outstanding alumnus" in 1989. Stackhouse has spent every study leave and sabbatical in India, Southeast Asia, or Eastern Europe, where he has been especially interested in the role of religions (and secular ideologies that serve as belief systems) in the formation of modern civilizations. He has received grants for his research from the Harvard-MIT Joint Center for Urban Studies, from the Lilly Foundation through the

Association of Theological Schools, and from the United Church Board for World Ministries. His written or edited books, several of which have won national awards, include *Ethics and the Urban Ethos* (1973), *On Being Human Religiously* (1976), *Creeds, Society and Human Rights* (1984), and *Apologia* (1989).

Gary Tobin is director of the Center for Modern Jewish Studies at Brandeis University. He has published extensively in the areas of planning, Jewish population research, social policy, and fund raising in the Jewish community. He is the author of numerous books, articles, and planning reports on a wide range of subjects. His areas include Jewish demography, fund-raising planning in Jewish organizations, and anti-Semitism. Tobin's most recent book is *Jewish Perceptions of Antisemitism* (1989). Currently, he is writing a book entitled *Fundraising in the Modern Jewish Community* and editing a volume (with L. Sternberg) entitled *Changing Jewish Life: Service Delivery and Social Policy*.

Murray S. Weitzman is a consultant to INDEPENDENT SECTOR. He was with the U.S. Bureau of the Census from 1962 to 1981. He was head of the bureau's research activities in three areas: the Soviet economy (in the Foreign Demographic Analysis Division), the Socio-Economic Statistics Program (in the Population Division), and Social Indicators (in the Center for Demographic Studies). Among his contributions to various publications are *Social Indicators III* (1978), *Dimensions of the Independent Sector: A Statistical Profile* (1985), *Giving and Volunteering in the United States* (with V. A. Hodgkinson, 1988), and *From Belief to Commitment: The Activities and Finances of Religious Congregations* (with V. A. Hodgkinson and A. D. Kirsch, 1988).

James R. Wood is professor and chairperson of the Department of Sociology at Indiana University, Bloomington, and director of the Project in Governance of Nonprofit Organizations of the Indiana University Center on Philanthropy. He is the author of *Leadership in Voluntary Organizations: The Controversy Over Social Action in Protestant Churches* (1981) and *Organized for*

Action: Commitment in Voluntary Associations (with D. Knoke, 1982). His current research focuses on religion and the third sector.

Robert Wuthnow is professor of sociology at Princeton University. In addition to numerous articles on American religion and culture, he has published most recently *The Restructuring of American Religion* (1988) and *The Struggle for America's Soul* (1989). He is currently writing a book on the culture of altruism in the United States and directing a comparative project on the voluntary sector in advanced industrial societies.

Faith and Philanthropy
in America

Part One

Understanding the Links Between Religion and Giving

The links between religion and giving are perhaps stronger in the United States than in any other modern industrialized society. We have a strong tradition of giving money and time to voluntary associations, philanthropies, and other charitable organizations. We also have an exceptionally rich tradition of religious voluntarism — a bewildering supermarket of faiths, denominations, sects, and cults. Despite the fact that ours is an increasingly secular society, religious bodies compete actively and effectively for contributors' loyalties, dollars, and time.

Why is this? Why does religion flourish so well in our society, and why does it contribute to the overall vitality of the voluntary sector? Is it simply historical accident? Is it something ephemeral that may be withering away as time passes?

The chapters in Part One provide historical and theoretical perspective on the contemporary links between religion and giving in American society. They provide an overview of the extent of religious activity: the numbers and variety of religious organizations, how much of the American population is involved in these organizations, what these members believe, and how much money they donate. The chapters survey the theological and organizational connections that solidify the link between religion and charitable giving. And they provide an unusual glimpse into the arguments that relate spirituality and altruism among the nation's wealthy.

These chapters also set the American experience in perspective by tracing some of the links that theorists and histo-

1

rians have detected between religion and giving. As it happens, there is a long tradition of speculation about the importance of free religious organizations for a free society in general and about the role of religion in fostering beliefs and values that favor voluntary caring as a distinct enterprise to be protected from the coercive powers of government and the profit orientation of the marketplace. Understanding these arguments helps us not only to appreciate the value of religion and giving in American society but also to see more clearly some of the dangers presently facing these activities.

Chapter 1

Robert Wuthnow

Religion and the Voluntary Spirit in the United States: Mapping the Terrain

America's churches, synagogues, meeting houses, and fellowship halls constitute a vast and often perplexing feature of our nation's collective life. Equally vast—and at times equally perplexing—are our nation's philanthropic and charitable activities: voluntary donations of time and money to a wide variety of organizations, social causes, and individual needs. Throughout much of our history, religion and giving have been closely linked; indeed, the identity of the latter could seldom be sharply distinguished from the former. At present, these connections remain close. But philanthropy has become a more clearly defined institution in its own right, and the relations between religion and giving have become more complex and more diverse.

An understanding of the specific manifestations of charitable activity within the various traditions that compose American religion requires the mapping of some general contours of the relevant terrain. A broad overview of the distinctive characteristics of American religion, paying particular attention to the dimensions of its beliefs and practices that may facilitate altruistic behavior, will provide a context in which to consider the varieties of charitable activities in religious institutions. A consideration of these activities in conjunction with the larger

3

societal forces affecting American religion will suggest some of the challenges currently facing these activities and institutions.

Distinctive Characteristics of American Religion

On the whole, religion in the United States is characterized by enormous organizational and cultural resources and by the diversity evident among them. Neither of these features by itself is unique among the nations of the world. Many countries in the Middle East and in Latin America, for example, rival the United States in intensity of religious commitment. Pronounced levels of religious diversity also characterize a number of countries, for example, India and the Malaysian region. The combination of the two is, however, unique. Among advanced industrialized countries, none equals the United States in overall levels of religious commitment and the range of religious diversity.

Among commonly cited indicators of the strength of organized religion in the United States are the sheer numbers of churches and church members reported in annual censuses and surveys. Estimates for the United States as a whole generally put the number of local congregations at around 250,000 to 300,000; that is, at least one congregation for every 1,000 members of the population, although in some states this number is as high as one per 300 population. Many of these congregations have long histories in their communities. However, as the population has expanded and new communities have emerged, vast numbers of new congregations (perhaps as many as 45,000 over the past quarter-century) have been founded as well. Thus, scarcely any segment of the American population is more than a few miles away from a local house of worship of one kind or another. Moreover, despite the fact that actual membership lists are notoriously inaccurate, very high proportions of the population actually claim to belong to a church or synagogue. Surveys conducted in recent years, for example, place these proportions at somewhere between 65 percent and 71 percent of the adult public (Gallup, 1988).

Not all who profess membership in religious organizations, of course, are currently active in these organizations.

Nevertheless, estimates from opinion surveys indicate that approximately 42 percent of the adult population can be found in church or synagogue on any given weekend (Gallup, 1988). According to other survey information, about 49 percent attend religious services at least once a month, and 24 percent attend every week (Miller, 1985, p. 347). Many Americans also devote much more of their time to religious organizations than simply attending worship services. Approximately 22 percent of the adult public claim to be involved in prayer groups or Bible study groups, for instance, and approximately 20 percent say they do some kind of volunteer work for a religious organization (Gallup, 1988; Hodgkinson and Weitzman, 1988). In addition, religious organizations in the United States have been relatively successful in evoking monetary giving from their members. Total giving to religious congregations in recent years has been estimated at approximately $50 billion, of which more than 80 percent comes from individual donations (Hodgkinson, Weitzman, and Kirsch, 1988). Other estimates suggest that this giving includes contributions from 52 percent of all U.S. households — a higher proportion than give to any other type of charity — and that the average household contribution (among those who give anything) was about $715 in 1987 (Hodgkinson and Weitzman, 1988).

These contributions, together with endowments and other earnings, have enabled religious organizations to employ large numbers of personnel, construct extensive facilities, and sponsor a wide variety of programs. The total number of clergy reported by religious organizations in the United States typically exceeds 500,000, of whom approximately two-thirds are currently employed in local parishes; approximately $2 billion is spent every year on new church construction; the number of local churches operating Sunday school programs for adults and children each week is nearly as large as the total number of congregations; and hundreds of day schools, colleges and seminaries, and hospitals are sponsored by religious organizations — the Roman Catholic church alone operates more than 7,000 elementary schools, 239 colleges and universities, and 731 hospitals (Jacquet, 1989).

All this constitutes the public or visible face of American religion. But there is a less visible dimension as well, one located in the hearts and minds of its practitioners and in their private devotional behavior. As is often reported, surveys consistently reveal that upward of 90 percent of the American public believe in the existence of God. A large majority, 86 percent, also pray regularly, presumably to this same God (Gallup, 1982). High percentages of the public affirm belief in other religious tenets, for example, in the reality of heaven and an afterlife. Many claim to read the Bible and other religious literature. High proportions say that religion is important in their lives — 53 percent say it is "very important," and another 31 percent say it is "fairly important" (Gallup, 1988).

These levels of religiosity in the American population take on added significance when compared with similar statistics from other modern countries such as England, France, and West Germany. For instance, a recent study showed that 61 percent of the American public think that following God's will is a very important value in their lives compared with only 35 percent who said this in Great Britain; 40 percent of the U.S. sample said that taking part in church-related activity is very important compared with only 15 percent in Great Britain. Another study showed that two-thirds of the American public think that daily life should be governed by religious commandments, whereas the proportions who think this in West Germany and France are about 40 percent and in Great Britain and Canada closer to 30 percent. In addition, figures on church attendance, belief in God, confidence in organized religion, and sales of Bibles all show much higher levels of religiosity in the United States than in any of these other countries (Wuthnow, 1987, pp. 30–31).

The diversity within American religion can be seen most clearly in its numerous denominations and faith traditions. More than 200 major denominations and faiths populate the religious landscape, while as many as a thousand smaller organizations, sects, and cults add to this number. Although some bodies have been absorbed into larger ones through mergers (or have simply died), the rise of new independent churches, sectarian schisms, and continuous importing of religious traditions from other cultures have been more than effective in keeping the spirit of diversity alive. Within the major Protestant denominational families, for example, there have been more than fifty major schisms resulting in new denominations during the twentieth century. A huge proliferation of meditation groups, communes, cults, and spiritualist fellowships has taken place since the 1960s. In the 1970s and 1980s, the diversity in American religion was further expanded by the emergence of numerous religiopolitical, moral, pseudoscientific, and avocational special-purpose groups. Among the most notable of these were gay caucuses, feminist groups, abortion rights groups, prolife activists, supporters of prayer in public schools, religious lobbyists, creationists, and associations of religious professionals.

This diversity, of course, has always interacted with the overall intensity of religious commitment in the United States, strengthening it and creating pockets of vitality to replace other forms of religious association whose attractiveness has diminished. If some sectors of the religious landscape — for example, liberal Protestant churches or inner-city churches — show decline, others — such as gay churches, Hispanic parishes, suburban evangelical churches, television ministries — manifest growth. As in the economy, the free market in American religion seems to encourage spiritual entrepreneurs to compete with one another to provide the most attractively packaged and most appealing varieties of religious commodities. Thus, on the whole, the religious sector constitutes one of the strongest and most dynamic segments of the entire voluntary effort in American society.

Religious Belief and Altruistic Motivation

All the religious traditions that have sunk roots in American soil embrace teachings about believers' responsibilities to their fellow human beings. The admonition found in both the Hebrew and Christian scriptures to love one's neighbor as oneself is widely known. Other teachings prescribe an ethic of care for fellow believers, for sojourners and resident aliens, and for those with physical and spiritual needs. Many of these prescriptions have been codified in the highly memorable dictums and narratives of religious tradition, such as the Golden Rule, the Beatitudes, and the parable of the Good Samaritan.

The specific expectations that follow these teachings are as varied, however, as are the denominations and faiths of which American religion is comprised. Some traditions levy standard fees on their members in the form of pew rent or temple membership, others enter into moral contracts with their members by asking them for annual pledges, and still others operate entirely from spontaneous donations and specialized solicitations. Expectations also vary greatly concerning overall levels of giving and the degree to which giving should be focused on the local congregation or fellowship. Although the tithe is still presented as an explicit guideline in many traditions, some groups present it as a minimum contribution, others as an archaic practice that needs to be revised downward radically; in most organizations the individual adherent is given wide latitude in deciding whether donations should be calculated on gross earnings or after-tax income and whether donations of time should or should not be regarded as substitutes for monetary giving. The variations in expectations concerning the role of the local congregation range from those asking that priority be given to the local congregation exclusively for its programs and needs, to those that emphasize local giving as a conduit to a wider array of agencies, to those that openly encourage giving to national and secular charities as well as the local congregation.

The degree to which religious teachings are assimilated into the life-styles and practices of their adherents is also quite variable. Although most believers give lip service in opinion polls to ideals of caring for others, some say that these ideals are very important in their lives while others admit that they have other priorities. As a result, practitioners vary widely in the frequency with which they attend religious services, pray, tell others about their faith, and consciously try to act in charitable ways. For example, although 73 percent of the respondents in one national survey said that they had prayed or engaged in personal Bible study during the past year, only 38 percent said that they had done any kind of volunteer work. The same study showed that even among people who felt that they had tried very hard to follow the example of Jesus, only 8 percent said that this example had helped them to be more compassionate; in comparison, more than twice as many had gained a sense of comfort or happiness for themselves by thinking about Jesus (Gallup and O'Connell, 1986, p. 114). In addition, those who express deep commitment to religious organizations are divided as to whether their main duties are to God first, to their fellows, or to both equally. According to one study, 64 percent of the American public think it is best to love God and then your neighbor, while 17 percent feel they should love God and their neighbor equally, and 11 percent say it is better to love your neighbor and then God (Gallup and O'Connell, 1986, p. 113).

Not surprisingly, empirical studies have resulted in no simple or consistent conclusions about the particular motivations that may provide the strongest and most effective links between religion and altruistic behavior. Some experimental research suggests that guilt may enhance the likelihood of someone engaging in altruistic behavior; other research indicates that a minority of believers view God as a wrathful deity to be feared or a stern disciplinarian who demands conformity to a host of moral injunctions; thus, by implication, it may be that for some believers religiously instilled guilt serves as a motivation for good deeds. Other theories have argued that altruism is more likely to stem from personal security, affirmation, and a strong conviction of self-worth. Abraham Maslow (1962), for example, argues that people are more likely to respond generously to others when their own basic needs for security and safety have been met and they are able to concentrate on "higher" needs for fulfillment and transcendence. Accordingly, such theories suggest that religion may be a better motivator of good deeds when it instills a sense of divine grace and acceptance; or as Maslow (1970) suggests, a "peak experience" characterized by an ecstatic sense of communion with God, nature, or some other transcendent being may be especially powerful in motivating one toward altruistic behavior. Some evidence has tended to support these claims. In one study, those who had experienced this kind of ecstasy or communion with God were significantly more likely to value helping others; this held both among the college educated (79 percent to 54 percent) and among those without a college education (65 percent versus 48 percent). They were also less materialistic and less likely to be concerned about social status (Wuthnow, 1978, p. 113). In another study, a national survey of the American public, 74 percent of the respondents who scored high on a standard self-esteem scale said they had donated money to a charitable cause compared with 57 percent of those who scored low on the scale. This study did not indicate whether these differences might have been contaminated by difference in income, education, age, or other personal characteristics. It did, however, reveal that people who feel close to God and affirmed by God were more likely to score high on the self-esteem scale, while those who feel afraid of God or guilty before God scored lower on self-esteem (Gallup, 1983).

Because of the difficulties in finding entirely consistent evidence for any of these arguments, some people have suggested that motivation is situationally specific. That is, the charitable impulse may be triggered by a variety of motivations (even selfish ones), but much depends on what one's peers are doing, how busy one is, and where the opportunity arises (for a literature review, see Hodgkinson, 1988). Still another way of reconciling the various theories has been to suggest that people respond from different motives depending on the kind of moral and religious reasoning to which they are used. Thus, some people may respond better to cut-and-dried "thou shalt" or "thou shalt not" statements, while others require highly complex philosophical systems that involve wide latitude in deciding when altruistic behavior is appropriate (see especially, Kohlberg, 1984; Fowler, 1981; and Stokes, 1982).

One thing that seems clear from the available research on religion and altruism, however, is that religion is more than a simple (or even complex) set of moral and ethical dictums. It is a richly symbolic language that embodies historical specificity, a high degree of intertextuality, and frequent usage of narrative genre. As such, much is lost when it is reduced either to moral admonitions or to styles of moral reasoning. Its implied mode of dissemination is through story; thus, not surprisingly, sermons, oral religious communication, and religious literature are replete with stories. These are likely to be the most salient connections between religious traditions and charitable behavior: the narrative discourse that concretizes, objectifies, and above all personifies what it means to be charitable. Certainly biblical parables such as the story of the Good Samaritan provide vivid examples of this style of discourse. Within popular culture and our own experiences—from the morning newspaper's human interest story about a contemporary Good Samaritan who helps AIDS patients to a friend in our community who is "always there" for others—these narratives from religious tradition are also played out and retold repeatedly in American culture.

Religious Practice: Mobilizing Giving

If teachings and stories that reinforce altruistic values constitute one of the significant connections between religion and philanthropy, the other important link consists of the organizational contexts that religion supplies and the ways in which these contexts help to mobilize voluntary giving behavior. Indeed, religion is particularly strong in this respect because of its extensive infrastructure at the grass-roots level and its various hierarchies of coordination and administration at state, regional, and national levels.

At the local level, as noted previously, somewhere between 250,000 and 300,000 congregations make up the bottom layer of American religion. Some of these congregations are quite small, numbering fewer than a hundred active members; others (an increasing number, it appears) involve thousands of members at various levels, drawing them in through television and radio ministries, slick Sunday morning services with live entertainment and a talk-show format, fleets of school buses, and specialized ministries for all ages and interest groups. In either case, the congregation provides many of the resources necessary for the possibility of any kind of charitable behavior: a facility in which to hold meetings and engage in planning and from which

to launch efforts into the community; one or more professionally trained clergy who can organize activities; a visible
entity that people in the community can drive by or find listed
in their telephone book should they be interested in volunteering time and money or have needs themselves; and a legal entity
that can solicit and disseminate funds.

None of this should be taken for granted when it is argued
that the church provides people with a sense of community;
community depends on tangible resources as much as it does on
a sheer sense of attachment among an aggregate of people. But
community is also more than physical, human, and legal resources. Congregations generally involve groups of several hundred people who meet regularly for worship and other services.
Within these communities, personal ties develop and become
the first-order mechanisms of caring: help when someone is
hospitalized, support in times of bereavement, and so on. In
addition to the actual caring provided, these relationships
model or exemplify standards of giving and volunteering. Like
verbal narratives, they ritually personify it. Beyond this, of
course, the local congregation also provides the occasion for
sermons about caring and stewardship, a place to hear about
needs in the community, social networks that can be used to
recruit volunteers, and subgroups that plan helping activities
either within the congregation or in the wider community.

Beyond the local congregation, American religion is also
well organized at the regional, national, and even international
levels to mobilize giving and to channel it in effective directions.
Presbyteries, dioceses, and other regional assemblies exercise
control over, coordinate, or provide legislative bodies for local
congregations. National headquarters provide higher levels of
administration and coordination and typically staff bureaus,
such as publishing, training, and visitation, that transfer services back to the local level. Other specialized organizations,
such as the National Council of Churches and the National
Council of Christians and Jews, integrate activities across denominations and faith traditions.

One important service that these agencies provide is disseminating information to local congregations. Such informa-

tion is likely to enhance awareness both of needs in other parts of the country or world and of opportunities for service, such as denominational fund-raising drives to support or petitions to sign.

A second way in which these agencies mobilize helping behavior is through direct organizational activities. Most of the large denominational bodies, for example, maintain lobbyists in the nation's capital to make their views known on important pieces of legislation. Many of these bodies also staff media news bureaus that disseminate resolutions and policy positions of the denomination to the general public. Through national bureaus, many religious bodies also participate in the work of other nonprofit organizations.

The other means of facilitating altruistic behavior through national religious organizations is by utilizing donations and endowments for charitable services themselves. A proportion of local giving is typically channeled directly to these services. A vast network of colleges and seminaries, hospitals, relief agencies, and foreign missions has developed over the past century and a half through these gifts.

The Varieties of Religious Philanthropy

The combination of American religion's extensive resources, its diversity, and its doctrinal commitment to altruistic concerns has resulted in an array of philanthropic activities nearly as varied as the broader nonprofit sector of which these activities are a part. Nearly every kind of secular philanthropy has its religious counterpart, except for some that are prohibited by law, and in many cases these religious counterparts developed first and provided the models for their secular successors.

Perhaps the greatest share of religious caring and giving takes place, as already noted, through the informal relationships nurtured within the local congregation. In an otherwise atomized and commercialized society, churches and synagogues remain one of the few places in which members of different families, age-groups, occupations, and neighborhoods can interact at a deeply personal level over extended periods of time.

They also provide one of the few places (other than therapy groups) in which frank discussion of the problems and gratifications associated with caring relationships within the family, the congregation, and the wider community can occur.

A considerable share of financial giving to local religious organizations goes directly or indirectly for the support of these informal caring relationships. The two single items that generally comprise the largest budget expenditures for local congregations are clergy salaries and building costs, both of which make possible the regular meetings, as well as exceptional gatherings such as funerals and weddings, around which social relationships in the congregation cohere.

Historically, the main philanthropic activities sponsored by religious organizations other than those within local congregations included foreign and domestic missionaries, Bible and tract societies, colleges and seminaries, hospitals, and various kinds of relief work, such as poor houses and orphanages. By the end of the nineteenth century and during the first two decades of the twentieth century, these traditional activities were enlarged in an effort to meet the demands of an increasingly urban and industrial society. Groups such as the Salvation Army and YMCA began ministering to the needs of urban immigrants; colleges were founded in increasing numbers; more specialized programs for women and youth were founded within churches and synagogues; chaplaincy programs and nursing schools were expanded, especially during the First World War; and of course temperance societies grew rapidly in both urban and rural areas, especially among women, as a means of responding to the growing tide of alcoholism, desertion, and child abuse.

Over the next half-century, especially during the Great Depression, religious groups found their efforts to cope with poverty, illness, and the growing demand for higher education falling increasingly short and thus turned more and more to supporting government initiatives to solve those problems. Charitable efforts also came to include greater participation in the legislative process to combat lynchings and other forms of racial discrimination and to make the voice of conscience heard on atomic weapons, tax policies, and foreign relations. The extensive participation of religious groups and individual clergy in the civil rights movement and protests against the Vietnam War in the 1960s and early 1970s can be seen in retrospect as the outgrowth of this longer tendency toward philanthropy being turned in a political direction.

In the years since World War II, religious organizations have also participated in a wide variety of new voluntary and service activities. Nonprofit retirement communities and nursing homes built and operated by churches for their members and in many cases for the wider public represent one response to the needs of a society with a growing number of elderly members. Meals-on-wheels programs, transportation services, and visitation programs represent other responses to this need. Pregnancy clinics, foster home programs, and shelters for battered women have been established in large numbers by local churches and synagogues to meet the needs of changing family relationships, as have church-subsidized counseling centers. An increasing number of religious groups have also participated actively in initiating and providing facilities for alcoholism and substance abuse support groups, gender awareness groups, gay fellowships, and training programs for the jobless. With cutbacks in government programs in the 1980s, many churches also opened soup kitchens and shelters for the homeless.

At the international level, religious organizations continue to sponsor a wide variety of medical missionary programs, emergency relief services, agricultural development projects, and schools. After the Vietnam War, churches and synagogues played an active role in resettling Vietnamese and Cambodian refugees, and approximately 300 local congregations have declared themselves "sanctuaries" to assist political refugees fleeing persecution in Central America. Local peace fellowships, extensive clergy involvement in nuclear disarmament campaigns, and watchdog groups monitoring human rights violations, supporting liberation efforts in Latin America, and opposing apartheid in South Africa also reflect the continuing interest of religious organizations in international philanthropic activities.

At present, then, churches and other religious congregations are involved in an exceptionally wide variety of charitable and benevolent activities that reflect both traditional commitments and responses to recent concerns. According to data gathered by INDEPENDENT SECTOR (Hodgkinson, Weitzman, and Kirsch, 1988), 79 percent of all congregations provide family counseling, 71 percent send relief somewhere abroad directly or indirectly, 56 percent support voluntary care in health institutions such as hospitals and nursing homes, 46 percent claim involvement in some kind of community development effort, 42 percent sponsor activities in culture and the arts, 32 percent list housing or shelter for the homeless among their activities, 31 percent provide day-care services, and 19 percent provide some form of housing or housing assistance for senior citizens.

Challenges from the Wider Society

Although philanthropy in its numerous varieties remains connected to religion in the ways we have considered, neither religion nor philanthropy exists in isolation from the rest of society. Both face the challenge of adapting to sweeping changes in the social milieu. Particularly important are the changes that have been identified by observers of American religion in four areas: secularization, religious restructuring, political and economic changes, and cultural influences.

Secularization, in the simplest sense, has been conceived of as an erosion in the absolute level of religious commitment in a society. According to this definition, the United States has in fact witnessed some secularization along certain dimensions in recent decades. For instance, the proportion of the public expressing confidence in the church or organized religion dropped from 66 percent in 1973 to 54 percent in 1989, and the proportion who believe religion can answer all or most of today's problems dropped from 62 percent in 1974 (after a high of 81 percent in 1957) to 57 percent in 1989 (Wuthnow, 1989). According to other data, the proportion of the public who say religion is very important in their personal lives has also dropped — from 70 percent in 1965 to 53 percent in the most recent polls

(Gallup, 1988). Such trends point to a possible erosion of religion's capacity to facilitate philanthropy as well. To the extent that religious involvement is a positive reinforcement to charitable and voluntary activity, then declines of this kind may signal declines in the latter as well. As yet, though, these declines have not been serious. Indeed, some analysts claim that they reflect an artificially high level of religious commitment in the 1950s and 1960s rather than evidence of long-term erosion. Moreover, other indicators suggest stability in religious commitment rather than change. Church attendance rates, membership rates, the proportions believing in heaven, and percentages of the population who pray regularly have remained relatively constant over the past two decades (Wuthnow, 1989).

A different conception of secularization, however, points toward more serious changes. This view emphasizes the *relative* decline of religion's influence in society. According to this argument, many of the functions that religion used to perform are now filled by other, distinctly secular institutions. The separation of taxation from tithing, giving government rather than the church primary control over the coercive aspects of societal giving, constitutes an example that developed relatively early in the modern era. More recently, the emergence of counseling and social work as professions separate from the clergy provides another example. Most relevant to the question of giving and volunteering, of course, is the gradual and pronounced development in American history of secular nonprofit organizations. Colleges, hospitals, orphanages, educational foundations, cultural associations, fraternal organizations, and public interest groups of all kinds have either shaken off earlier religious ties or emerged without sectarian affiliations from the beginning. As a result, it now makes sense to speak of religion, in a way it did not a century ago, as a component (among many others) of the voluntary sector. It also makes sense to ask whether religion will continue to be a vital component of this sector or whether it will increasingly run into competition from secular alternatives.

In addition to the impact of sheer secularizing tendencies, the voluntary spirit in America is also being affected by the internal restructuring presently taking place within religion

(Wuthnow, 1988). Even among the religiously active, loyalties to particular denominations have diminished greatly. As a result, many of these entities appear to be having difficulty meeting operating budgets and are having to cut back charitable pro-grams they once sponsored. At the same time, secular and nondenominational agencies can appeal for money and time through direct-mail campaigns and television programs. A large number of special-purpose groups have also sprung up on re-ligious turf. Some of these groups continue to sponsor charita-ble activities such as missionary work and relief for the needy. An increasing number, however, are concerned with the special interests of their own members: youth organizations, gay cau-cuses, professional organizations for church administrators, hobby groups for religiously minded enthusiasts, and so on.

The restructuring of American religion has also involved numeric losses among liberal mainline religious bodies, sub-stantial growth among conservative groups, and heightened competition between the two. The result for charitable activities has been mixed. On the one hand, liberals have continued to work for social justice and broad humanitarian concerns; con-servatives have focused efforts on evangelism, missions, and family issues; and competition between the two factions has sometimes invigorated the efforts of both, even resulting on occasion in borrowing and imitation. On the other hand, this competition has sometimes drained each side of resources for charitable outreach and presented an image of rancor to the wider public rather than a vision of reconciliation and redemption.

Beyond the religious domain itself, the character of re-ligious giving remains highly vulnerable to the political and economic winds that blow across the social landscape from various directions. Periodic revisions of tax and reporting laws for religious organizations always create uncertainties for the programs of religious organizations. Sharp swings in levels of economic growth, inflation, and unemployment create similar uncertainties, especially in view of the fact that no simple or straightforward effects of economic conditions on charitable giving have been documented for the full range of religious organizations. Of special importance as well are the vagaries of government expenditures on social, educational, health, and welfare services. At one moment, religious organizations find themselves in direct competition with government programs; at another, government officials call on religious leaders to take up the slack created by cutbacks in government programs.

Finally, the voluntary spirit in American religion is subject to the influences of changing cultural forces in our society. Over the past half-century, rapid growth in higher education and the mass media has created new possibilities to arouse charitable sentiments in the public at large. Television preachers, United Way, rock concerts staged as benefits, teach-ins about South Africa, and courses that focus on poverty and discrimination are all examples. These channels have also enhanced opportunities to confront Americans with problems and needs in the wider world, such as famine and oppression, and religious organizations have sponsored such information campaigns both directly (as in the case of appeals by televangelists) and indirectly (through contributions to secular coalitions). Nevertheless, much of the growth in higher education and the mass media has been driven by narrowly careerist, technical, and consumerist agendas. Accordingly, social observers point to the individualism prevalent in our society and question whether religious communities themselves can withstand these pressures let alone promote a more general spirit of giving. If American culture is becoming more narcissistic, they argue, people will have neither the motivation to become involved in charitable activities nor the familiarity with needs and opportunities for involvement that has traditionally been fostered by churches, synagogues, and other community organizations.

On balance, then, American religion near the end of the twentieth century remains a vital feature of our society, one with a long tradition of respectability and with vast resources to use both in ensuring its own survival and in nurturing the charitable programs that have always been part of its mission. Despite changes in the nature of faith and in the wider society, religious organizations remain one of the most effective mechanisms in our society for motivating, organizing, and disseminating charitable giving. At present, though, American religion is also subject to internal strains and to changes in the broader society. These developments render its future as a supplier of philanthropic services more precarious than ever before. Without the motivating and mobilizing contributions of religion, the voluntary spirit itself would surely wither.

References

Fowler, J. *Stages of Faith*. San Francisco: Harper & Row, 1981.

Gallup, G. *Jesus Christ in the Lives of Americans Today*. Princeton, N.J.: Gallup Organization, 1982.

Gallup, G. *Survey of Self-Esteem*. Princeton, N.J.: Gallup Organization, 1983.

Gallup, G. "Trends in U.S. Religious Life Show Considerable Stability." *Emerging Trends*, Dec. 1988, *10*, 2.

Gallup, G., and O'Connell, G. *Who Do Americans Say That I Am?* Philadelphia: Westminster Press, 1986.

Hodgkinson, V. A. *Motivations for Giving and Volunteering: A Selected Review of the Literature*. Washington, D.C.: INDEPENDENT SECTOR, 1988.

Hodgkinson, V. A., and Weitzman, M. S. *Giving and Volunteering in the United States: Findings from a National Survey*. Washington, D.C.: INDEPENDENT SECTOR, 1988.

Hodgkinson, V. A., Weitzman, M. S., and Kirsch, A. D. *From Belief to Commitment: The Activities and Finances of Religious Congregations in the United States*. Washington, D.C.: INDEPENDENT SECTOR, 1988.

Jacquet, C. H., Jr. *Yearbook of American and Canadian Churches, 1989*. Nashville, Tenn.: Abingdon Press, 1989.

Kohlberg, L. *The Psychology of Moral Development*. San Francisco: Harper & Row, 1984.

Maslow, A. *Toward a Psychology of Being*. New York: D. Van Nostrand, 1962.

Maslow, A. *Religions, Values, and Peak-Experiences*. New York: Viking, 1970.

Miller, W. E. *American National Election Study, 1984*. Ann Arbor,

Mich.: Inter-University Consortium for Political and Social Research, 1985.

Stokes, K. (ed.). *Faith Development in the Adult Life Cycle*. New York: Sadlier, 1982.

Wuthnow, R. *Experimentation in American Religion*. Berkeley: University of California Press, 1978.

Wuthnow, R. "Indices of Religious Resurgence in the United States." In R. T. Antoun and M. E. Hegland (eds.), *Religious Resurgence: Contemporary Cases in Islam, Christianity, and Judaism*. Syracuse, N.Y.: Syracuse University Press, 1987.

Wuthnow, R. *The Restructuring of American Religion: Society and Faith Since World War II*. Princeton, N.J.: Princeton University Press, 1988.

Wuthnow, R. *The Struggle for America's Soul: Evangelicals, Liberals, and Secularism*. Grand Rapids, Mich.: Eerdmans, 1989.

Chapter 2

Max L. Stackhouse

Religion and
the Social Space
for Voluntary Institutions

The idea of an "independent sector" did not originate in the Garden of Eden. It is not an integral part of Creation; nor is it evidence of a Fall from a Golden Age of Innocence. It may, however, help preserve us from certain evils and contribute to the well-being of the common life. It is an idea that has become partly embodied in some societies slowly and painfully in the course of human history, an idea that is based on certain aspects of the religious heritage of the West and that calls us to new horizons.

Simple and Complex Societies

Primal societies seldom have independent sectors. It is one of the marks of the "simple" society — "simple" is of course relative, for anthropologists tell us that such societies are incredibly difficult to understand — that all parts of the society are presumed to be integrated into an organic unit. The family system is integrally related to the political system, the cultural system, the economic system, and the religious system. A certain complexity of organization, which the sociologists call differentiation, seems to be the first precondition for the formation of an independent sector. Independence tends to occur, in other words, not among the wandering bands or in the settled village

22

but in the city—in urbanized cultures with diversified institutions and complex divisions of social function.

But urbanization in the demographic sense of density of population and complexity of organization is not a sufficient base for an independent sector. The great cities of the ancient world, like many of the new cities now exploding in the emerging countries of the world, did not develop voluntary associations, although they may have developed medical, educational, technological and other complex professional institutions not present in simple societies. Nor is it the case that the independent sector automatically grows from or in reaction to the public sector or government and the private sector or corporations once these are well developed.

Indeed, the "third sector," as we find it, for example, in Levitt's book by that title (1973), may be a misnomer. It assumes that what drives civilizations, what makes them work the way they work, is fundamentally economics and politics, the corporation and the government, and that the formation of the third sector is a rather peculiar creation of modern populist reformism, once economic and political conditions are "ripe." Such a view may be the product of both historical amnesia and a lack of comparative social awareness no longer possible in a globally interdependent world. Indeed, it may be precisely the other way around: Certain kinds of social, intellectual, and moral factors have to be in place to form an independent sector. *Then* an open, dynamic, and pluralistic political economy can emerge.

Max Weber demonstrated three-quarters of a century ago in the conclusion to his master work, *Economy and Society* ([1914–1922] 1968), "The City," that only under certain conditions, under the influence of a distinctive kind of religious influence, are the basic patterns generated that produce what we today call "voluntary associations," "nongovernmental organizations," "not-for-profit corporations," or "mediating institutions." Indeed, he traces the roots of these structures to the impact of Christianity as it legitimated the shattering of closed genetic groupings and fixed social hierarchies in the medieval cities. Several volumes of comparative analysis of other civilizations—

India (Weber, [1920] 1951) and China (Weber, [1921] 1951), especially—confirmed his argument.

Weber did not write as a believer, nor did he draw all the conclusions that his work implied. However, he did demonstrate that such institutions as today make up the "independent sector" have very deep roots. Only some social histories developed the patterns of "consociation," "bonding," or "federation," or developed the legal structures to enhance these; only some civilizations opened the door to the intentional formation of voluntary, community-based and community-serving bodies that are, in principle, not dependent on other dominant sectors of society. Further, he showed that the social patterns that generated these possibilities were formed by the interaction of multiple factors, including religion, and were not only political or economic ones, as important as these are.

Where a social history brings the institutions of the independent sector into prominence, civilization has a distinctive shape. It is an ordered pluralism, based in both balances of power *and* kinds of cooperative mutuality that are rooted in religious or ethical principles of an enduring kind. Human wills are freed and guided to work cooperatively with others—neither swallowed in a sea of collectivism nor required to stand in the mean isolation of egoism.

One of the greatest modern theorists of this cluster of institutions, James Luther Adams (1976, 1986a, 1986b) has extended Weber's view. He has pointed out that such organizations are only "voluntary" and "independent" in certain respects, and they easily fall into the perils of bureaucratization, or self-interestedness. But Adams has also shown, more clearly than did Weber, how the "social space" for these possibilities in the West was created out of the distinct history of certain religious organizations.

What we now see is a plethora of groupings active in modern pluralistic societies—unions, caucuses, and lobbies; advocacy, cultural, educational, and artistic organizations; hobby, sports, and social clubs; professional, charitable, and philanthropic institutions. While every complex society has various kinds of fraternities, gangs, clubs, fellowship circles, and interest groups (many of which are secret in closed or traditional societies), they play a relatively minor role in shaping the future of most civilizations. They normally stand only at the margins of historical significance.

Modern, pluralistic, democratic societies, however, are distinguished by the "social space" carved out for groups. They are given wider scope; they take on a deeper character, in part because of a series of developments that have religious roots. In the final analysis, they cannot be understood without reference to the relation of church history to social history.

Religious Roots

Drawing in part on the work of Weber's colleague Ernst Troeltsch ([1914] 1931), Adams shows that it was often the heretical sects, the advocates of marginalized faiths, the conventicals of true believers demanding the right to practice their faith without the constraint of crown or miter and appealing to godly principles of justice who were decisive for this feature of our modern existence. They formed solidarities in the West that authoritarian forces could not control. At other times, it was followers of great prophetic visions or the bearers of priestly compassion who wanted to mediate their view of divinity to the consciousness and habits of the people. At still other moments, there came to dominance religious groups that focused entirely on the transcendental world and left this world to the powers that be (who often approved of this view and supported them against other perspectives). But even these groups claimed the right to exist beyond the power of any to control.

Such groups insisted, in the name of all that was holy, that no one could prevent them from joining together "for religious and charitable purposes." Some matters were outside the control of all earthly authorities. In the name of God, they claimed the right to be, to organize, to care for the neighbor, and to set forth their views publicly. This had a decisive impact on Western history. The ancient and now obscure battles between pope and emperor (or preacher and magistrate) and at other times between economic elites and ecclesiastical leadership, or between pagan crafts and pious arts proved to be fateful to the West. To put the matter in its strongest form, ecclesiology (the theory and practice of church organization) is a decisive clue to the meaning of Western social history precisely because that is where religious ideas become most concrete in regard to the social, political, economic, and cultural sectors of society.

Wherever religious communities won their case, wherever civilizational leadership accepted such claims—because they believed them, or because they had no choice due to the fact that the population was persuaded that they were valid and would not accept any leadership that denied them—a new kind of "social space" was carved out of the ordinary patterns of civilizational formation. Other institutions were viewed as important, but not ultimate. Thus, an additional, peculiar "separation of powers" took place in the West, making the differentiation of complex society even more complex. What religious communities fought for was eventually institutionalized: The right of people to form intentional religious associations outside an established religion was more and more tolerated, acknowledged, celebrated, and subsequently expanded to include nonreligious charitable and ethical organizations.

People do not have to agree on everything or belong to the same institution to exist peacefully together in the same society. Indeed, people could belong to several groups— some chosen, some required, some casually, some seriously, some sacred, some secular. From these roots came both the notion of the human person as a "joiner," with multiple, chosen memberships, and a conception of society as an "association of associations." The pluralistic definition (as opposed to both the ancient Greek and the modern socialist definitions) of democracy and the idea of the corporation separate from household or regime were born of this womb. These ideas were nurtured in the beliefs of the people, in custom, and in law, by generations of clergy from the nonestablished faiths, until today the right to freely participate in—or to refuse forced membership in—such organizations has come to be seen as one of the most basic human rights. We now believe what would have seemed incredible in primal, traditional, or feudal societies and seems strange still in many lands of the East and South: A society without an independent sector is an undeveloped or an oppressed society.

Biblical Sources

Adams's colleagues and students have traced the history of these developments and developed the bibliographic resources to establish their point (Robertson, 1966). The evidence is quite convincing, as is his contention that a decisive influence is the biblical idea of "covenant." This notion, present in most branches of Judaism and Christianity and sometimes implicit in Islam, holds that while individual integrity and pious regard for that which is beyond all time is important, the only God worth worshiping is also present in the struggles of history, in the shared commitment to justice, love, and peace that binds humans together and looks toward social salvation.

Humans are most devout when they voluntarily choose to belong to and be accountable for communities of faith under a sovereign God who is greater than any other authority. In spite of the pharaohs of Egypt; in spite of the efforts of the wise and the rich and the strong to control all sectors of civilization; in spite of patriarchal, ethnic, and sex-role stereotypes that define from birth what people can or cannot be and do, people called of God—Israel, the "New Israel" of the early Christian community, and reforming groups of many stripes—feel compelled by conscience to join in communities of mutual care and discipline beyond the control of conventional powers. They establish a "free zone," from which they can simultaneously govern themselves according to a higher law than the civil code and address the problems of the world in terms of a more ultimate justice and compassion.

Nothing stops such groups. They have a message, a purpose, a mandate that, in principle, pertains to the whole of humanity. They live to serve, not to master. Such a covenant is not simply a contract, for in a contract, humans construct their own principles by agreement and calculated advantage. Rather, in a covenant, ethical principles are seen as prior to any human agreement, and sacrifice is sometimes demanded. Yet obedience to these terms renders true freedom. And when a degree of liberation and independence is reached, it is precisely the ethical content of this covenant that provides the guidelines for the governance of the common life. It supports the reformation of the law to permit pluralism but limit chaos; it brings the virtue of service to the center of leadership; it sacrificially supports "unofficial" communities with "time, talent, and tithe"; it simultaneously frees the will and draws the free will into relationships of discipline and mutual care. At least, that is the intent; it is sometimes nearly realized.

Modern Results

Many are today familiar with the part of the West's religious history that grows from these roots: The formation of the Jewish synagogue, the rise of the Catholic church, the Protestant Reformation, and so on. However, many also believe today that democracy derives from movements that have nothing to do with these religious movements—perhaps, from the French Revolution or the Enlightenment with their tendencies to repudiate religion as a positive force in social history. Those in the heritage of Troeltsch, Weber, and Adams argue against this common view and suggest instead that it was the recovery and recasting of the idea of the covenant in the "orders" and among the "sects," as they interacted first with Calvinism and then with other branches of the biblical heritage, that brought these ancient themes into modernity. These, they argue, created what we now mean by democracy, precisely because they created the "social space" for today's independent sector with all its "blooming, buzzing confusion" of people doing worthwhile things together. (Similar cases have been argued by A. D. Lindsay, J. H. Nichols, A. S. P. Woodhouse, G. H. Williams, and a host of other historians who recognized the significance of this history in contrast to the religious and cultural traditions influencing the social philosophies of Hitler and Stalin on the one hand and the great classic philosophies of Asia on the other. Their assembly of the evidence when democracy has been under threat in the twentieth century dare not be lost.)

Clearly, several parts of Europe and America were early influenced by the "independence" movement that grew from these religious roots and generated, over time, the fierce defense of the rights to assemble, speak on matters of the common life, and publish, without the approval of anyone else. They saw a certain "sovereignty of sphere," as some Dutch scholars call it (Kuyper, 1931). Many other lands have developed or are developing parallel traditions today, although the struggles are not ended at home or abroad.

It is not really an accident that "civil rights" in America, "solidarity" in Poland, "anti-apartheid" in South Africa, "fair elections" in the Philippines, or "base communities" in Latin America have taken place under the mantle of the church (each sometimes with resistance from established religious leadership) (Fagan, 1980; NCCB, 1989).

These chapters in church history from the past, or now being written, in other words, are what has made modern, Western societies more or less safe not only for religious pluralism — the denomination, the sect, the synagogue, the temple, the mosque, as well as the monastery and the cathedral — but for the service club, the charity institution, the private school, the nonprofit corporation, the union, the committee, the professional association, the opposition party, the foundation, the advocacy movement, the neighborhood improvement organization, the political action committee, and all their "networks." The evidence seems rather clear: Without some understanding of this background, it is unlikely that we will understand what it is that brought the "social space" for the independent sector into being and what, ultimately, must guide it.

In this regard, it is important to point out that these developments are not distinctively "conservative" or "liberal" in the conventional senses, in part because these terms often refer today to social *policy* or *party*. The key point behind the independent sector is one of *polity*, of how the social order is structured so that open, vigorous debate over policy matters by multiple parties is possible. Nor do the fruits of this history bias society toward one religious or political orientation. The Ku Klux Klan can find space in an open, pluralistic society, as can a revolutionary popular front and the Hare Krishna, so long as they do not destroy the capacity of other groups to exist and do not use coercive force where they cannot persuade.

More obviously within the framework of the social polity, contemporary neoconservatives and neoprogressives both see that the independent sector is vital for all they hold dear. And that fact suggests that, for all the dissonance and pluralism and diversity that many experience as moral crisis in this society, the main point out of this heritage remains a secure and central point of normative consensus. (See Berger and Neuhaus, 1977; Evans and Boyte, 1988.)

What Is a Sector, Anyway?

My own research in this stream of scholarship has drawn on the foregoing historical insights and tends to confirm them; but it has been more analytical and comparative in focus. That is, for several years I have tried to understand why, in terms of social analysis and comparative religion, social history has tended to work this way (Stackhouse, 1984, 1988). Further, as a theological ethicist, I have tried to figure out whether it ought to work this way (Stackhouse, 1987). Let me summarize some of my chief findings.

In every society five "sectors," each populated by institutions, are necessary. In simple societies, these sectors are intimately integrated, as already suggested. In complex societies, they are more clearly differentiated. But no society continues to exist without them, although each sector can take a quite distinctive form and be variously related to the other sectors. The indispensable sectors of society are familial, political, economic, cultural, and religious.

Family. Everyone is born out of a sexual relationship and as a male or female (although all may have both "masculine" and "feminine" characteristics or sentiments in varying degrees). Thus, everyone has a rather significant genetic identity that is fateful for many aspects of life. Further, each has relatives of some description who socialize us into rather prescribed gender roles. We may struggle against these in some measure, but the associations are, for the most part, involuntary. We did not choose them and cannot, fully, choose to opt out of them. If large numbers of society, for any reason, do not perpetuate these associations and produce a new generation to carry them on, society falls.

To support these relationships, every society has familial institutions, which in most societies include not only several generations but extended relationships such as clan, tribe, caste, and ethnicity, for it is mostly within these relationships that we marry. The ideal for familial relationships can vary, of course; but no society is without one, and every society thinks that they are sacred. Woe be to those who attempt to undercut its holy values.

Politics. Every society experiences threats of violence from within and threats of invasion from without. To contain and resist this violence, every society develops political institutions, legitimized authorities who adjudicate disputes, control crime, are responsible for evoking commitment to the common good and demanding it by force where it is needed but not present, and holding "foreign" threats at bay. The political order may be as simple as a (primarily ceremonial) clan chief or as complex as an empire's bureaucracy, with its inevitable satrapies, client states, and standing armies. But if a society does not have any structures for regime, it is quickly subject to lawlessness from within or defeated by invaders from abroad. And, indeed, it is true that the peace and continued survival of the community depends no less on well-ordered politics than it does on a sexuality that involves fidelity and integrity.

We do not choose the politics into which we are born. We may become, at a certain stage of sophistication, opposed to the powers that rule and turn to reform or revolution. However, such actions are ordinarily undertaken in the name of patriotism — to restore the "true order" forsaken by incumbent leaders or to undertake those policies that can meet the challenges of the future in contrast to those decadent or venal leaders who are stuck in the past or who while away national purpose and sov-

ereignty. Indeed, the accumulation, exercise, preservation, and
extension of political power are the stuff of heroism, the stuff
that makes men gods. There is a majesty, like unto holiness, in
political power, and no few of the caesars, tsars, and kaisers of
the world have been quite sure of that and ready to claim their
divine rights.

Economics. Everyone is also born into a class. Not only familial
and political relationships are largely defined for us before we
exist; but economic ones are as well. Of course, certain aptitudes
for certain kinds of work may come with our genes, and we may
be socialized into certain skills from the moment we can crawl.
The kind of regime in which we live may also enhance or limit
economic options. A gift for securities analysis is economically
of less significance in China than in Japan today, but a capacity
for security studies could be more significant. Nevertheless,
much of everyone's economic prospect is deeply influenced by
the place in the structure of the economic system into which one
is born.

It is surely possible to structure economies so that pre-
determined "stations in life" are not permanent, neither over the
generations nor in the course of a lifetime. It may also be
possible to reduce the enormous gaps that, historically and
today, separate the very rich from the very poor. Yet there is little
doubt about the fact that every society must have a viable economic system and that in every system not everyone can do every
job or can be rewarded on the same basis for the work that the
society needs to have done. Every society will have some reward
system for important work well done, some material indicators
that mark class ordering, with some wealthier and others
poorer, and some spillage of these categories onto those who do
not deserve what they get.

Culture. Each of us also has a mother tongue. That fact is a
simple indicator that we are also born into a cultural-linguistic
system that has its own grammar, its own songs, its own styles, its
own ways of naming sexual, political, and economic reality, and
its own characteristic channels of thought about the cosmos. We

can learn new languages, we can translate from one to another, we can invent new words and abandon old expressions; but every society has a dominant cultural system that sets the standards for all members of that society. Incapacity in the cultural system, lack of fluency, alienation or exclusion from its terms leaves people out—the children learn foreign tongues, they are less effective in gaining political influence, they succeed less often economically, and they do not marry well.

Religion. Finally, everyone is born into a faith (or a humanist tradition that functions, today, much as a religion in this regard). However, religion is not always centered in what is clearly the independent sector. As often as not, it is attached to one or another of the other sectors or some combination of them. Indeed, in much of the world and in most of world history, the four sectors of social life listed above are taken to be holy or inviolable. They are at or near the center of religious meaning for most people. Individuals give their ultimate loyalties to these four primary or "axial" sectors of society. For instance, the mystery of fertility, the rites and rituals of marriage, knowledge of sacred genealogies, and loyalty to clan totems, tribal spirits, or caste loyalties, with all their resistances to too much intimate contact with someone not of "the right kind," mark the boundaries of familial religions. Such loyalties exist not only in faraway jungles or ancient texts but in every family reunion and meeting of a prospective bridegroom.

Similarly, many people dedicate themselves religiously to their nation. Government service is sometimes seen to be the highest calling. Warriors are accorded the highest honors when they give "the supreme sacrifice" to defend the nation. What state does not find its most monumental memorials dedicated to the rulers of days gone by who saved, by force, the regime from peril? It is not at all an accident that political leaders have usually been addressed in history as "My Lord." Indeed, even in a democracy, the flag is, for many, the most sacred symbol to which they pledge allegiance.

And so on we could go. Similar analyses could be given to the alliances of religion and economic class or religion and cultural-linguistic ways of construing the world. Not a few think that the material interests or the poetic expressions of their own group are divine. Frequently, religion only appears to be a fifth sector; it is really the ecstatic expression of the mysterious potencies of the other dimensions of life. That is why social scientists can analyze it in terms of its psychosexual, its political, its economic, or its cultural bases and biases. And they are surely correct at least to some degree. Often enough a given religion is simply the ritual and ideological support system for those sectors of society that, in their negative forms, we know by other names: tribalism (sexism, nationalism, or racism), political power (militarism, colonialism, or imperialism), economic interest (greed, corruption, or ressentiment), or ethnocentrism (idolatry or cultural imperialism).

Independence and Religion?

What is most remarkable is that we can find in some traditions, such as some of those indicated above, suggestions that religion is *not* to be identified with but is to be distinguished from precisely these sectors of life, even if it is to be related to these areas as an independent factor. Indeed, it is also to be distinguished from those peculiar "new sectors" of complex civilization that are beyond our present discussion: education, medicine, technology, and the like. Religion sometimes claims to be based on something other than these and, indeed, to be capable of reforming these and experimenting with new methods of meeting basic human needs. Where that begins to happen, we are on the brink of a social change more profound and more enduring than anything that the familial, political, economic, and cultural sectors can bring about on their own.

We can, perhaps, see this at long distance more easily than we can see it up close. When Buddhism entered China, its monks challenged the family structure with their celibacy, the political regime with their notion that the Buddha was higher than the emperor, the economy with their begging, and the hegemony of classical Chinese culture with their translations of Sanskrit texts. They created an independent sector, at least for a time, until the

Confucian renaissance incorporated and partially domesti-
cated their contribution. Similarly, when Protestant missionaries entered India, the clergy challenged arranged marriage
with a vision of love marriage; they argued for a government of
law, not of maharajas; they claimed that the caste system, especially the servitude of outcaste peoples, was evil; and they
made both Western science and classical Hindu texts (that had
long been accessible only to the elites) available to all. These
influences had a wide impact, eventuating in the Hindu renaissance. The movements initiated by Mahatma Gandhi and taken
up in a distinctive way in another context by Martin Luther
King, Jr., where the churches were the only arena of voluntary
social space for some, are the late consequence. In these and
other cases, we find the formation of an independent sector
based in comparable religious traditions to be the basis of both
social redefinition and social renewal.

It is not, however, only *explicitly* religious groups that contribute to such a redefinition or renewal. Many people who feel
they have "outgrown" the church or synagogue or temple as they
knew it in their youth or who are victims of incompetent or
arrogant religious instruction or leadership invest a similar
kind of moral intensity and spiritual creativity in things that,
today, are considered nonreligious. Counseling services, PTAs,
and community improvement committees, advocacy groups
and collectors clubs, and even foundations and political parties
are kept vibrant by those commitments, convictions, and principles that echo profound religious sensibility and thereby preserve the moral rudders of civilization. Indeed, it is almost an
axiom that to get something done in a community without the
use of coercive authority, get the granddaughter of a rabbi, the
son of a preacher, the nephew of a priest, or the niece of a
missionary to organize it.

We do not yet know what the current resurgence of interest in the independent sector means. Neither are we sure
whether or not it is coupled with the new vigor that seems to be
evident among evangelical and Catholic Christians and among
several other of the world's religions (Kopf, 1969; Koyama, 1984;
Sanneh, 1989; Stackhouse, 1982). It may be only a rather pale

ethical echo of earlier religious commitment, essentially a negative resistance to "statist" approaches to social problems without a positive basis.

That is not altogether bad. The Hebrew scriptures say that "the sins of the fathers are visited unto the children unto the third and fourth generations." It is also true that the blessings of the elders are visited unto the subsequent generations for a good many years. And much social good can come of it. Many people are helped and much evil is avoided. Moral character, ethical commitment, and principled behavior can carry us for decades, perhaps centuries. They have a validity and integrity of their own.

Without religious renewal, however, the zeal for the kind of commitment, principle, and service that opens the social space on which independence feeds begins to run dry. It loses its inner coherence because the transcendent foundation is lost. Beneficiaries of the blessings of generations begin to depend on agendas written less on the deepest foundations for moral existence than on the preferences of familial, political, economic, or cultural authorities as they stand. Slowly but surely the independent sector becomes no longer independent but dependent—generating ideological support for things as they are, without an independent reference point by which to assess and guide society from the inside.

If that happens, we shall lose the social space so painfully won and forfeit the distinctive contributions of a tradition that both frees and calls to a discipline of voluntary service. It would be a great loss.

References

Adams, J. L. *On Being Human Religiously*. (M. L. Stackhouse, ed.) Boston: Beacon Press, 1976.

Adams, J. L. *Voluntary Associations*. (R. Engel, ed.) Chicago: Exploration Press, 1986a.

Adams, J. L. *The Prophethood of All Believers*. (G. Beach, ed.) Boston: Beacon Press, 1986b.

Berger, P., and Neuhaus, R. *To Empower People: The Role of Mediating Structures in Public Policy*. Washington, D.C.: American Enterprise Institute, 1977.

Evans, S., and Boyte, H. *Free Spaces: The Sources of Democratic Change in America.* New York: Harper & Row, 1988.

Fagan, P. W. *Bibliography on Human Rights.* Washington, D.C.: Library of Congress, 1980.

Kopf, D. *British Orientalism and the Bengal Renaissance: The Dynamics of Indian Modernization.* Berkeley: University of California Press, 1969.

Koyama, K. *Mount Fuji and Mount Sinai.* Maryknoll, N.Y.: Orbis, 1984.

Kuyper, A. *Lectures on Calvinism.* Grand Rapids, Mich.: Eerdmans, 1931.

Levitt, T. *The Third Sector.* New York: AMACOM, 1973.

NCCB (National Conference of Catholic Bishops). "A Word of Solidarity (with the Churches in Eastern Europe)." *Origins,* 1989.

Robertson, D. B. (ed.). *Voluntary Associations: The Study of Groups in Free Societies.* Atlanta: John Knox Press, 1966.

Sanneh, L. *Translating the Message: The Missionary Impact on Culture.* Maryknoll, N.Y.: Orbis, 1989.

Stackhouse, M. L. "The World Religions and Political Democracy." *Religion and Society,* 1982, *29,* 19–49.

Stackhouse, M. L. *Creeds, Society and Human Rights.* Grand Rapids, Mich.: Eerdmans, 1984.

Stackhouse, M. L. "Politics and Religion" and "Christian Social Movements." In M. Eliade and others, eds., *Encyclopedia of Religion.* New York: Macmillan, 1987.

Stackhouse, M. L. *Public Theology and Political Economy.* Grand Rapids, Mich.: Eerdmans, 1988.

Troeltsch, E. *The Social Teaching of the Christian Churches.* (O. Wyon, trans.) New York: Harper & Row, 1931. (Originally published 1914.)

Weber, M. *The Religion of China.* (H. Gerth, trans.) New York: Free Press, 1951. (Originally published 1921.)

Weber, M. *The Religion of India.* (H. Gerth and D. Martindale, trans.) New York: Free Press, 1951. (Originally published 1920.)

Weber, M. *Economy and Society.* (G. Roth and others, eds.; E. Fishoff and others, trans.) New York: Bedminster Press, 1968. (Originally published 1914–1922.)

Chapter 3

Peter Dobkin Hall

The History of
Religious Philanthropy
in America

Of the 916 projects listed in the 1986–87 compendium of research in progress compiled by INDEPENDENT SECTOR
(Hodgkinson, 1988), only 43 (4.7 percent) deal specifically with
religion. Only 2 (1.5 percent) of the 130 working papers produced by the "flagship" nonprofit research enterprise (Program
on Nonprofit Organizations, 1988) specifically address religion
or religious organizations, and of these, only one deals with
American religious organizations, doing so in terms of the
technical question of how churches are treated under the
federal tax code.* Daphne Layton's (1987) listing of 2,195 books
and articles on philanthropy and voluntarism includes only 57
(2.1 percent) that deal specifically with religion.

Quite clearly, the scholarship of philanthropy has given
religion remarkably short shrift. This deficiency is particularly
striking in view of the fact that churches and denominationally
tied institutions command nearly two-thirds of all the contribu-

* The research on which this paper is based was made possible by the
support of the Lilly Endowment and the Program on Non-Profit Organizations, Yale University. I am especially grateful to Michael Lipsky, whose 1985
PONPO seminar first made me aware of the distinctions between eligibility
and need-based criteria, and to Charles Perrow, whose recent work on the
AIDS crisis illuminated for me some of the internal contradictions of modern philanthropy. My greatest debt is to Carl Milofsky, whose work gave me
the courage to articulate ideas that when first conceived, seemed too unset-
tling to put in writing.

tions, 34 percent of all volunteer labor, 19 percent of all the wage earners, and 10 percent of all wages and salaries in the nonprofit sector (Rudney, 1987).

This oversight is curious, not only because of the quantitative significance but also because of a number of compelling qualitative reasons for treating religious organizations as a part of the nonprofit sector: As organizations, they share many processual and structural similarities with secular nonprofits, in particular a strong mission orientation; historically, secular and religious nonprofits have been closely associated; and in the contemporary setting, there is suggestive evidence that churches play an important role in stimulating nonreligious voluntarism whose impact is community-wide.

Why has religion been overlooked in efforts to understand voluntarism and philanthropy? Part of the answer may involve the fact that few scholars are likely to possess firsthand knowledge of what churches do and how they do it. The nature of funding for nonprofit research may also play a role, since less than 2 percent of foundation grants are awarded to religious organizations and of these, only a minuscule proportion for studying religion (Clinton, 1987). The organization of nonprofits as an industry may also play a role in diminishing attention to the role of religious nonprofits: of the 600 members of INDEPENDENT SECTOR in 1985, only 25 (4 percent) were identifiable as religious organizations, including 10 nondenominational but religiously oriented agencies, 5 Jewish, 4 Catholic, 4 Lutheran, 1 each from the Methodists, Evangelicals, Churches of Christ, and Seventh-day Adventists (INDEPENDENT SECTOR, 1987). Notably absent were such major denominations as the Baptists (the nation's third largest denomination), the United Church of Christ (fifth largest), the Mormons (seventh largest), Eastern Orthodox (eighth largest), and the Episcopalians (ninth largest). Interestingly, the amount of research devoted to religious nonprofits is roughly proportional to the representation of religious organizations in INDEPENDENT SECTOR (IS) and to the number of foundations that have religion as a field of interest.

While it is clear that the mainline nonprofits have had

little interest in religion, it is equally evident that religion has had little interest in the mainline nonprofits. When the great circling of the wagons of nonprofitdom began in the 1960s, the churches, on the whole, stayed clear of the trade association impulse. Some may have believed themselves immune from the sanctions that were being imposed on foundations. Others may have found the trade associations' stands in favor of such things as affirmative action, participatory governance, and public accountability incompatible with their own convictions. Whatever the cause, the aloofness of religious organizations complemented secular scholarship's indifference to the role of religion in American philanthropy and voluntarism.

The Origins of Modern Philanthropy

The wariness with which organized religion and organized philanthropy regard each other today has deep historical roots. These involve not only the contention of religious and secular institutions for "the high moral ground" but, more fundamentally, differences of conviction and outlook. In order to grasp these differences, it is necessary to review briefly the origins of organized philanthropy in America and its relation to organized religion.

Modern American philanthropy came into being in the last third of the nineteenth century, when the dislocations incident to rapid industrialization and urbanization outstripped the capacity of existing institutions to care for the poor and dependent. In particular, the rising tide of crime, violence, and social disorder in the years 1877–1893 led many Americans to think seriously about the ties between progress and poverty.

To some, it seemed quite clear that traditional forms of charity and almsgiving were not only inadequate to the task of alleviating misery but actually aggravated it. The strongest proponents of this viewpoint were those influenced by Darwinist social theories, especially those of the British political economist Herbert Spencer. Spencer's leading American spokesperson also happened to be the nation's wealthiest industrialist, Andrew Carnegie. It was Carnegie who gave clearest expression to the modern conception of "scientific" philanthropy in his famous 1889 essay "Wealth." "Those who would administer [wealth] wisely," wrote Carnegie ([1889] 1962c, pp. 26–27),

> must indeed be wise; for one of the serious obstacles to the improvement of our race is indiscriminate charity. It were better for mankind that the millions of the rich were thrown into the sea than so spent as to encourage the slothful, the drunken, the unworthy. Of every thousand dollars spent in so-called charity today, it is probable that nine hundred and fifty dollars is unwisely spent—so spent, indeed, as to produce the very evils which it hopes to mitigate or cure.
>
> The best means of benefiting the community is to place within its reach the ladders upon which the aspiring can rise—free libraries, parks, and means of recreation, by which men are helped in body and mind; works of art, certain to give pleasure and improve the public taste; and public institutions of various kinds, which will improve the general condition of the people; in this manner returning their surplus wealth to the mass of their fellows in the forms best calculated to do them lasting good.

Carnegie's radical scheme called for nothing less than the use of private wealth to attack the causes of poverty and dependency rather than merely using it to alleviate their symptoms.

Carnegie's proposals were based on a carefully reasoned Darwinist reinterpretation of society and the place and purposes of the individual within it. As a Darwinist, Carnegie viewed the life of the community as a collective phenomenon, in which the struggle for existence, more than merely ensuring the survival of the fittest, created a hierarchy of relationships of mutual dependency. The "men of affairs," as he referred to the administrators of industry and its wealth, were inevitably tied to and dependent on their employees, as their employees were dependent on them (Carnegie, [1886] 1962a). In this setting, "the life of the race"—the good of the community—involved society's capacity for continuous self-renewal, through the preservation of conditions that encouraged individual initiative continuously to create and re-create enterprises. In this process, philanthropy played a vitally important role, not only by "placing within their reach ladders upon which the aspiring can rise" but also by continuously redistributing wealth. Carnegie's comment "he who dies rich dies disgraced" was more than an injunction to charity; it was a pragmatic acknowledgment of the extent to which economic and social progress depended on the circulation of wealth, and he took it seriously enough to suggest the imposition of confiscatory inheritance taxes and progressive income taxation.

Carnegie's view of society, which was the framework that shaped his ideas about philanthropy, rested on quantitatively based concepts of efficiency (Chandler, 1977). Just as in his business he had pioneered cost accounting, so in looking to the larger problems of society, he sought to relate calculable inputs to calculable outputs. From this economistic approach followed a number of significant departures from traditional charitable practice. Since values of philanthropic investments were to be calculated in terms of their measurable effectiveness, philanthropists must, of necessity, shift their attention from the symptoms of poverty and dependency (suffering) to the causes. This in turn implied a shift of attention from alleviating the suffering of individuals to the impersonal and abstract problems of systems and institutions. Finally, it implied a shift from attending to the subjectively defined *needs* of individuals to the *eligibility* of individuals for assistance: Were they "worthy" or "unworthy," were they potentially good investment vehicles?

Despite their radicalism, Carnegie's ideas were, on the whole, well received. This doubtless stemmed from the extent to which they meshed with the thinking of those who, by the 1880s, had given the greatest attention to the problems of maintaining social and economic order in this especially turbulent period. Certainly the most important of these groups were the "charity organization societies," which, beginning in the late 1870s, were

striving to rationalize charitable services and promote cooperation among charitable agencies.

Though influenced by social Darwinism, this movement's
preoccupation with "lavish, uninformed, and aimless" charity
that "encouraged pauperism and imposture" was actually an
outgrowth of the secularized social reform activities of the antebellum decades (Warner, 1908). These had originated in a religious movement, the second Great Awakening, which had
sought to redeem America from "those Errors in matters of
Religion and Government, and that declention in manners,
which so much prevail, and which greatly endanger the well-
being of the State" ("An Act for the Support of Missionaries,"
[1798] 1953, p. 266; Foster, 1961). Over time, these efforts had
become increasingly secular in emphasis, focusing less on religion than on character formation. The Bible and tract, moral,
missionary, and sabbatarian societies of the 1820s gave rise to
nondenominational temperance, abolitionist, and young men's
associations, as well as more focused activities directed to the
poor and disabled, to public health, and to the abolition of
slavery (Ryan, 1983). Despite this secular shift, the central theme
of the antebellum reform remained moralistic: Poverty, dependency, and ill health were products of defective character,
failures of "moral prophylaxis." Since democratic government
was, by definition, incapable of exercising a moral influence, the
role of voluntary associations was to supply the moral dimension that would otherwise be lacking.

By the 1850s, voluntary charitable efforts were so ubiq-
uitous that reformers had begun to worry about inefficiency,
waste, and duplication of effort (Eliot, 1845, pp. 149–150).
Underlying this economistic rhetoric, however, was a more profound anxiety about the charitable elite's failure to stem the tide
of democracy (Fredrickson, 1965). The United States Sanitary
Commission, a private organization to which the government in
1862 entrusted coordination of relief, sanitary inspection of
army camps, and provision of nurses, hospitals, and ambulance
services, became the paradigm for the reformulation of charitable activities in the postwar period.

Drawing its members from among "men brought up in

luxury, with all the advantages of high and generous culture," the commission was less concerned with the alleviation of suffering than with reducing the costs of the war for the taxpayer and preserving the soldier or "producer" when he "returned to the industrial pursuits of civil life" (Fredrickson, 1965, p. 104). Even more important than this, the members of the commission regarded its work as "a matter of teaching order and discipline":

> Men like Bellows, Strong, and Stille welcomed the sufferings and sacrifices of the hour because they believed they served the cause of discipline in a broader sense than demanded by purely military requirements. An unruly society, devoted to individual freedom, might be in the process of learning that discipline and subordination were good in themselves, and the commissioners wanted to play their role in teaching this lesson [Fredrickson, 1965, p. 105].

In line with this, the commission

> regarded the spontaneous benevolence of the American people, not as something embodied and expressed in their own work, but as a great danger to the discipline of the army which it was their business to limit and control. The desire of people at home to bring comfort and relief to the soldiers was regarded by the conservatives on the commission in much the way they had regarded the reform impulse before the war. If not limited and controlled, it would be a danger to established institutions [Fredrickson, 1965, p. 106].

The charity organization societies were based on the same rationale as the Sanitary Commission and, in many cases, were set up by veterans of the commission. Like its wartime predecessor, a charity organization society was

a semi-official body of prominent citizens who inspected public institutions such as poor houses and
work houses—much in the way the Sanitary Com-
missioners had inspected the camps—and made
recommendations, based on "scientific" principles.
Like the commission, it placed members of the
upper classes in positions of influence which were
immune from the pressures of democratic politics.
If the Sanitary Commission had been devoted to
military efficiency at the expense of purely humanitarian ends, the State Charities Aid Association
was apparently more interested in the efficiency of
the labor force than in the relief of suffering. It
opposed public relief as "undermining the self-
respect of recipients, fostering a spirit of dependence opposed to self-support, and interfering
with the laws governing wage and labor" [Fredrick-
son, 1965, p. 212].

Not surprisingly, the charity organizers found social Darwinism
a congenial doctrine; and it became the common ground for
alliances with pragmatic "men of affairs" like Carnegie, whose
vast wealth could be harnessed to higher purposes than mere
conspicuous consumption.

The third strand of modern American philanthropy led
from the thought of the classic political economists of the late
eighteenth and early nineteenth centuries. Beginning with Mal-
thus's 1798 "Essay on Population," English social thinkers had
devoted considerable attention to the problems of poor relief,
the need for reforming the Elizabethan poor law, and the conditions of industrial labor. Though the political economists, who
upheld free trade and abhorred government interference, and
the philanthropists, who advocated government action to protect factory operatives, were at loggerheads for decades, by the
1870s, the spokespersons for "the dismal science" and the "humanity mongers" had drawn together (Warner, 1908, pp. 3–32).
Once again, social Darwinism was the medium of accommodation between these two seemingly incompatible viewpoints. The

communitarian and perfectionist concerns of the philanthropists meshed with the Darwinists' interests in the "life of the race" and evolution. Their particular meeting ground was the process of selection, which in human societies was clearly subject to rational control. Both agreed that natural selection was "not only a harsh, but an expensive way of improving the species"; and both came to agree that by rationally ordering the environment, the process of selection could become more efficient and less costly (Warner, 1908, p. 25).

The significance of this accommodation was more institutional than intellectual. In the 1860s, political economy was the concern of only a handful of academics. Essentially a deductive philosophical enterprise, the field had languished, in large part because of the resistance of college benefactors, many of whom were staunch advocates of tariff protection of American industry, to its free trade doctrines (Mason, 1982; Buck, 1965). Social Darwinism, in providing a rationale for empirical and inductive social and economic research, created an opportunity for academic careerists; the economic and social crisis of the 1870s underlined the importance of this shift of emphasis. The formation of the American Social Science Association in 1868 was the first tangible sign of the eagerness of political economists to make themselves indispensable in "fighting the wilderness, physical and moral" that Americans found themselves facing in the decades following the Civil War (Eliot, 1869; Haskell, 1977). The creation of this cadre of highly trained, university-based professional specialists was the cornerstone in the foundation of "scientific" philanthropy.

When social Darwinist ideology, industrial wealth, and academic expertise came together in the 1890s, modern American philanthropy was born. Underwritten by the millionocracy and guided by the academic enterprise that the industrialists so generously funded, philanthropy was part and parcel of the broader movement that one historian has called "the corporate reorganization of American life" (Sklar, 1984). Though employing a rhetoric of benevolence, "scientific" philanthropy's desire to put charity on a businesslike basis was anything but humanitarian. Far more concerned with efficiency and "race progress" than with alleviating suffering, one leading writer on philanthropic subjects (Warner, 1908, pp. 23–24) commented:

> The most obvious result of charity as a selective force has been to lengthen the lives of the individuals cared for. There are many who believe it to be in and of itself a uniformly desirable result. They hold that no spark of human life can be extinguished without greater indirect loss than the direct gain which comes in freedom from the necessity of supporting the individual. They would care with all tenderness for the most misshapen, physically and morally, until death could no longer be postponed. As the author has stood by the beds of consumptive or syphilitic children, he has wondered if it was a kindness to keep life in the pain-racked body. Cure was out of the question so far as medical science now knows, and one wonders why days of pain should be added to days of pain. The same questions recur as one passes through the incurable wards of an almshouse, especially as one studies the cases of cancer patients. The answer of religion to such questions is easy, and it seems very sure that without religious incentive we should not have entertained our present views regarding the sanctity of human life.

According to this writer, because religion stood in the way of putting the unfit out of their misery, the only alternative to extermination as a cure for pauperism was "preventative measures." "[I]n proportion as the burden of the dependent has increased and the standard of care risen, the search has spread from symptoms to causes, from causes to conditions of poverty, and culminated in a concerted demand for prevention rather than relief" (Warner, 1908, p. 25).

Such preventative measures included forbidding the marriage of insane and idiotic people, those afflicted with syphilis and gonorrhea, and epileptics. The same writer also urged the castration and "permanent isolation" of the "essentially unfit":

> The movement to establish philanthropic monas-
> taries and nunneries for the feeble-minded is be-
> coming the substitute for natural selection. The
> prevention of marriage of the unfit, the steriliza-
> tion of criminals, and the custodial care of the
> imbecile are initial steps in prevention—that the
> unfit may cease to be produced and to pro-
> duce. . . . Certain it is, that while charity may not
> cease to shield the children of misfortune, it must,
> to an ever increasing extent, reckon with the laws of
> heredity, and do what it can to check the spreading
> curse of race deterioration [1908, p. 31].

Though the rise of fascism made this kind of thinking unfashionable, it is important to remember that through the 1930s, such social Darwinist brutalism remained perfectly respectable and continued to dominate the thinking of many grantmakers and the charities that benefited from their largesse.

Religion and Philanthropy

Amos Warner's ill-concealed contempt for "the unfit" and for those who would care for "the most misshapen, physically and morally" not only expressed the sentiments of the emerging cadre of secular philanthropists but those of a Protestant mainstream. As early as the 1850s, a vigorous pamphlet battle had been waged between churchmen who favored institutionally based "scientific" approaches to social problems and those who argued that "the work of the real disciples of Christ must be performed by them individually, and not by the church. The love for men which ought to glow in the bosom of individual Christians could never dwell in a corporation or ecclesiastical organization" (Smith, 1957, p. 166).

The institutionalists of the 1850s became the Sanitary Commission boosters of the 1860s, who by the 1870s were setting up charity organizations societies and arguing, as did Henry Ward Beecher, that any workingman unable to support his family on a dollar a day was morally deficient and that railroad strikers should be subdued with "bullets and bayonets, canister and grape" (Cross, 1967, p. ix). Anti-institutionalism never really achieved any large-scale organizational expression; it merely remained as a persistent but troubling reminder that the mission of the church might not be as easily translatable into programs of social action in the world as some seemed to believe.

To say that this spiritual emphasis did not achieve organizational expression is not to say that it was without significance. The younger clergy—those entering pulpits during the turbulent period between the panics of 1873 and 1893—as well as many in the laity, responded to the tide of suffering and disorder as a distinctly spiritual challenge. Walter Rauschenbusch, who served an immigrant congregation in New York's Hell's Kitchen in the 1890s, described the impact of seeing good men go into disreputable lines of employment and respectable widows consent to live with men who would support them and their children. One could hear human virtue cracking and crumbling all around (Rauschenbusch, 1964, p. 238). Confronting suffering as an immediate human issue rather than as a set of textbook abstractions or newspaper alarums forced ministers like Rauschenbusch to rethink their theology, to ponder the meaning of charity, and to recast the role of the church and its ministry as a social force.

Certainly one of the most touching and widely read accounts of this process is Charles M. Shelton's novel *In His Steps* ([1897] n.d.). Its protagonist, the Reverend Henry Maxwell, presides over a wealthy inner-city congregation. In the midst of a Sunday service, a "dusty, worn, shabby-looking young man" appeared in Maxwell's church. This unemployed printer challenged the parishioners:

> "I was wondering. . . if what you call following Jesus
> is the same thing as what He taught. What did He
> mean when He said: 'Follow me!'" Here the man

turned and looked up at the pulpit. "The minister said that it is necessary for the disciples of Jesus to follow His steps, and he said these steps are obedience, faith, love, and imitation. But I did not hear him tell you what that meant, especially the last step. What do you Christians mean by following the steps of Jesus?

"I've tramped through this city for three days trying to find a job. In all that time I've not had a word of sympathy or comfort. . . . What I feel puzzled about is — what is meant by following Jesus? What do you mean when you sing 'I'll go with Him, with Him, all the Way?' Do you mean that you are suffering and denying yourselves? Are you trying to save lost and suffering humanity as I understand Jesus did? What do you mean by it?

"Somehow I get puzzled when I see so many Christians living in luxury and singing 'Jesus, I my cross have taken, all to leave and follow Thee,' and remember how my wife died in a tenement in New York City, gasping for air and asking God to take the little girl too. Of course I don't expect you people can prevent everyone from dying of starvation, lack of proper nourishment, and tenement air. But what does following Jesus mean? I understand that Christian people own a good many of the tenement houses. A member of the church was the owner of the one where my wife died, and I have wondered if following Jesus all the way was true in his case" [pp. 16–19].

The tramp then fell forward and died on the communion table while everyone stood in horrified silence. This event, as Shelton noted, was destined to make "a remarkable change" in the "definition of Christian discipleship" for the Reverend Maxwell and certain members of his congregation — as well as for the community in which they lived.

Though this immensely popular book proceeded to spin

a rather fantastic millenarian tale in which businessmen, newspaper editors, lawyers, and doctors began putting their Christian principles into practice and ultimately reforming American society, there was nothing imaginary about its starting point—the stark confrontation between Christian ideals and the realities of suffering. As Shelton took pains to point out, the moralistic pronouncements of the social Darwinists and the charity organization society advocates simply did not apply to the immediate human realities of suffering. Blaming the poor for their poverty in an economy in which human destinies were so profoundly affected by technological change and global markets simply did not make sense. Explaining the causes of poverty "scientifically" and formulating programs for its eradication did nothing to alleviate the hunger, fear, and humiliation of those who suffered from it.

A minister with a background in social work, Shelton directly challenged the social Darwinism of philanthropists like Carnegie. Serving as a minister of a Congregational church in Topeka, Kansas, a state where the catastrophic decline of commodity prices after 1873 had impoverished a once staunchly Republican farming population and converted it into a bulwark of Populism, Shelton knew that poverty and dependency were more than a matter of moral deficiency. For him, as for many others who knew the facts of poverty firsthand, the impersonal and parsimonious solutions of Warner and the other "scientific" philanthropists made no sense in terms of the facts of poverty.

But more to the point, Shelton and others found it difficult to reconcile the "scientific" philanthropists' view of the "essentially unfit" to their reading of the Scriptures. In the parable of the Good Samaritan and in other texts, Christ seemed to be demanding a kind of brotherly love that did not calculate, that did not draw distinctions between the "worthy" and the "unworthy," the "fit and the "unfit." Love of one's neighbor, like one's love of God, had to be absolute and unconditional.

This reading of the Gospels had a number of rather startling implications. On the practical side, it implied that one could not separate one's work in the world from one's beliefs. This was precisely the point Christ seemed to be making in Mark

X:17–30, when he drew a distinction between obeying the commandments, a merely legal exercise, and faith. Shelton,
Rauschenbusch, and their contemporaries were sophisticated
enough to understand that Christ was not merely condemning
wealth and urging the virtues of poverty. Rather, he was asserting
the primacy of spiritual over worldly obligations. More importantly, he was challenging his questioner to make a choice between one and the other; and as the subsequent discussion with
the disciples indicates, it was the capacity to make that choice, to
love truly both God and one's neighbor, that constituted the core
of "walking in His steps." This was, of course, the very choice that
confronted Shelton's protagonist, Rev. Henry Maxwell.

Shelton, Rauschenbusch, and the other ministers who
rejected "scientific" philanthropy were not alone in believing
that Christian charity involves far more than the economical
provision of services. As, if not more, important was the creation
of a community of feeling, a set of human bonds, which are in
themselves perhaps more valuable than the services themselves.
Jane Addams suggested as much in her 1892 essay "The Subjec-
tive Necessity for Social Settlements" ([1910] 1961, pp. 95–97),
when she wrote of "the impulse to share the lives of the poor, the
desire to make social service, irrespective of propaganda, express the spirit of Christ."

> Christianity has to be revealed, and embodied in
> the line of social progress is a corollary to the
> simple proposition that man's action is found in his
> social relationships in the way in which he connects
> with his fellows; that his motives for action are the
> zeal and affection with which he regards his fellows.
> By this simple process was created a deep enthusi-
> asm for humanity, which regarded man as at once
> the organ and the object of revelation; and by this
> process came about the wonderful fellowship, the
> true democracy of the early Church, that so capti-
> vates the imagination. . . . The spectacle of the
> Christians loving all men was the most astounding
> Rome had ever seen. They were eager to sacrifice

themselves for the weak, for children, and for the aged; they identified themselves with slaves and did not avoid the plague; they longed to share the common lot that they might receive constant revelation. It was a new treasure which the early Christians added to the sum of all treasures, a joy hitherto unknown in the world—the joy of finding the Christ which lieth in each man, but which no man can unfold save in fellowship.

It is difficult to imagine Addams accommodating herself to the economistic motives and methods of "scientific" philanthropy. She described her attempts at cooperation with Chicago's newly organized Bureau of Organized Charities in the bitterest terms, telling how, in attempting to conform to its "carefully received instructions," she had refused relief to a shipping clerk who had lost his job (Addams [1910] 1961, pp. 122–123). A white-collar worker forced to work outside in the winter as a manual laborer, the man contracted pneumonia and died. "I have never lost trace of the two little children he left behind him," Addams wrote (p. 123), "though I cannot see them without a bitter consciousness that it was at their expense I learned that life cannot be administered by definite rules and regulations; that wisdom to deal with a man's difficulties comes only through some knowledge of his life and habits as a whole; and that to treat an isolated episode is almost sure to invite blundering."

In spite of this experience, Addams could never wholly reject the ideas of the "scientific" philanthropists, for the sheer magnitude of the problems she faced seemed to require a wholesale rather than a retail approach to charity. As Henry Steele Commager so artfully put it (1961, p. xiv): "More and more she came to feel like Alice with the Red Queen: no matter how fast she ran, she was still in the same place; the poverty, the slums, the crime and vice, the misgovernment, the illiteracy, the exploitation, the inhumanity of man to man—all these were still there." Overwhelmed, she persuaded herself that "scientific" philanthropy could be humanized, and the union of the two traditions was symbolized in 1905, with her election as president of the National Conference on Charities and Corrections and the merger of the journals of the charity organization and settlement house movements into *Charity and the Commons*.

Though Addams never ceased to believe that "scientific" philanthropy could be humanized, in her eagerness to be politically and organizationally effective, she may have traded away those aspects of her work that made it so distinctive. As welfare historian Michael Katz (1986, pp. 160–162) points out, in exchange for the Progressive's adoption of a social legislation plank authored by Addams (who also seconded Theodore Roosevelt's nomination as the party's presidential candidate), "Addams and her colleagues decided to swallow their liberal convictions and accepted the convention's refusal to seat black delegates, and they set aside their pacifism when they failed to protest the platform's calls for rearmament." Later efforts to reassert these moral claims came too late. By the 1920s, "social work" as a profession carried on in the framework of public bureaucracies and privately funded universities and social service agencies had supplanted personal and religious commitment as the basis for charitable activity.

Although its rhetoric owed much to Addams, in practice social welfare work as it emerged in the 1920s was more firmly rooted in the economistic than the religious traditions of charity. This is especially clear in volumes like *Recent Social Trends*, the 1933 compendium that, among other things, sought to summarize the social welfare achievements of the previous three decades. The chapter on "privately supported social work," written by Sydnor H. Walker of the Rockefeller Foundation (1933, p. 1169), was sharply critical of charity in the 1890s for its "marked obtuseness to the existence of any personal feelings or of a defined personality among the recipients of social work." While asserting that "the private social agencies were approaching the old problems of poverty and delinquency in a new positive spirit," Walker's use of a humanized rhetoric fails to mask the fact that the old economism was alive and well. The chapter devotes most of its attention to standards, coordination, centralization, and other professional issues.

By the 1930s, it was quite clear that the religious spirit that had informed much of the charity of the 1890s had succumbed to mere fact-finding. According to Michael Katz (1986, pp. 170–171), "In the end the reformers' path to professionalism tied the management of social change to the development of their own careers. Along with university based social scientists, who had faced similar career problems a few decades earlier, they made the trip from 'advocacy to objectivity' by resting the case for their authority and importance on the capacity of neutral experts to find technical solutions to complex problems. Somehow, those neutral technical solutions usually supported whoever it was that paid the bill."

Religion and Philanthropy in the Postliberal Era

The gradual assumption of social welfare responsibilities by government that began with the Progressive Movement of the early twentieth century obscured the differences between religion and philanthropy that so concerned Americans a century ago. Christian conceptions of brotherly love and secular conceptions of charity and philanthropy have become almost indistinguishable. And yet, beneath the rhetoric, tensions have remained: The "literature gap" referred to at the beginning of this chapter is only one symptom of a far more fundamental unease that, in recent years, has begun to reemerge.

In the 1960s, an increasing federal commitment to social welfare and health care services, combined with the use of private nonprofit vehicles for providing services, fueled demands for greater efficiency and effectiveness and the elimination of duplication, waste, and overlap. The spiraling inflation of the 1970s and the budgetary austerity of the 1980s not only forced care-giving agencies to do more with less but to justify their programs, procedures, and policies to an increasingly competitive array of public and private funders. On the organizational level, evaluation and assessment, strategic analysis and planning, managerial professionalization, and sophisticated accounting systems were put in place in the hope of making philanthropy more businesslike. On the system level, ambitious plans were drafted to encourage cooperation, cost and facilities sharing, and a rational division of funding, labor, and markets in the hope of eliminating duplication and waste.

Though few failed to give lip service to efficiency and effectiveness as ideals, efforts to restructure voluntary organizations have been less than successful, often bringing about a rediscovery of the long-buried differences between "scientific" and religious philanthropy. Rationalization, whether on the system or the organizational level, has been especially problematic for denominationally tied social service and health care agencies, where commitment to services has always been more important than budgetary considerations and where quality of service has tended to be defined in less than calculable ways. The supporters of one Pennsylvania hospital that bowed out of efforts to create a regional health care system a decade ago succinctly summarized the issue: To Sacred Heart doctors and nurses, medical philosophy included more than higher degrees, a sharp scalpel, and a sharp mind. It included TLC—tender loving care. And the hospital became known for it. No matter what a patient's faith, a nun was supposed to visit every patient every day. Staffers saw the atmosphere as homey. Doctors, nurses, staff and patients were "a family": "'This hospital was known for tender loving care,' said one Sacred Heart doctor. That view meshed with Sacred Heart's religion. The hospital had 'the Guardian Angel flying over the building,' said one doctor. And Sacred Heart loyalists said that faith in God was what made for better medicine. At Sacred Heart, Msgr. Fink wrote, 'Faith and Science walked strongly forward.' Each was as important as the other" (Harrington, 1979, p. 9).

Though at first perceived as an essentially political effort by the denominations to maintain control of their institutions, it now seems increasingly clear that this debate over the qualitative distinctiveness of religious care giving was really a reiteration of the old debate between "scientific" philanthropy, with its economistic concerns and its preoccupation with the "worthiness" of clients, and religious philanthropy, which wanted to relieve suffering first and ask questions later. This became apparent as unhappiness with management professionalization and organizational and system restructuring spread from religiously tied to other kinds of organizations, particularly neighborhood and community-based voluntary agencies, which placed mission over methods (Weiss, 1981; Hunter, 1983; Friedman, 1986; Milofsky, 1988).

Though nonprofits scholarship has been dominated by economistic concerns with efficiency and effectiveness, an important literature that gives serious attention to the qualitative dimensions of philanthropy and voluntarism has begun to emerge. Though not explicitly addressing itself to the religious aspects of helping and care giving, this work in effect legitimates the religious contention that "brotherly love," the building of community and identity among both care givers and the cared for, is as important as the services provided. Interestingly, this body of literature has not developed merely in response to contemporary tensions between marketing and mission, but has come out of the effort to create a case-based theoretical understanding of organizations. Tracing its roots to Chester Barnard's classic, *The Functions of the Executive* (1939), this enterprise offers a view of organizations that is both richer and more complex than that offered by the economists and more compatible with the view of human behavior as ethically governed.

The purpose of organization theory was not to criticize the inefficiency of organizations but rather to point out that what had been considered inefficiencies were really central to their activities and might even comprise their raison d'être. Only recently, however, has organization theory begun to reconnect itself to more traditional concerns about social ethics and purposes, specifically addressing itself to contemporary efforts to make voluntary organizations more effective and efficient.

Few have been more eloquent than sociologist Carl Milofsky, who underlined the creation of community values and social bonds as positive and desirable outcomes of voluntary action. "Community is an ideology or abstraction that does not automatically develop in an area," Milofsky (1987, p. 288) has written, "it is a sense of identification with and commitment to a place, and must be constructed through the efforts of individual actors and organizations." More than merely articulating this broadened viewpoint, he sought out its historical antecedents, pointing out the extent to which social welfare pioneers like Jane Addams dissented from the narrow economism of the "scientific" philanthropists of her own time. Finally, Milofsky (1987, p. 291) has discerned the bureaucratic and community-based models of voluntary organizations as distinct and possibly incompatible ethical traditions:

> Roland Warren once argued that when thinking about social change people orient themselves toward one of two general values, which he characterized as "truth" and "love." The truth orientation, he explained, refers to "the impassioned conviction of the zealot," the person who is convinced that he has come upon some fundamental moral value and wishes to see it embedded in the warp and woof of events. The love orientation, in contrast, is used "roughly in the sense of the Latin *caritas* and the Greek *agape*, and 1 Corinthians. I am using it not in the affective sense, but in the appreciative sense as a relationship of infinite appreciation and respect, perhaps best expressed by Stoic and Jew and Christian alike in the concept that men are all brothers, being children of the same loving Father." Warren claimed that, in their purest form, these values tend to conflict with each other.

"Pragmatism, as opposed to truth and love," Milofsky (1987, p. 291) has written, "tends to produce certain distinctive organizational structures that close off broad-based participation and crystallize a division of labor in a way that reifies expertise."

Conclusion

Where does this leave us? It does seem clear that "scientific" philanthropy, public and private, did little more than sequester poverty and suffering, putting it out of sight and out of mind, and propagate the illusion that delegating the tasks of care giving to specialists and institutions absolved us of personal responsibility for the poor and dependent. But now the hungry, the homeless, and the incurably ill confront us daily, literally demanding that we respond personally to their evident needs. More jails and more police will not help. Nor can we expect that AIDS will solve the problem of poverty by exterminating the "unworthy" and "essentially unfit."

In pondering the problem of bridging the steadily widening chasm between the haves and the have-nots and the inadequacies of our methods, we would do well to consider the words with which Jacob Riis concluded *How the Other Half Lives* (1957, p. 226): "The sea of a mighty population, held in galling fetters, heaves uneasily in the tenements. . . . The gap between the classes in which it surges, unseen, unsuspected by the thoughtless, is widening day by day. No tardy enactment of law, no political expedient, can close it. Against all other dangers our system of government may offer defense and shelter; against this not. I know of but one bridge that will carry us over safe, a bridge founded upon justice and built of human hearts." The courage — the foolhardiness — needed for this was not then and is not now within the capacity of the calculating. Without discovering its religious roots, American philanthropy is unlikely to play a significant role in the building of such a bridge.

References

Addams, J. *Twenty Years at Hull House*. New York: New American Library, 1961. (Originally published 1910.)

"An Act for the Support of Missionaries to Preach the Gospel in the Northern, and Western Parts of the United States, and Among the Indian Tribes." In *The Public Records of the State of Connecticut*. Vol. 9. Hartford: State of Connecticut, 1953. (Originally published 1798.)

Barnard C. B. *The Functions of the Executive*. Cambridge, Mass.: Harvard University Press, 1939.

Buck, P. (ed.). *The Social Sciences at Harvard*. Cambridge, Mass.: Harvard University Press, 1965.

Carnegie, A. "An Employer's View of the Labor Question." In

E. C. Kirkland (ed.), *The Gospel of Wealth and Other Timely Essays*. Cambridge, Mass.: Harvard University Press, 1962a. (Originally published 1886.)

Carnegie, A. "Results of the Labor Struggle." In E. C. Kirkland (ed.), *The Gospel of Wealth and Other Timely Essays*. Cambridge, Mass.: Harvard University Press, 1962b. (Originally published 1887.)

Carnegie, A. "Wealth." In E. C. Kirkland (ed.), *The Gospel of Wealth and Other Timely Essays*. Cambridge, Mass.: Harvard University Press, 1962c. (Originally published 1889.)

Chandler, A. D. *The Visible Hand: The Managerial Revolution in American Business*. Cambridge, Mass.: Harvard University Press, 1977.

Clinton, J. "Trends in Foundation Giving." In *The Foundation Directory, Eleventh Edition*. New York: Foundation Center, 1987.

Commager, H. S. "Foreword." In J. Addams, *Twenty Years at Hull House*. New York: New American Library, 1961.

Cross, R. D. (ed.). *The Church and the City*. Indianapolis, Ind.: Bobbs-Merrill, 1967.

Eliot, C. W. "The New Education." *Atlantic Monthly*, 1869, *23*, 203ff.

Eliot, S. A. "Public and Private Charities in Boston." *North American Review*, 1845, *61*, 149ff.

Foster, C. I. *An Errand of Mercy: The Evangelical United Front, 1790–1837*. Chapel Hill: University of North Carolina Press, 1961.

Fredrickson, G. M. *The Inner Civil War: Northern Intellectuals and the Crisis of the Union*. New York: Harper & Row, 1965.

Friedman, M. "The Elusive Problem of Management Cooperation in the Performing Arts." In P. DiMaggio (ed.), *Nonprofit Enterprise and the Arts: Studies in Mission and Constraint*. New York: Oxford University Press, 1986.

Harrington, W. *The Hospital Memoirs*. Allentown, Pa.: Call Chronicle Newspapers, 1979.

Haskell, T. *The Emergence of Professional Social Science and the Nineteenth Century Crisis of Authority*. Urbana: University of Illinois Press, 1977.

Hodgkinson, V. (ed.). *Research in Progress, 1986–87: A National Compendium of Research Projects on Philanthropy, Voluntary Ac-

tion, and Not-for-Profit Activity. Washington, D.C.: INDEPEN-DENT SECTOR, 1988.

Hunter, S. "Failure Factors in Multi-Institutional Systems." *Health Care Management Review,* 1983, *8,* 2.

INDEPENDENT SECTOR, *Annual Report, 1986.* Washington, D.C.: INDEPENDENT SECTOR, 1987.

Katz, M. B. *In the Shadow of the Poorhouse: A Social History of Social Welfare in America.* New York: Basic Books, 1986.

Layton, D. N. *Philanthropy and Voluntarism: An Annotated Bibliography.* New York: The Foundation Center, 1987.

Mason, E. S. "The Harvard Department of Economics from the Beginning to World War II." *Quarterly Journal of Economics,* 1982, *97,* 386–433.

Milofsky, C. "Neighborhood-Based Organizations: A Market Analogy." In W. Powell (ed.), *The Nonprofit Sector: A Research Handbook.* New Haven, Conn.: Yale University Press, 1987.

Milofsky, C. (ed.). *Community Organizations: Studies in Resource Mobilization and Exchange.* New York: Oxford University Press, 1988.

Program on Non-Profit Organizations. *Research Report 6.* New Haven, Conn.: Program on Non-Profit Organizations, Yale University, 1988.

Rauschenbusch, W. *Christianity and the Social Crisis.* New York: Harper & Row, 1964.

Riis, J. *How the Other Half Lives.* New York: Sagamore Press, 1957. (Originally published 1892.)

Rudney, G. "The Scope and Dimensions of Nonprofit Activity." In W. W. Powell (ed.), *The Nonprofit Sector: A Research Handbook.* New Haven, Conn.: Yale University Press, 1987.

Ryan, M. P. *The Cradle of the Middle Class: The Family in Oneida County, New York, 1790–1865.* New York: Cambridge University Press, 1983.

Shelton, C. M. *In His Steps.* Springdale, Pa.: Whitaker House, n.d. (Originally published 1897.)

Sklar, M. J. "Periodization and Historiography: The Corporate Reconstruction of American Society, 1896–1914." Paper presented at the annual meeting of the Organization of American Historians, Los Angeles, 1984.

Smith, T. L. *Revivalism and Social Reform: American Protestantism on the Eve of the Civil War*. New York: Harper & Row, 1957.

Walker, S. H. "Privately Supported Social Welfare Work." In *Recent Social Trends in the United States*. New York: McGraw-Hill, 1933, pp. 1168–1223.

Warner, A. G. *American Charities*. New York: Crowell, 1908.

Weiss, J. A. "Substance versus Symbol in Administrative Reform: The Case of Human Services Coordination." *Policy Analysis*, 1981, 7, 21–45.

Chapter 4

Paul G. Schervish

Wealth and
the Spiritual Secret
of Money

They [the wealthy] get to the point where their money is
like their God. They've got to hoard it.
— Beverly Geiger (Miami)

I reject the notion that living at the lowest level is God's
intended solution. In many instances in life, we are
where we are because it was part of God's plan.
— Donald Mason (Atlanta)

Do not lay up for yourselves treasures on earth, where
moth and rust consume and where thieves break in and
steal, but lay up for yourselves treasures in heaven, where
neither moth nor rust break in and steal. For where your
treasure is, there will your heart be also.
— Matthew 6:19–21

An ever-expanding literature exhorts or documents the connection between religion and philanthropy, yet the *process* by which
religion actually induces charitable outcomes remains largely
unexamined.[1] In this chapter, I seek to take a modest first step in
this direction. My purpose is to take a fresh look at the fundamental meaning of wealth and religion and to explore how and
under what conditions religion opens the wealthy to a more

generous and encompassing care for others.* What is distinctive about the wealthy and their approach to the world? What is religion as a particular type of normative consciousness, and just what is it about religion—and certain nontheistic spiritualities—that helps to mobilize attention to the needs of others? In addressing these questions, I draw on the findings from the recently completed Study on Wealth and Philanthropy, in which intensive interviews were conducted with 130 millionaires distributed over twelve metropolitan areas.[2]

The leading question is how in fact religion contributes to translating the worldly empowerment of wealth into a strategic practice of philanthropy. The concomitance of religious and philanthropic commitment has been documented by a number of important surveys studying the activities of individuals (Hodgkinson and Weitzman, 1988) and religious congregations (Hodgkinson, Weitzman, and Kirsch, 1988). What remains to be explained is the inner logic of this connection, a concern, I am pleased to note, that is taken up in an important way by Wuthnow in his research on the virtue of compassion in human interactions.

I argue that religion or spirituality encourages philanthropy by explicitly linking givers to the concerns and needs of others. My analysis follows a three-step logic: (1) if *wealth* affords individuals the ability to have what they want (at least in the material realm) and (2) if *philanthropy* can be understood as the transformation of time and money from a pool of wealth into a disposable gift to others, (3) *religion*—as it takes form in what I call the spirituality of money—motivates or spurs philanthropy, in amount and type, by shaping the quality of the wants or desires among the wealthy. If the wealthy generally can have what they want, it is the realm of spirituality that directs their wants into a bond of care for others.

In the first section, I describe how wealth provides the

* I am grateful to the T. B. Murphy Foundation Charitable Trust for supporting the research reported here, to Andrew Herman, with whom I developed a number of the ideas in the paper, and to Ethan Lewis, who graciously and competently assisted in the preparation of this chapter.

basis for the wealthy to shape the world according to their desires. Although all members of society to some extent create the world around them, the wealthy are most able as individuals to exercise agency in determining what happens to and around them. In the second section, I explore the meaning of religion as a *tie* or *bond*, both to God and others. Religion or spirituality brings into the purview of the wealthy a set of wants or desires having to do with the welfare of others who live beyond their immediate horizons. This also helps explain the sometimes comparable effect of nontheistic forms of spirituality that encourage bonds of care between people. In the conclusion, I discuss the implication for how donors mobilize or transpose resources from a pool of wealth into disposable gifts for others. Although it does not always occur, the major positive effect of religious consciousness is its potential to affect not just the amount of giving but the quality of the care and involvement of the donor.

Where Your Treasure Is:
The Worldly Empowerment of Wealth

The first step in tracing the path through religion from wealth to philanthropy is to demarcate the distinctive characteristic of wealth in this context and to understand how it positions the wealthy in regard to the other two terms, religion and philanthropy. The most fundamental finding derived from the Study on Wealth and Philanthropy in regard to wealth is that at least in the material realm, the wealthy can have what they want. By this I do not mean that they become released from the laws of gravity or aging. Rather, in the dialectic of socialization and social construction, they are masters of social construction. As such, what the wealthy want and do for others is fused to what they want and do for themselves.

Freedom, Empowerment, and Hyperagency:
"Them with the gold makes the rules."

With varying degrees of explicitness, the wealthy describe the distinctive attribute of wealth as a reciprocal or twofold set of freedoms. The first is the freedom *from* necessity, especially from having to depend for their material well-being on people or circumstances outside their control. The second is the freedom *to* determine circumstances or at least to choose freely among those handed to them. "That the freedom to choose is a privilege," reflects Bradley Stark,[3] a thirty-two-year-old heir of a distinguished American family, "is the single most important fact. It's the nature of privilege itself." In everyday practice, the two forms of freedom go hand-in-hand and flow easily into each other. "What I do I want to do," says Paul Goetz, a Los Angeles philanthropist. "Money buys you complete mental freedom," adds Walter Adams, an exceptionally successful real estate speculator. "When you have money you can do whatever you want. You could buy the White House for yourself if you wanted to."

This attribute of freedom is a potent form of *empowerment*—the capacity of the wealthy to shape the world and themselves according to their wishes. Wealth enables the wealthy to be efficacious agents in the unfolding of their lives, to live in the world more as constructing subjects than as socialized objects. Often this empowerment is taken on gradually. It usually emerges in the fullest sense only after the wealthy pass through one or more phases of personal self-development in which they undergo a moral education in regard to money. They struggle in the public sphere to establish a business, to wend their way up the corporate or professional hierarchy, or to take up family civic obligations or philanthropic commitments. Privately, they may seek to come to grips with the guilt, expectations, and responsibilities of their inheritance and earnings. In so doing, they transform their identities just as they transform the world around them. At the end of these formative trials, the wealthy emerge with an enhanced capacity to shape their fortunes. For Allison Randall, it took an emotional battle with her father over legal custody of her inheritance to proclaim her personal declaration of independence. Launching her career as a progressive political activist is just one of an abundance of possibilities. "I'm free, you know. I'm free of financial restrictions. It's wonderful. What more could I want? I have money that I can do things with—for myself and for the causes I feel are important. My next career could be anything. I have that freedom and I'm not afraid to sort of think, 'Well, maybe you *could* do that.'"

Of course, most individuals enjoy some ability to dispose over the world in accordance with their wants. Few are without some autonomous capacity in society. What distinguishes the wealthy in the reciprocal process of shaping and being shaped by the world is that they can do more than deflect social pressures. They need not settle simply for finding a more or less compatible place within prescribed limits. In more ways and in more institutionally profound fashion than the nonwealthy, they can shape the very constraints and requirements in which they live. What the nonwealthy can accomplish only by mounting a social movement, the wealthy can implement single-handedly. "I can pick up the phone and call a congressman who's heard my name and have the impact of one million votes on the issue with a phone call," claims Graham Reynolds, an outspoken missionary of wealth. Reynolds unabashedly extols what numerous other respondents care to recount only in more reserved terms. This distinctive additional capacity of the wealthy not simply to find a favorable place within the institutional limits of everyday life but to transcend and remake this place is *hyper-agency*. This is just "the Golden Rule," explains David Stephanov, a shoot-from-the hip real estate magnate: "Them with the gold makes the rules."

The notions of freedom, empowerment, and hyperagency capture worldly capacities of wealth at a general level. In actual practice, freedom and hyperagency become incarnated in three interrelated yet distinct manifestations: temporally, spatially, and psychologically.

Temporal Empowerment: "I never washed my daughter's hair."

Temporal empowerment entails the capacity to overcome or avoid the limits imposed by time, to bring the past and future under the control of the present and to expand the present by substituting money for time. As to the past, the wealthy are able to accentuate the beneficial aspects of their biographies and to deflect or redeem what they regret. In regard to the future, the wealthy do not simply await passively what is to come but intervene in the present efficaciously. They initiate or set the contours of the institutional life within which they and others live. As Michael Hodson explains, his great-grandfather's financial legacy shapes his thinking even as he ensconces himself as a young artist in England: "When you know that there's money left to you by your great-grandfather who's been dead God-knows-how-many-years before you were born, that gives you the sense that it isn't your money. It's the family's."

In addition to reconstituting the past and shaping the future, the wealthy expand the present. They hire others to perform tasks for them—what entrepreneur Brian Riley describes as "spending money to buy my time back." They also exert enough clout to get things done quickly on their own terms. "People want to come and see me," explains Paul Goetz. "I don't see them because it takes time away from what I want to do." When you are wealthy, says Graham Reynolds, "You always have the upper hand in negotiating, and you can do in one-tenth the time what it would take someone else ten times the time to do—because of the credibility they'd have to develop." The wealthy also spend less time on mundane tasks. This frees them up to pursue those things they like to do rather than have to do. "I never washed my daughter's hair," reveals Rebecca Austin, a West Coast attorney who has hired a nanny. On his part, Reynolds tells how he buys ten suits at a time, racing "to see how quickly I can get into the store and out." "The real value I have in my life is time," he confides; "that's the only limiter. It's certainly not money."

Spatial Empowerment: "You give me Mexico; that's what I want."

Spatial empowerment is the ability of the wealthy to extend themselves and their influence geographically or territorially. The most localized aspect concerns the individual as a *physical being*. The spatially empowered insulate themselves from the demanding presence of others. They move relatively unimpeded through the world, procuring for themselves an efficacious social presence at meetings, vacation hideaways, and charity events. They obtain all needed medical care and have the where-withal to attend to their psychological and physical fitness. They gain access to people and places — what Reynolds calls "power to get through time and red-tape barriers"—even as they restrict access to themselves. And when they wish to be in contact even with prominent people, they bring them in for audiences. Boasts Stephanov, who once bought a bank simply "to learn how bankers thought": "When I want something, the people I can get it from come here and meet me for breakfast, and I tell them what I want. When I have to convey a message to the governor, he comes here or he'll have his top two or three aides come down, and I'll tell them what I think should be done, and then we'll go from there."

In addition to projecting and protecting their own phys-ical beings, the wealthy exert spatial empowerment by construct-ing a *base of command*. A base of command is a material site in the form of a company branch, social organization, or staff person-nel through which the wealthy exert control over people, organi-zations, and policies located geographically beyond their bodily presence. Such territorial self-extension can be intensive (the degree to which individuals saturate an area with their pres-ence) or extensive (the degree to which such control expands geographically). For Rebecca Jacobs, a Detroit-based importer, the growth of her business is the flourishing of her dream: "First I had one outlet, fifteen outlets, twenty outlets, then I had fifty outlets, a hundred outlets; I had two hundred outlets and I just couldn't believe it. Now I'm supplying a thousand outlets on a weekly basis in the United States alone, and I haven't even stopped. I figure I'm in my infancy right now. This is just gradual growing. Turning point? No. There have just been a lot of dreams."

As business owners, philanthropists, investors, political contributors, and board members, the wealthy create for them-selves a series of "outposts" or franchises of their worldly power — conveyors of their will by which they exert control even when not physically present. Establishing such outposts is not just a material undertaking; it becomes a kind of personal manifest destiny. Jacobs, for instance, relishes her success in cornering the Upper Midwest, Canada, and the Northeast. Being "closed out" of Cleveland and California is only a tempo-rary setback in her grand design. "I'll tell you what," she declares. "You give me Mexico; that's what I want."

A third manifestation of spatial empowerment is through *artifactual re-presentations* such as art collections, homes, busi-nesses, real estate empires, personal foundations, or other visi-ble constructs that make the selves of the wealthy present even at a distance. Such physical constructs empower the wealthy by literally re-presenting or visibly interjecting their tastes, inter-ests, and priorities over a wider geographic realm. For example, many individuals extend their spatial empowerment by self-promotion through advertising and press releases. The most explicit expression of artifactual re-presentation occurs among those who bestow their family names on their businesses, es-tates, or charitable gifts. So it is for Michael Hollander, an East Coast media and food entrepreneur, who explains, "I have been very happy to have my family name on things because I think it is very meaningful to children coming along in the family to see and understand that their family was responsible and is a re-sponsible family in the institutions where it had people and involvement." The family name thus becomes "a visible exam-ple," something "under their nose" that they will "have to live up to."

Psychological Empowerment: "To affect the lives of forty million people"

While temporal and spatial empowerment are capacities by which the wealthy project and exert themselves in the world, *psychological empowerment* refers to the corresponding mode of consciousness by which the wealthy perceive themselves as both efficacious and entitled to be so. "My goal, long term, is to affect the lives of forty million people—and those forty million will affect the rest of the world," proclaims Reynolds, who again differs from his colleagues only in the scope of his expectations, not in their content. Because psychological empowerment oper-ates ultimately as an inner capacity, it proves to be less ex-clusively the preserve of the wealthy or powerful than temporal and spatial empowerment. Many nonwealthy, including those on a quest for wealth, display this quality of self-assurance. As the basic ingredient for building a worldly domain, psychological empowerment exists as a key precondition and not just a consequence of being wealthy.

Such psychological empowerment is apparent in the determined vision of many entrepreneurs who confidently discount—indeed even celebrate—the element of risk in their transition from the safe harbor of salaried employment to the uncharted waters of self-directed enterprise. "It's a lot different from the corporate executive who works his way up from the ground floor and never really took a risk other than a career risk," remarks Walter Adams. "It's the lone wolf who's never really comfortable in a General Motors type structure. Clearly, the most dominant force in my success has been pure instinct." This same egoism leads many inheritors to aggressively claim positions of authority and stewardship in progressive community foundations or in more conventional cultural institutions. Despite his progressive politics, for instance, Bradley Stark readily describes his philanthropic orientation as a "charitable posture right out of Dickens." It is "a classic example of the 'haves' acting on behalf of the have-nots without help or involvement."

Psychological empowerment is the personal disposition on the part of the wealthy that they can entertain "great expectations," that they can be efficacious in achieving those expectations, and that their wants or goals are socially productive. "When it came to Boston," reports Jacobs, "when they said 'you can't do that, you can't pay that much money for the district,' I said, 'I'm paying that, and that's it.' I knew that it was right for me, and I bought it. And I was never sorry. I paid that bank loan back in two years." It is the complex conviction of entitlement—the wealthy's realization that they can have what they want and, imbued with the ethos of the invisible hand, that their pursuit of private interest promotes the public good.

There Shall Your Heart Be Also: The Spiritual Secret of Money

It is clear that attaining the full empowerment of wealth as the capacity of self-construction and world building does not necessarily preclude even extensive philanthropic involvements. In fact, one of the most important findings from the Study on Wealth and Philanthropy is that for many wealthy individuals, philanthropy is little more than an extension of the moral disposition and worldly control by which they approach their everyday activities. Despite its aura of moral selflessness and public contribution, philanthropic commitment frequently reflects the push of social, family, and business obligation and the impulses of temporal, spatial, and psychological empowerment already described. This is how Carol Layton, a New York interior decorator, seems to view it. Once you have succeeded in business and saturated your consumption needs, she explains, "that's when you come into the idea... of what do you do with the money. First you have children and you want to help make them financially secure. Then if you're like me, I have a need for ongoing things. I want the business to go on. I want to build something that doesn't die when I die. So we're building something that I hope will have continuity. Now I can indulge in certain kinds of fantasies where you get active in certain kinds of philanthropic organizations."

It is also clear that religion is not the exclusive path to a spiritually committed philanthropy. Our interviews reveal how various nontheistic modes of consciousness or spirituality can induce a comparable internal transformation. However, my intent here is to uncover what is going on in those instances where religion does in fact forge a link between wealth and morally committed philanthropy. If survey research highlights the general statistical importance of the religious factor,[4] our interviews provide insight into how religion helps translate worldly empowerment into philanthropic commitment.

The Second Mode of Psychological Empowerment: "How can I be counted on somehow?"

The first task is to identify that moral ethos by which the wealthy move from being able to have what they want to being concerned about the quality of their wants. "I love having money," says Carol Layton. "It makes it possible for me to do whatever I want to do." But what is that quality of will, emotion, and affection that moves the wealthy from a concern about the quantity of their interests to a concern about the quality of their wants? Our research reveals that for many respondents—both those who earned and those who inherited their wealth—a major transformation in consciousness takes place at some point as they come into that wealth. This point may arrive quietly and gradually or appear as a dramatic realization, "a cruncher," as Ethan Wright, a Chicago entrepreneur, describes it. The recognition that his business could now offer him financial security "was like a seizure. . . I could do anything I wanted to do. But I didn't know what the hell to do. So the first thing I did was hired myself a psychoanalyst." Soon after Wright set out on a European vacation with his wife and kids, recapitulating the classic motif of journey-quest. Upon his return he concentrated on identifying his deeper interests: "I had arrived at what the goal was, which was financial independence. My problem was that I had made it. In a sense, I had separated myself from my main business activity. . . . So I had to find something to do. And what you end up doing, I think, what I discovered is you go to those things that truly interest you, have been an interest of yours in your life."

At first Wright gained only an inkling of the spiritual secret of money, with his new-found freedom rekindling his musical interests. But as time went on he began to experience ever more fully the capacity financial security allows for turning consciousness inward and concerns outward. He came to evaluate the moral or spiritual content of his wants and to consider how he could recast or apply his worldly empowerment to a broader and deeper set of purposes. This is in effect a *second level of psychological empowerment* whereby the wealthy move beyond pursuing private interest as their public contribution to pursuing public needs as their personal concern. "I now see that I don't have to concentrate on my struggle to survive or grow, or get over being poor," explains Gregory Singer, a Detroit entrepreneur who has survived a series of business downturns. "I can now look with a lot more depth at who I am, what I need, what my purpose in life is, how can I give back to the system, how can I be counted on somehow."

Accounts of major shifts in consciousness like those reported by Wright and Singer suggest that for some wealthy individuals the two phases of psychological empowerment are sequential. For many others, however, the two modes of psychological empowerment coexist — either because the initial aura of the transformation wears off or, as with Todd Schlesinger, a Miami developer, because both modes of consciousness have advanced together and now overlap and even compete. "My interests probably run the entire gamut: from the things that pull at my heartstrings, to the things that I see as pure need, to coming from a desire to pay back a little bit to the community, going all the way to the other extreme — ego, prestige, *et cetera.*"

Whether sequential or congruent, the second mode of psychological empowerment is not limited to any particular doctrine or specific activity. It is a disposition that undergirds a wide range of specific religious and spiritual ideas and that includes the conscious dedication to worldly efficacy on behalf of others. Even though there is no single orientation or activity that encapsulates the religious content of the second mode of psychological empowerment, it is possible to identify from our interviews a fundamental core.

Religion: "When I'm vertically in tune, then I'm horizontally in tune."

Although often derived from nonreligious experiences and expressed in nontheistic language, what gets enunciated is remarkably close to the most basic experience of religion, namely, *an empathetic bond to others.* The etymology of the term *religion* in Latin is somewhat uncertain, having three possible derivations (Schiffers, 1975, p. 1359). But because the meanings are complementary rather than contradictory, it is less important to single out a particular one. According to Schiffers, the verb *relegere* means "to constantly turn to" or "to conscientiously observe" some worthy object of attention. The verb *reeligere* means "to choose again" this origin or goal.

Yet the most encompassing meaning, as well as the most commonly cited source, is *religari*, denoting "to tie together," to bind, or "to form a bond." In this basic way, then, the second level of psychological empowerment in which individuals become sincerely conscious of their bonds to others can be united to the notion of religion. A tie to the transcendent is a tie to the earth. In theistic terms, this entails the experience of a tie of duty or love to God along with a corresponding tie to other people. "When I'm vertically in tune, I'm horizontally in tune," reports Mark Heller. "Whenever I take seriously God's word and follow in my faith, I'm positioned to deal with the problems on a satisfactory basis." In nontheistic terms of spirituality, the transcendent plane is deemphasized or eliminated though the importance of affective concern remains highlighted. That is, psychological self-actualization or humanism still cultivates empathetic social identification or attention to the lives of individuals. This connection is especially crucial to the wealthy, actor Gene Sanders points out, because "through wealth there is a way to become isolated, not only a way to protect yourself financially, but a way to isolate yourself personally and emotionally, closing off consciousness and closing oneself off to the needs of others."

Transforming Consciousness:
"How the hell do you get that blind up?"

The issue is the same no matter how it is expressed, insists Boston businessman Charles Dore. "There are so many people that are just into themselves and can't seem to get out of themselves, can't seem to see the broad picture. People don't want to see. They draw the curtain. You start to tell them about Ethiopia or poverty and—and these people basically are good, but they tend to pull the blind. How the hell do you get that blind up?"

How indeed do some of the wealthy "get that blind up"? And what do they say to explain how a committed bond to God, to principles, or to other people becomes a dynamic, constructive force in their lives? Sara Elster, a savvy progressive philanthropist in New York, helps provide an answer. She views her life as a "spiritual journey" in which she draws on her personal religious experience to carry out the worldly vocation of "co-creativity" with God: "I have a lot of distance to go in my spiritual development. But I have a very, very strong sense now that I really am on a spiritual journey. And that when you do let go and hand yourself over to that, you are no longer in control and at the same time you use all of your intelligence. What I'm trying to work out for myself is how do you use your intelligence, how do you use your contacts in high places effectively? It's not handing everything over to God and saying, 'What will happen, will happen,' sort of in an apocalyptic sense. It's that you are very much a co-creator and this is what you've been given. And I've been given a lot and therefore it's my responsibility to give my best in every way whether it's money or intelligence."

Sara Elster articulates the inner meaning of religion and spirituality more concisely than many of our respondents. Nevertheless, her words reflect the religious experience of a broad cross section of those we interviewed. Her emphasis on being a co-creator characterizes the nontheistic spiritual consciousness of many others.

Participative Agency. The first point to note is Elster's *reverse insight* — as philosopher Bernard Lonergan terms it — into the meaning of wealth at the second level of psychological consciousness. Empowerment is not the ability to create a world in accord with her will but the ability "to let go and hand yourself over." It is acceptance of the fact that "you are no longer in control." This does not imply simple disinvestment of wealth or power but a rechanneling of it. Through hyperagency the wealthy become self-determined and efficacious agents. Religious consciousness, as defined here, rather than destroying such agency makes it a *participative agency* linked and responsive to the agency of God and other people.

"It's not handing everything over to God," cautions Elster, but the devotion of "money and intelligence" to a more encompassing agenda than her own. She remains a subject and retains her temporal and spatial empowerment. What is different is that she now experiences her subjectivity as tied to the subjectivity and empowerment of God in a relation of what she calls "co-creativity." Wealth is not eschewed but mobilized.

Taken with Gratitude. This worldly vocation becomes embedded in Elster's consciousness through a second insight inversely related to the first. Just as she recognizes that she is "no longer in control," she acknowledges too that she has "been given a lot." Theologian Robert Ochs has remarked that there are three ways to take a gift: It may be taken for granted, taken with guilt, or taken with gratitude. For Sara Elster and numerous other respondents, including many who are not religiously dedicated, taking their fortune with gratitude is the single most crucial aspect of their consciousness. Gratitude sets them apart from those who stay locked within the first-mode psychological empowerment. They recognize that their wealth and abilities are unearned gifts—that despite their worldly capacities, they are not demigods determining their own and others' fates but beings who are themselves humbly abiding within a gracious dispensation.

How the wealthy understand the story of their own agency is inextricably connected to how they act in regard to the stories of others. The etymology of religion as "conscientiously observing one's origins" here comes to the fore. Such knowledge never produces a fatalism or quietism. Rather, as Susan Aldrich puts it, the experience of wealth as a gift leads the wealthy to "take their money very seriously." This means placing the hyperagency engendered by wealth at the service of the goals engendered by spirituality: "The best thing about being wealthy is the access, the ability to make choices, to not be bogged down in long mundane things. I have a tremendous amount of creative potential to do things that a lot of people don't have the time or the ability to do. There is a spiritual quality to it, too, because you know, you feel tremendously fortunate to have this gift and you want to do something with it. At least I do. Most of the people I know that have wealth feel that way too. Most of the wealthy people I know take their money very seriously and have a spiritual connection with it to do something with it."

Describing his spiritual awakening, Paul Moore says, "The first thing that really happened to me was when I discovered quite by accident. . . that I really couldn't do everything myself. People tend to equate wealth with power. I've gotten in touch with the fact that I really don't believe I have any power that I don't get from God, and that's a lot different idea than what I had when I was in business. I used to think that I was generating all of it."

If religion is one path to a less self-encumbered life of wealth, the recognition of a life graced by unearned opportunities, unachieved benefits, and ultimate contingency is at the core of the transformative capacity of religion to bring about this result.

Religion and Responsibility:
"I wasn't put on this planet to play it safe."

The experience of wealth as gift never produces an ascetic quietism. The respondents in our survey are too American for that. Although only a minority of them report that riches impose a gnawing burden of guilt, virtually all disclose an apprehension about the amount or source of their wealth. This uneasiness spurs the wealthy to work out a range of words and actions that sanction their advantage. Such justifications invariably revolve around a discourse of responsibility. Entrepreneur Gary Newmann rejects the possibility of living comfortably with his wealth. He is driven in business and philanthropy by "that hungry feeling" of "obligation" that makes him realize that he "wasn't put on this planet to play it safe." "I've a responsibility and obligation to really do that which nobody else can. . . . [We wealthy must] make the most of this God-given gift of being able to live dangerously with what we are given."

Despite this and similar testimonies about the link among gift, religion, and responsibility, it is not particularly apparent how this connection occurs. Because of its high ethical overtones the discourse of responsibility can obscure the fact that religious consciousness may be marshaled simply to reinforce rather than transform what the wealthy view as the nature of their responsibilities. The philosopher Jules Toner defines care as loving others in their true needs. The question is whether religiosity provides a sacred canopy, as Peter Berger calls it, for the wealthy to do what is just in their own interest rather than what people need. Once again, religious consciousness is inde-terminate. It can play a distinctive role in either bolstering or prodding the believer beyond what I have described as the first level of psychological empowerment.

One set of such justifications concerns why it is futile, misguided, or even counterproductive to disinvest wealth. It is argued that there is no obligation to share what is properly obtained; that even if wealth were shared it would in short order become reconcentrated in productive hands; and, more funda-mentally, that the concentration of wealth is needed to finance and reward the entrepreneurial initiative that is so crucial to the vitality of a free society.

How religious sentiments shore up these orientations and fail to induce bonds of care for others will be addressed in a moment. But first I want to discuss the nexus between financial responsibility and religious consciousness when religion makes a relatively autonomous contribution to the economic morality of the wealthy. To begin with, even under the influence of a more challenging religious perspective, the wealthy do not necessarily abandon the pursuit of making and controlling wealth. What changes, however, is that religious consciousness moves their "getting and giving" of wealth onto a plane where logics of legitimation not dictated by market criteria come into play.

Stewardship as a Vocation: "He's only got our hands."

The paramount religious justification, embraced by progres-sives and conservatives alike, revolves around the vocation of stewardship. Simply stated, the contention is that wealth is not evil; only squandering it is. "We are where we are because it was part of God's plan," explains Donald Mason, the owner of a publishing firm. "Paul writes to Timothy and says, 'As for the wealthy, encourage them to be generous and do good works.' He doesn't say, 'As for the wealthy, tell them to get rid of it because

they can't go to heaven.' He's saying that they have a stewardship."
God's "only got our hands," adds Dore, explaining what inspired
his funding of a halfway house for black alcoholics. Exasperated
by a friend's callous suggestion that he not support a program
for blacks, Dore asks, "Don't they listen to what Jesus said to
them — 'Help my people'? — that's all he said."

A close look at the inner logic of stewardship helps explain the compelling feelings of "responsibility" that Dore and
others report and takes us a step closer to uncovering the distinctive contribution of religious consciousness in marshaling
bonds of care. To begin with it is important to distinguish the
impulse of *stewardship* from that of *noblesse oblige*. Although the
orientation of noblesse oblige has a contemporary application,
it is an ethic of economic responsibility derived from the paren-
talism of the feudal dispensation, just as stewardship is an ethic
of responsibility born of capitalism. Without going into detail
here, the major difference is that the cultural logic of noblesse
oblige proffers a doctrine of distribution while that of stewardship furnishes a code of production. Regardless of how one
views the moral status of capitalism, the ethos of stewardship
focuses attention on how wealth is concentrated and put into use
as an engine of production and employment rather than consumption and leisure. It is for this reason that, almost to a
person, even religiously oriented respondents couch their philanthropic commitments of wealth in the productive language of
investment, systemic change, "making a difference," and social
entrepreneurship. Time and again they repeat some version of
the adage that to provide a fish is to feed someone for a day, but
that to teach someone how to fish is to provide food for a
lifetime.

As a form of religious discipleship, the productive ethic of
stewardship imbues its followers with what Max Weber calls
worldly asceticism. This discipline requires from its devotees a
dual consciousness capable of discerning the interstices between God and world. Other-worldly asceticism draws direction
for daily life from a knowledge of God's will as embedded in
scripture and dogma. In contrast, a nonreligious, this-worldly
humanism obtains its bearings by observing patterns of histor-

ical causality. The distinguishing characteristic of worldly asceticism, however, is that it attends to and intersects with a
cognizance of both Divine will *and* social structure.

Attending to the two realms of religion and history as
sources of data means that the worldly ascetic incorporates a
duality and not a *dualism* of consciousness, to borrow a distinction from Anthony Giddens (1984). As such, religiously inspired
uses of money must heed the realities of both the City of God
and the City of Earth. The two realms impinge upon and mutually shape each other while not being collapsed into each other.
Gregory Singer exemplifies the duality of consciousness of those
respondents who take seriously not just the intersection of the
will of God and the course of history but their relative autonomy.
On the one hand, Singer's religious conviction dictates a realm
of responsibility that goes beyond just giving money, namely, a
personal relationship with those whom he helps. Singer states
his version of how a tie to God implies a special bond of care: "I
feel like I've studied enough about the Christian principles of
giving. . . that I think I have a responsibility to a higher involvement than to just give funds. Unless I get involved myself, it
doesn't really mean very much. It's just money; it's from my hand
to somebody else's. That doesn't put me in a relationship to the
need. It doesn't put the recipient in any kind of relationship with
me or understanding of who I am or of the source of my feelings
or beliefs or of where the giving comes from. And I feel that if
one does give, that he somehow connect the source of the gift to
the receiver of the gift."

But Singer also takes seriously his earthly citizenship.
While his religious devotion proffers an ethic of care, his historical consciousness stipulates the kind of worldly responsibilities
needed to put this care into actual practice. "I don't believe in
just giving money," he insists, "but in putting legs on the money."
He commits his money toward achieving those productive outcomes dictated by the ethic of stewardship, including making
stewards of others: "We very often overlook the fact that when we
give someone something we also give them a responsibility to
use that gift in its most productive fashion. If we just hand
somebody ten bucks and walk away, that person isn't going to

feel very responsible because all someone's done is kept him in that same receiver mode. He hasn't lifted the guy up, corrected that problem or that need. I feel that there is a quality to putting legs on the money and getting involved and letting people know that a little more effort on their part makes a lot of difference."

Laura Madison likewise brings religious and historical consciousness to bear in charting the use of her inheritance. The fruit of her fifty-year trek from Long Island debutante to central Manhattan activist is the simple injunction that she must be "totally loving." Invoking the metaphor of listening, Madison demonstrates how a vocation of worldly asceticism involves being attuned to the logic of human personality: "I listen and I go where I think I'm needed. I do whatever I hear about that seems to be working towards helping humanity, which is my prime goal. It's the only thing I'm interested in in the world — the health of humanity: human beings having an opportunity to be truly human, which very few people are. Most people don't even know what it is to be human, which is to be a spiritual person as well as a physical, mental, emotional person. And to really relate to other human beings all over the world, whoever they are, wherever they are. And in making a oneness that's there but isn't seen by most people." It is a matter of "healing the earth, healing the rifts between people," she continues. Turning to the meta-phor of healing, she manifests the underlying sensitivity that religious orientations operate within rather than against the workings of human nature. She implicitly answers in the affir-mative the question that Einstein said was crucial for discerning the meaning of human existence: whether the universe is friendly.

Although I have indicated some ways by which religious engagement with God inspires personal engagement with oth-ers, just how this happens always remains partially hidden from our respondents — something Gabriel Marcel (1950) would call *mystery*. The mystery of being always remains unfathomable and can never be fully deciphered. Mystery is to be entered into, participated in. This does not mean that we are excused from trying to comprehend what is going on, only that we not treat this spiritual transposition, in Marcel's terms, simply as a secret to be found out or a problem to be solved. It is therefore not surprising that our respondents eventually turn simply to enunciating their spiritual sentiments in the form of paradoxes—all of which say in one way or another that to give is to get, to care for others is to care for oneself, to die is to live. "You let go of your ego, and you can be more loving than in any other way. It's all the letting go that brings everything to you in every way, for yourself, and for everybody else," explains Laura Madison, who struggled much of her life to surmount the hurdles imposed by her inheritance and movingly recalls the key incident in this struggle as follows: "I heard a voice and the wind almost blew me down as I came into the alley, and the voice said, 'If you really believe what you think you believe, then you've got to let go.' Life is all letting go of your children, letting go of your ego, letting go of your money, letting go of everything that you think is contributing to you. . . . Finding out who you are and coming from what is inside of you . . . is everything you need."

To commit oneself merely to the quest for empowerment is to distort one's life. "My role is to attempt to harmonize my activity with the roles that the Creator would like to see born," reflects Brendan Dwyer, a Detroit wholesaler. "To the extent my activity harmonizes with the role he sees for me, then I'm going to have a peace and tranquility in exercising that [role] and in living that you can't get in any other way. And when I'm in conflict with that, then I'm going to have a certain tension and disunity."

The Shadow Side of Religion: "Money is trouble."

A frequently stated sentiment is that money is a two-edged sword—unless wielded properly it can prove dangerous. "Money is trouble," says Mark Heller, reflecting on the temptations of wealth. "God is interested in the material, but he's more interested in the spiritual, because you see all of us are terminal cases. It isn't just a cancer patient who has been diagnosed with advanced cancer who is terminal. We're all terminal." But not only in money trouble; religion can be trouble too. Religion not only fails at times to provide a path to the second level of psychological empowerment—it can also keep the wealthy from the path of care altogether—or lead them into self-righteousness.

Religion becomes trouble, for instance, when the experience of wealth as a gift is missing. Without such humility, religion ceases to be transformative, becoming instead an occasion for proud willfulness. Such is the tendency described by Beverly and Ross Geiger, whose own vocation involves converting the wealthy to born-again Christianity and encouraging them to practice philanthropy. The Geigers remark that the wealthy are especially difficult to convert because they are already "upstanding people...sufficient unto themselves," people who say, "'I'm me, I made it, and I don't need anything.'" The wealthy can all too easily "get to the point where their money is like their god. They've got to hoard it."

Religion becomes trouble as well when the bond or partnership with God ceases being one of participative agency and turns into an outright appropriation of Divine authority. Rather than remaining humble participants in the *mysterium tremendum*, the wealthy too readily become dispensers of God's will. Instead of learning what to do by unraveling how things work and what people need, the wealthy can too readily become dogmatic purveyors of scripturally deduced morality. "We usually ask the Lord; he shows us," says one respondent whose narrative of her spiritual autobiography recounted no instance where God's will challenged her or was not in accord with her own. God wanted her to have the very same estate she wanted all along. God rewards her for being charitable; and she presents her personal reading of the Bible as God's literal word. To point this out is not to judge harshly. It is merely to recognize an instance where the first mode of psychological empowerment has become substituted for the second mode.

Even though a language of stewardship continues to occupy their narratives, those who violate the relative autonomy of history and heaven end up substituting a dualism of consciousness for the duality of consciousness that makes philanthropists examine not just "what God wants" but what needs to be done. Atlanta publisher Mason warns of the danger in substituting what we want for what God wants. But he fails to warn against the danger of substituting "what God wants" for what needs to be done: "I think there is a delusive glamour of sin that the apostle Paul talks about in the early chapters of Romans. He refers to these people: 'They gave up God and therefore God gave them up to be the playthings of their own desires.' And I think that when we give up our sense that we are creatures of a creator God who has a plan for our lives and loves us and cares for us, and we turn our backs on that—whether it's for physical lust or material lust or whatever—to pursue what we want, we run the risk of becoming playthings of our own desire."

Ironically, Mason and others who verbalize an ethic of stewardship to bring salvation to the world, tend to underplay the dialectic tension between the logic of heaven and the logic of earth. Theology is substituted for anthropology, as Ludwig Feuerbach put it, in an effort to make sure that anthropology does not become substituted for theology. Although "we are creatures of a creator God," creation itself is not to be excavated as an historically available incarnation of God.

Conclusion

The narrator in Dylan Thomas's A *Child's Christmas in Wales* reports, "I can never remember whether it snowed for six days and six nights when I was twelve or whether it snowed for twelve days and twelve nights when I was six." Similarly, I can never remember whether the passage from Matthew and Luke reads "where your treasure is there will your heart be also," or "where your heart is there will your treasure be also." Perhaps like the snow it matters only that we remember—in this case that treasures and hearts go together. Because the treasures of the wealthy are large and affect the treasures and hearts of others, it matters how the wealthy come to define the relation between their treasures and their hearts.

My purpose in posing the relation of wealth and religion in biblical terms is not to write a brief for religion. My findings provide no evidence to conclude that religion is an exclusive or even an especially reliable path to the care for others. The findings do indicate, however, that an inner conviction about a tie to God often eventuates for the wealthy in the mobilization of their treasures on behalf of others. Yet the question remains what is going on when religious conviction is at work.

For Patrick Lockwood the major affect of religion on his philanthropy is quantitative. He reports no particularly creative involvements. His philanthropic aspirations are simply "to share with the Church or other institutions." But his religious conviction has inspired him to increase the percentage of his giving each year over the past thirty years to a point where it vastly exceeds the ten percent he speaks about here: "I was taught as a youngster from my mother's knee that tithing was the proper thing to do, giving ten percent of your income. Well, later on as I began to read the Bible for myself I discovered that giving ten percent is what is expected by God; that's just the minimum. . . . That's like giving God a tip. But when you are really interested in helping the work of God, and you want to do something to show your gratitude, you give more than ten."

Spiritual conviction can also induce the wealthy to break through the traditional limitations on their involvement with recipients. Benjamin Ellman expresses not just a bond of care for others but a reciprocal relationship with them. His early charitable engagements stimulated his interest but were strictly money based and impersonal. Yet all this changed after he began to participate firsthand in the community projects to which he donated: "I then became very much involved. In many instances where you've done things, you can actually see concrete results where people have benefited. It was unbelievable what I learned about the numbers of people in this community whose life depended on that agency. I mean, if they didn't get the subvention so their kids could go to camps or day-care centers, while older people were taken care of and brought meals — their whole life depended on that institution. And you see instances where children have gone on from very humble beginnings to become major contributors not only to themselves but back to the community. I think that those are things that you get personally. You feel real good about that. I think the minute someone starts to help, they make a difference — they make a difference in their own lives, you see."

It is rare that religion creates a worldly vocation that is as distinct as Lockwood's or Singer's. Yet religion did so in these two instances and does so to a lesser extent in the lives of many other respondents. In the course of their daily dealings with money, all wealthy individuals arrive at the first level of psychological empowerment by uncovering the rules and exercising the capacities of temporal and spatial empowerment. Less frequently, however, do the wealthy unearth the *spiritual secret* of money — that paradoxical capacity of money to be turned to the service of others.

The capacity of the wealthy to exercise hyperagency in building both a worldly and an inner domain eventuates for all our respondents in the encounter with what the Hindus refer to as Kalpataru or "wishing" tree (Smith, 1958). At least in the material realm, the wealthy, far more than any others, can heed the inscription on the Kalpataru tree that promises "you can have what you want." The question is the quality of those wants. Although we have no way of knowing how many of the wealthy self-critically attend to the quality of their wants, our findings persuade us that financial security bestows on all wealthy the opportunity to do so. Not least among the reasons why the wealthy come to harbor "great expectations" about what they should or would like to do on behalf of others is the fact that they can actually accomplish much of what they envision as their calling.

The spiritual secret of wealth, then, is that riches can offer their proprietors an avenue to deeper meanings and purposes. Wealth offers an opportunity for conversion to care for others just as it offers an opportunity for steadfast adherence to ingrained behavior at the first level of psychological empowerment. The wealthy can have what they want not only in the material realm but in the spiritual realm as well, not only for themselves but on behalf of others also — provided they choose "appropriate" wants. Like wealth itself, the spiritual secret of money is both constraining and empowering, both socializing and enabling. The empowerment of wealth that grants individuals the capacity to pursue their interests guarantees *nothing* about the quality of those interests or about the degree of

selflessness with which they are pursued. The meaning and
practice of economic morality differs for the wealthy not because they are inherently more (or less) spiritual or can learn the
spiritual secret of money better than others. Nor is it simply
because hyperagency, along with other resources and responsibilities of empowerment associated with the possession of
wealth, opens a *broader panorama* of potential empathetic involvement than would otherwise be the case. Rather, economic
morality differs for the wealthy largely because wealth has the
potential to relieve the material insecurities of everyday life, to
awaken sensibilities of gratitude, to provoke questions about the
quality of wants, and to provide the wherewithal for an economic vocation.

Notes

1. For instance, Hall (in Chapter Three of this volume) docu-
    ments how "scholarship of philanthropy has given religion
    short shrift" and argues that this is due in large part to the
    uneasy history of critical encounters and accommodations
    between religious consciousness and efficiency-oriented
    philanthropy. A comprehensive account summarizing what
    we now know theoretically and empirically about the rela-
    tion of philanthropy and religion still needs to be compiled,
    although some good beginnings have been made (Hodgkin-
    son, this volume; Layton, 1987; Fraker, 1989).
2. The study was conducted by the Social Welfare Research
    Institute at Boston College and was funded by the T. B.
    Murphy Foundation Charitable Trust. With only a few ex-
    ceptions, respondents possessed a net worth well in excess
    of $1 million and included several who appear on lists of the
    most wealthy Americans. For a detailed description of the
    sample, methodology, and interview protocol, see Scher-
    vish and Herman (1988). A comprehensive presentation of
    the findings in regard to the practice of philanthropy
    among the wealthy appears in Schervish (in preparation).
3. All names, along with any geographic or organizational
    descriptions that could be used to identify specific indi-

viduals, have been changed to preserve the anonymity of the respondents.

4. It is true that survey research indicates that on average religiously committed people give more time and money. It remains unclear, however, what percentage of this disproportionate inclination toward charity reflects giving to support buildings, personnel, and activities from which givers directly benefit as church members — what we call consumption philanthropy (Schervish and Herman, 1988) — and what percentage derives from the specific kind of religious concern for others I describe below. Moreover, all such statistics are summary measures that state the overall impact of religion as averaged over the lives of many individuals, some of whom embody a substantial effect of religion and some of whom embody little or no effect. Therefore, without the assistance of other information, statistical findings alone are incapable of filling in the causal linkages by which religious concern encourages other-directed giving.

References

Fraker, A. T. *Religion and American Life: Resources.* Champaign: University of Illinois Press, 1989.

Giddens, A. *The Constitution of Society.* Berkeley: University of California Press, 1984.

Hodgkinson, V. A., and Weitzman, M. S. *Giving and Volunteering in the United States: Findings from a National Survey.* Washington, D.C.: INDEPENDENT SECTOR, 1988.

Hodgkinson, V. A., Weitzman, M. S., and Kirsch, A. D. *From Belief to Commitment: The Activities and Finances of Religious Congregations in the United States.* Washington, D.C.: INDEPENDENT SECTOR, 1988.

Layton, D. N. *Philanthropy and Voluntarism: An Annotated Bibliography.* New York: The Foundation Center, 1987.

Marcel, G. *The Mystery of Being.* Chicago: Regner, 1950.

Schervish, P. G. *The World of Wealth and the Vocation of Charity:*

Strategies of Philanthropy Among America's Rich. San Francisco: Jossey-Bass. In preparation.

Schervish, P. G., and Herman, A. *Final Report: The Study on Wealth and Philanthropy*. Boston: Social Welfare Research Institute, Boston College, 1988.

Schiffers, N. "Concept of Religion." In K. Rahner (ed.), *Encyclopedia of Theology: The Concise Sacramentum Mundi*. New York: Seabury Press, 1975.

Smith, H. *The Religions of Man*. New York: Harper & Row, 1958.

Part Two

Patterns of Giving and Volunteering in the Major Faith Traditions

One of the hallmarks of American religion is its diversity. We speak of religious pluralism; indeed, we pride ourselves on the heterogeneity of our faith traditions and religious organizations. It is this diversity, many observers believe, that keeps religion strong in an otherwise secular society. Diversity promotes health because it forces religious organizations to compete for members and contributions. Diversity also provides a heterogeneous society with a variety of alternatives from which to choose. People can select membership in terms of their national origins, family background, ethnic identity, or spiritual inclinations.

Although the vast majority of religious organizations in the United States reflect the Judeo-Christian tradition and therefore agree fundamentally on the importance of charity and benevolence, each of the major faith traditions has distinctive teachings and distinctive organizational characteristics that shape its practices. In a volume of this nature it is not possible to survey all or even a large fraction of these various traditions. We have, however, attempted to provide overviews of the distinctive teachings and practices with respect to giving for several of the major faith traditions.

The chapters in this section provide, first of all, an overview of the relations between religion and giving for the major traditions based on recent national studies and, second, evi-

91

dence on the ways in which giving is currently taught and practiced within the Roman Catholic tradition, among American Jews, within liberal Protestant denominations, among Protestant evangelicals, in the Mormon faith, and among black churches. The chapters differ by virtue of their authors' backgrounds and experience as well as the nature of evidence available. The chapter on Roman Catholic giving, for example, presents an impassioned argument by a leading member of the Roman Catholic clergy for a clearer understanding of the theological tradition itself. The chapter on Jewish giving, in contrast, focuses largely on the results of recent quantitative research. Yet each of the chapters in this section presents evidence both of the historic understandings that have shaped views of giving within a particular tradition and of the ways in which giving is currently practiced. These chapters also point to some of the current dilemmas facing religious leaders and, indeed, the voluntary sector in general.

Chapter 5

Virginia A. Hodgkinson
Murray S. Weitzman
Arthur D. Kirsch

From Commitment to Action: How Religious Involvement Affects Giving and Volunteering

Americans have been described as both a generous and a religious people. In 1988, 71 percent of households (65 million) contributed to charity, and 45 percent of Americans (80 million) volunteered. Sixty-five percent reported that they were members of religious organizations, and 61 percent reported that they had attended religious services in the past six months (Hodgkinson and Weitzman, 1988). For many years, nearly half of the total giving from all sources has been contributed to religious organizations (AAFRC Trust for Philanthropy, 1988), and surveys of individual giving and volunteering have shown that at least two-thirds of all individual contributions and almost half of all volunteers give time to religious organizations (Hodgkinson and Weitzman, 1986). The purposes of this chapter are to explore what relationship exists between religious involvement and giving and volunteering to charitable causes of all types and to determine whether there is any connection between the activities of religious institutions and patterns of giving and volunteering to other charities by members of these institutions.

In order to explore these relationships, we conducted special analyses from two recent national surveys sponsored by the INDEPENDENT SECTOR and conducted by the Gallup Organization.

Giving and Volunteering in the United States (Hodgkinson and Weitzman, 1988) involved in-home personal interviews conducted from March 8 to March 22, 1988, with 2,775 individuals eighteen years of age and older to determine the level and extent of giving and volunteering. This sample included oversamples of African-Americans, Hispanics, and affluent Americans (household incomes over $50,000) in order to have enough respondents to carry out statistically reliable analyses of these groups. The sampling procedure is not representative of the very wealthy (those with incomes above $200,000) because they constitute such a small percentage of the population. Weighting procedures were used to ensure that the final sample was representative of the adult population in the United States in terms of age, education, marital status, occupation, size of household, region of the country, and household income. This survey also explored behaviors, such as religious involvement, and motivations for giving and volunteering to determine whether these behaviors or motivations were reflected in actual giving and volunteering.

From Belief to Commitment: The Activities and Finances of Religious Congregations in the United States (Hodgkinson, Weitzman, and Kirsch, 1988) presents the findings from a national survey of 4,200 congregations in a multistage study to determine the types of activities they engaged in, the level of giving and volunteering of congregations, and the allocation of time and resources to these various activities.

The methodology of the congregational survey was complex. After an unduplicated count of 294,271 religious establishments (including churches, synagogues, temples, and mosques) listed in telephone directories in the continental United States was obtained, a fixed sample of 4,200 congregations was derived by stratifying the sampling frame by census region, and within region by standard metropolitan or nonmetropolitan areas. The development of the large fixed sample ensured that congregations randomly selected within each area were proportional to that area by type of congregation representing more that a hundred denominational and nondenominational institutions. Representatives of the 4,200 congregations were asked several questions relating to demographics of their congregations by telephone and further asked to answer a longer written questionnaire.

The written questionnaire portion of the survey was conducted in three stages to assure an adequate response rate and a national representation in the sample. The first long questionnaire that was sent out elicited 648 responses. Because of the difficulty respondents had in answering this long questionnaire, it was shortened somewhat; the modified, or second, questionnaire, elicited 704 responses. After nonrespondents were studied to determine the response rates of the total sample, a third telephone survey was conducted among nonrespondents to increase the representation of specific quota groups and denominations within them that were relatively underrepresented in the set of questionnaires completed up to that time. The goal for this final interviewing phase was 500 completed interviews, and 510 were completed. The total number of completed surveys over the three stages was 1,862, yielding an overall response rate of the more detailed questionnaires of 44.3 percent. Since the original sample of 4,200 institutions was more than twice as many as needed, the more detailed institutional responses were adequate to develop a representative national sample of religious institutions.

Our analysis of the two surveys for this chapter involved comparing giving and volunteering behavior among members and nonmembers of religious congregations by utilizing the national survey on giving and volunteering. We then analyzed the patterns of giving and volunteering among members with the activities in which congregations were engaged to determine whether there were similarities between member giving and volunteering behavior and the activities of the congregations.

The Activities and Finances of Congregations

One of our major questions in the national survey of the activities and expenditures of religious congregations (Hodgkinson, Weitzman, and Kirsch, 1988) was how donations from individuals to religious organizations were used. One of the major findings was that approximately half (46 percent) of donations to religious institutions were used to support a range of activities other than religious ministry and education, activities ranging from human services to improvement of the environment. These donations were used to support activities within the congregation and also were given to other organizations. Volunteer time in congregations followed similar patterns.

An estimated 294,000 congregations not only engaged in religious ministry and education but were deeply involved in serving their members and communities across a broad area of activities. The natural affinity between religious belief and improving the human condition is probably much stronger than most people think. Almost as many congregations offered programs in human services, 87 percent, as offered religious services and religious education. Nearly 42 percent of all the hours that clergy, other employees, and volunteers spent in serving their congregations were devoted to human service activities other than religious services and education.

Congregations participated in a wide variety of programs and activities in addition to religious ones. Approximately 87 percent of all congregations reported one or more programs in human services and welfare, including 80 percent in family counseling programs; 79 percent reported one or more programs in international activities, including 71 percent in relief-abroad programs; 70 percent reported programs for public or societal benefits, including 46 percent in community development programs; 68 percent reported programs in health, including 56 percent involved in institutional care, such as hospitals, nursing homes, or hospices; 43 percent reported programs in arts and culture; 38 percent reported programs in education, including 38 percent in elementary education; and 27 percent reported programs for the improvement of the environment.

Nine out of ten congregations reported that they used volunteers to perform work in their congregations. There were 253,000 volunteer clergy who gave an average of seventy hours per month. Overall, 10.4 million volunteers other than clergy worked an average of ten hours per month in congregational

programs. Fifty-two percent of those volunteer hours were devoted to religious programs and 48 percent to other congregational programs, including elementary, secondary, and higher
education (18 percent); human services and welfare (12 percent); health or hospitals (7 percent); public or societal benefit
(5 percent); arts and culture (6 percent), international activities
(5 percent); and environmental quality (1 percent). Overall,
volunteers represented 85 percent of the total employees in
religious congregations. The estimated value of volunteer time
in congregations was $13.1 billion in 1986, of which $6.8 billion
(52 percent) went to religious programs, and $6.3 billion (48
percent) went to other congregational programs. These findings
suggest that many Americans and their families get their first
introduction to voluntary service and responsibility to engage
in community activities through participation in a religious
congregation.

Congregations developed among their congregants the
habit of giving not only for religious purposes but for other
activities that support the community. Of the $41.4 billion do-
nated by individuals to congregations in 1986, $19.1 billion (46
percent) was allocated to activities other than religious programs or donated to other organizations. These figures do not
include the value of in-kind donations, such as food, clothing,
and shelter, which six out of ten congregations reported giving
to social services programs in their communities, or the value of
volunteer time contributed by members. Furthermore, congregations provided facilities to foster community participation. More than nine out of ten congregations reported that
their facilities were available for groups within their congregations, and six out of ten reported that their facilities were available to other groups in the community.

In 1986, the total expenditures of religious congregations
were estimated at $48.1 billion, of which $35.7 billion (74 percent) was used for current programs and activities, $8.4 billion
(17 percent) was donated directly by congregations to other
organizations and individuals, and $4.0 billion (8 percent) was
spent on capital outlays. Of the $8.4 billion donated by con-
gregations to other organizations and individuals, $5.5 billion

went to denominational organizations and charities, such as Catholic Charities; $1.9 billion was donated to other charitable organizations in the community; and $1.0 billion was given in direct assistance to individuals.

Congregations spent $48.8 billion on current programs and activities, of which $35.7 billion was for paid expenditures and $13.1 billion was for the assigned value of volunteer time. Of this $48.8 billion, 58 percent was for religious activities, including religious education, and 42 percent was for other program activities. These other program activities included education (14 percent), human services (9 percent), health and hospitals (6 percent), public and societal benefit programs such as human justice and community development (3 percent), arts and culture (3 percent), international activities (3 percent), and environmental quality (1.4 percent).

Congregations and Community Service

Congregations provided programs to serve families and members as well as assistance for some of the most difficult social problems facing communities today. In the national survey, two waves of congregations (1,353) were given more detailed questionnaires to answer about their activities. In order to determine how services that congregations offered were clumped together, we conducted a correlation analysis of the activities and then did a factor analysis of the correlations.

For this analysis, the responses of 1,192 congregations were analyzed by means of thirty-five direct questions about programs or activities. The factor analysis produced three separate clusters of activities or factors that are uncorrelated with one another but can be used to explain the activities of congregations. These three separate factors in which the factor loadings were above 0.4 clustered around (1) human services to those in need, (2) international and/or community concerns, and (3) educational programs. (Factor values, or loadings, can range between 1.00 and −1.00.)

Essentially, congregations that provided programs serving people in need were most likely to have a cluster of programs. The most common cluster was programs in child abuse (0.819); battered women (0.778), teenage pregnancy (0.690), housing for senior citizens (0.690), foster care (0.642), housing for the homeless (0.617), and to a lesser extent, after-school programs (0.593), day care for the elderly (0.553), migrant or refugee programs (0.527), family planning (0.483), programmatic assistance for the physically and mentally disabled (0.429), and meal services (0.418).

The second area of clustered activities in which congregations engaged was that of international and/or community concerns. Congregations that had activities on international programs both in the United States and abroad (0.654) were also likely to have similar activities in health (0.654), peace and security (0.648), civil rights and social justice (0.605), nuclear disarmament (0.592), relief abroad (0.580), promotion of friendly relations abroad (0.559), and refugee-related programs (0.539). To a lesser extent, congregations were also likely to engage in programs for public education on diseases, such as AIDS (0.506), community development (0.500), environmental quality protection (0.493), arts and culture (0.491), programmatic assistance for the physically and mentally disabled (0.465), and institutional care, such as hospices, clinics, and nursing homes (0.454).

Congregations interested in education were also most likely to offer several programs. Those most likely to be clustered together were secondary education (0.906) and elementary education (0.854), followed by adult basic education (0.743) and higher education (0.706).

These findings suggest that congregational activities other than religious services and religious education focus on three distinct groupings: services to those in need, international and community interests, and education. Moreover, if congregations focus on activities in any one of these areas, they are likely to offer a cluster of programs. For the sample, of the 93 percent that reported programs in human services, the largest group (41 percent) reported five or more activities in human services; in international programs, of the 75 percent of congregations that reported such activities, 27 percent reported five or more activities; in community and public or societal benefits, of the 72 percent that reported such programs, 21 percent reported five or more activities; and in education, of the 45 percent that reported such activities, 24 percent reported four activities. In terms of the proportion of congregations offering such programs, programs serving those in need were clearly most numerous.

Congregational representatives were asked what in their opinion were the three most important activities they engaged in other than religious services and education. The most frequent responses were recreation and camps for children (22.3 percent) and relief-abroad programs (11.5 percent). The other most frequently mentioned responses were human service activities (9.8 percent), day care for children (9.3 percent), public and societal benefit programs in general (9.3 percent), family counseling (8.9 percent), education (8.8 percent), meal services (8.6 percent), and food and clothing distribution (7.8 percent). Again, the programs most frequently mentioned by respondents were those involving activities that serve children and those in need.

We also examined the relationship of congregations' perceptions of the effect of recent changes in public policy (such as in health and welfare programs) on their members and the activities they provided, especially in relationship to the needs of the community. From the sample of 1,192 congregations, only 19 reported that as a result of recent public policy changes, their members were "considerably improved," while 149 responded that their members were "moderately improved," 708 reported "no change," 252 reported that their members were "moderately impaired," and 64 reported that they were "considerably impaired."

While the sample size of 19 congregational representatives who responded "considerably improved" would usually be too small to keep as a separate group for analysis, there was a large enough sample on the other end of the spectrum (64) who answered "considerably impaired" to keep the five groupings. (See Table 5.1.)

The most interesting pattern to emerge was the V-shaped

Table 5.1. Percentage of Congregations Reporting Activity
Based Upon Their Perception of the Effect of Recent
Public Policy Changes on Their Members.

Activity	Considerably Improved N(19)	Moderately Improved N(149)	No Change N(708)	Moderately Impaired N(252)	Considerably Impaired N(64)
Human Services/Welfare Activities					
Meal services	57.9	45.0	37.0	44.4	48.4
Day care (preschool)	36.8	32.2	29.8	36.9	43.8
Day care (elderly)	42.1	27.5	25.1	27.8	32.8
After-school programs	42.1	34.9	27.4	34.9	43.8
Battered women	31.6	31.5	21.8	29.4	34.4
Teenage pregnancy	42.1	35.6	25.1	34.9	37.5
Tutoring	31.6	31.5	22.3	32.9	37.5
Housing for the homeless	31.6	38.9	29.8	40.5	48.4
Housing for senior citizens	21.1	26.2	17.2	21.4	31.3
Migrants/refugees	15.8	26.9	19.5	25.4	37.5
Foster care	26.3	24.8	20.2	25.0	32.8
Public and Societal Benefit Programs					
Civil rights/social justice	57.9	44.3	37.6	57.5	68.8
Community development	63.2	52.4	40.8	55.1	70.3
Family planning/ abortion	36.8	37.6	27.0	36.5	48.4
Right-to-life	57.9	57.1	46.8	44.4	54.7
International					
Relief abroad	73.7	69.8	68.4	77.8	79.7
Refugee programs	36.8	37.6	30.8	42.1	53.1
Health and Hospitals					
Institutional care	73.7	56.4	48.7	59.9	70.3
Programmatic assistance (mentally and physically disabled)	57.9	48.3	38.6	51.6	64.1
Public education on diseases (AIDS, etc.)	42.1	35.6	31.5	44.4	48.4

Note: "No answer" or "don't know" responses were deleted before percentages were computed.

distribution, with those congregations on either end of the spectrum providing the most services. Even in cases such as "housing for the homeless," where the small size of 19 causes a change in this pattern, the middle or "no change" congregational representatives least reported offering the services or programs. These findings suggest that congregations that reported that their members were either improved or impaired by recent public policy changes were likely to be far more active in community services. This is particularly true among congregations reporting that the effect of public policy changes had impaired their members. They were most likely to offer programs in meal services, housing for the homeless, day care, afterschool programs, civil rights or social justice programs, and community development activities. They were most likely to support relief abroad and refugee programs and to engage in support for institutional health care programs and programmatic assistance for the physically and mentally handicapped. In most of these activities, congregations focused on programs for people in need, both at home and abroad. However, a significant proportion of congregations also engaged in activities that addressed long-term solutions, such as community development. What we do not know is whether these congregations have increased such activities as a result of changes in public policy.

Patterns of Giving and Volunteering by Membership Status in Religious Organizations

In the 1988 national survey of giving and volunteering (Hodgkinson and Weitzman, 1988), individuals were asked a series of questions to determine the level of individual giving and volunteering. In that survey, 65 percent of American adults reported that they were members of religious congregations and 35 percent were nonmembers. The survey showed that members of religious congregations were far more likely to report making contributions (80 percent) than nonmembers (55 percent). Members were also much more likely to volunteer (51 percent) than nonmembers (33 percent).

Scholars have commented that individuals who give to

religious organizations do not necessarily support other charities, or if they do, they may not support them at the same level as those who do not give to religious organizations. In order to examine these hypotheses, we separated the national sample into members and nonmembers and examined the patterns of their giving to other charities.

In 1987, out of 91 million households, 65 percent reported church membership and 35 percent reported nonmembership. Eighty percent of member households and 55 percent of nonmember households reported giving to at least one charity. Of member households, 38 percent reported giving to only one charity, 29 percent reported giving to two charities, and 33 percent reported giving to three charities. Among nonmembers, 46 percent reported giving to one charity, 28 percent reported giving to two charities, and 26 percent reported giving to three or more charities. It is clear from these findings that a larger proportion (both in actual number and percentage) of members than nonmembers are likely to give to more than one charity. Members were 50 percent more likely to volunteer than nonmembers.

Not only do more members give to more than one charity, but they give a higher percentage of their household income. Members who reported giving only to one charity gave an average contribution of $511, or 2.0 percent of average household income ($25,729); of those who gave to two charities, the average contribution was $679, or 2.1 percent of average household income ($32,368); of those who gave to three or more charities, their average contribution was $1,386, or 3.6 percent of average household income ($38,738). Nonmembers gave an average contribution of $277, or 0.8 percent of average household income ($33,035), to one charity; $229, or 0.6 percent of average household income ($37,882), to two charities; and $789, or 2.0 percent of average income ($39,280), to three or more charities. Although the amount of donations tended to rise with household income for both members and nonmembers, membership in a religious organization was more important as a determinant of the percentage of income given than income itself. In all cases, members with a lower average household income than nonmembers gave from two to three times as much as a percentage of household income than nonmembers.

Patterns of gift giving to various charities by membership status were analyzed to determine whether there were differences in gift giving by type of charity between members and nonmembers. Of the 52 percent of total households that gave to religion, 87 percent were members of religious organizations and 13 percent were not. When the number of total contributions to various charities was disaggregated by membership, between 60 and 69 percent of the total households that contributed to arts and culture, international causes, and public benefit causes were members of religious organizations; between 70 and 80 percent of households that contributed to education, health, human services, and youth development were members; and more than 80 percent of households that contributed to private and community foundations were members. Only in the area of the environment was there more of a balance: Of total households that contributed to environmental causes, 57 percent were members and 43 percent were nonmembers.

Another way of looking at the distribution of contributions by charity is to examine the proportion of giving among member and nonmember households that gave to particular types of charities. The highest proportion of members gave to religious organizations (88 percent) followed by human services (33 percent), health (32 percent), youth development (26 percent), and education (25 percent). Nonmembers contributed to health (38 percent), human services (35 percent), religion (35 percent), youth development (26 percent), and environmental causes (25 percent). While nearly twice as many member households (4.8 million) contributed to the arts as did nonmember households (2.5 million), as a proportion of total contributors in each group, nonmembers were somewhat more likely to give to the arts (14 percent) than were members (10 percent). Contributors to environmental causes among member households (5.5 million) and nonmember households (4.3 million) were much closer, but as a proportion of total contributors in each group, nonmembers were more than twice as likely to contribute to environmental causes (25 percent) than were members (12 percent).

Although members and nonmembers contributed to similar charities, members were far more likely to support religion and education than were nonmembers, who were more likely to support environmental causes and the arts. The patterns of membership also reflect the patterns of activities of religious institutions. Congregations spent most of their time and money on religion, education, human services (including youth development), and health. The largest proportion of members of religious congregations gave to these types of charities.

There were large differences, however, among the total percentage of income given between members and nonmembers who gave to all charities, particularly among those who gave to three or more charities. Member and nonmember households that gave to three or more charities were grouped by each type of charity and by the percentage of average household income contributed. Except for the arts and the environment, three to four times as many members as nonmembers contributed to all other charities. Twice as many members contributed to the arts, and a third more members contributed to the environment. Members who gave to three or more charities, one of which was human services, or youth development, or public and societal benefit, or international causes, gave 4 percent or more of their household income to charity, whereas nonmembers gave from 1.6 percent to 2.4 percent of their average household income. Members who gave three or more gifts to charity, one of which was health, or education, or the environment gave from 3.1 to 3.8 percent of their household income to charity, whereas nonmembers gave from 1.9 percent to 2.5 percent. Members were much more likely than nonmembers to be multiple givers.

A fairly common assumption prevails among the public and even in religious communities that women give more to religion than do men. The findings of the national survey do not confirm this assumption. Among the total population, females represent 51.6 percent and males 48.4 percent. Among the percentage of respondents reporting household giving by sex,

73.1 percent of females and 68.9 percent of males reported giving. The distribution of total givers was 53.1 percent females and 46.9 percent males. While females gave an average household contribution $790 (1.8 percent of household income), males gave $888 (2.1 percent of household income). Of total contributions, females represented 47 percent and males, 53 percent. In terms of total contributions, males tended to be slightly more generous than females, although the proportion of females giving was slightly higher than males.

This distribution of total giving was about the same for the distribution among males and females who reported household contributions to religion. Forty-seven percent of females and 43 percent of males reported contributing to religion. Of the total composition of giving to religion, 53.9 percent were females and 46.1 percent were males, which was similar to the breakdown for the total population of contributors. The average contribution of females to religion was $649 (1.9 percent of household income) and $791 for males (2.0 percent of household income). Of the total contributions to religious organizations, 49 percent came from females and 51 percent from males, which was only slightly different than for total giving.

The average amount given by type of charity varied by members and nonmembers. The average gifts to religion by members were two and a half times as large as those given by nonmembers. Members and nonmembers gave about the same average gift to education and health. Members gave higher average contributions to human services, youth development, and public and societal benefit programs than did nonmembers. Nonmembers gave higher average contributions to environmental and international causes. Nonmembers' average contributions to the arts were more than three times higher than those of members.

Overall, 42 million contributing household members had 62 percent of total household income in the United States in 1988 and gave 85 percent of total contributions in that year. The pattern of gift giving among members reflected the pattern of activities of congregations, where the greatest attention was given to health, education, and human services, including youth development. Contributions to other charities by members of religious institutions represented two-thirds of total giving to these organizations. By type of charity, giving by religious members accounted for 83 percent of total contributions to youth development, 81 percent to public and societal benefit organizations, 76 percent to education, 69 percent to human services, 69 percent to health, 66 percent to international causes, 44 percent to environmental organizations, and 40 percent to arts and culture.

Volunteer service among members and nonmembers followed similar patterns of giving. Members were five times as likely as nonmembers to volunteer to religious organizations, half again as likely to volunteer in education and human services, and equally as likely to volunteer in the arts.

Religious Involvement and Giving and Volunteering

Frequency of attendance at religious services was also analyzed to explore the relationship of religious involvement and giving and volunteering to other charitable causes. Respondents were asked how often they attended religious services — weekly, two to three times a month, less than once a month, within the last six months, within the past six to twelve months, within the last one or two years, or never. Responses were analyzed by the total sample, by members and nonmembers, by household income, and by levels of giving and volunteering.

Approximately 61 percent of American adults reported that they had attended church in the past six months. They gave an average contribution of $818, or 1.9 percent of their average household income ($30,775). Those 29 percent who attended church once a week gave 2.7 percent of their average income compared with the 14 percent who attended two or three times a month and gave 1.4 percent of their average household income ($29,788), the 15 percent who attended less than once a month and gave 0.8 percent of their average household income ($33,269), and the 7.2 percent who attended in the last six to twelve months and gave 0.7 percent of their average household income ($34,221). Another 32 percent of respondents who reported that they had not attended church in the last year or two or never attended gave only 1.1 percent of their average household income ($41,516).

The proportion of respondents who contributed and volunteered increased by frequency of church attendance. Of those households that reported weekly church attendance, 83 percent contributed and 62 percent volunteered; of those who attended services two or three times a month, 76 percent contributed and 58 percent volunteered; of those who attended once a month, 69 percent contributed and 51 percent volunteered; of those who attended in the last six months, 78 percent contributed and 58 percent volunteered. Of those who attended church within the past year or two years or who never attended, 60 percent contributed and 52 percent volunteered. The level of religious involvement increased the likelihood of both giving and volunteering.

Respondents who reported attending religious services once a week were also most likely to give and volunteer both to religion and other charities. Fifty-three percent of that group gave both to religion and other charities, and 73 percent volunteered. In comparison, 44 percent of those who attended two or three times a month contributed to both, and 69 percent volunteered. Of those who attended less than once a month, 34 percent contributed to both, and 54 percent volunteered. Finally, only 22 percent of those who attended within the last year to two years or never attended contributed both to religion and other charitable causes, and 62 percent of that group volunteered.

Although membership in religious organizations did not vary much by income group, attendance at religious services did. At least 60 percent of all income groups other than those over $100,000 reported that they were members of religious organizations. Approximately 49 percent of households with an income of $100,000 or more reported membership. From 28 to 35 percent of households with an income below $50,000 reported attending religious services weekly, while fewer than 20 percent of those households with an income of $50,000 and above reported attending religious services weekly. While fewer than one-quarter of all households with an income of up to

$50,000 reported attending religious services within the last one to two years or never, over half of all households with an income of more than $50,000 reported not attending or never attending. However, among those with a household income of more than $50,000, nearly two-thirds of those who professed membership gave to both religious organizations and other charities.

Weekly attendance at religious services (26.4 million households) was associated with a high level of giving and volunteering both to religious organizations and to other charities and appears to have an impact on total individual giving. The 22.0 million contributing households in this group gave 48 percent of total individual contributions, although they represented only 24 percent of total households (91 million). The 13.9 million of these households that contributed to both religion and other charities represented 37 percent of total giving, although this group comprised only 15 percent of total households.

Weekly attendees at religious services had a lower average household income ($30,532) than did those who attended once a month or less ($33,269), or those who attended in the last six to twelve months ($34,221), or those who had not attended in the last year to two years or never attended ($41,516). These findings suggest that active involvement in religious organizations leads to active involvement in other charitable activities. They also suggest that generosity with money and time is not so much determined by income as by level of religious commitment.

The Influence of Personal Goals on Giving and Volunteering

Respondents were asked a series of questions relating to their personal goals. These goals ranged from having a nice home to making a strong commitment to religion. Those respondents who reported that making contributions to charity (13 percent) or making a strong commitment to a religious life (28 percent) or giving time to charities (9 percent) was an absolutely essential personal goal gave and volunteered in much higher proportions than did respondents who reported other personal goals as absolutely essential. Nearly 80 percent of each of these groups contributed to charity, and 55 percent or more volunteered. As a percentage of household income, respondents who both contributed and volunteered and who reported that giving to charities was an essential personal goal gave 3.9 percent of their average household income, or nearly twice the national average household contribution (1.9 percent). Those who reported that making a commitment to a religious life was essential gave 3.8 percent of their average household income, and those who reported that giving time to charities was essential gave 3.0 percent. Those who did not volunteer but who contributed were still more generous than the average contributor, but not as generous as those who also volunteered.

Respondents who listed these personal goals as absolutely essential were far more likely to be members of religious organizations: Nearly 85 percent of those who reported that giving to charities and making a strong commitment to religious life were members, and 75 percent of those who thought giving time to charities was essential were members. Even in this very generous group, those who were members and both contributed and volunteered gave a much higher percentage of household income than nonmembers. For those who responded that giving time was absolutely essential, members gave 3.5 percent of their household income compared to 2.0 percent for nonmembers. For those who thought that contributing to charity was essential, members gave 4.3 percent of their household income compared with 2.9 percent for nonmembers; those members who thought that making a strong commitment to religious life was essential gave 4.3 percent of their household income compared with 1.6 percent of nonmembers.

Members seem to have more of a social orientation than nonmembers. When respondents were asked how they first started volunteering, members were three times as likely to state that they learned about their volunteer assignment through participation in an organization and 75 percent more likely to respond that someone had asked them. Members were three times as likely as nonmembers to report that they were very active in their communities and more than twice as likely as nonmembers to report that they were fairly active. While only one-third of members reported that they were not active at all in their communities, nearly three-fifths of nonmembers reported that they were not active at all in their communities.

Another indicator of the willingness to give and volunteer more was captured in a question that asked Americans what percentage of income they ought to give and how many hours a week they ought to volunteer. Although approximately half of all Americans responded that they did not know or gave no answer to this question, members of religious organizations were much more likely to respond that they should give from 5 to 10 percent of their household income to charitable causes (71 percent) than were nonmembers (29 percent). Members were even more likely to respond that they should give 10 percent or more of their household income (82 percent) than were nonmembers (18 percent). Members also were more likely to respond that they ought to volunteer from three to four hours per week (78 percent) than were nonmembers (22 percent), or four to five hours per week (71 percent compared with 29 percent), or five or more hours per week (73 percent compared with 27 percent).

The goals for both giving and volunteering were much higher among members than nonmembers. In terms of actual behavior, of the 9 percent of households that gave 5 percent or more of their household income to charity, 92 percent were members of religious organizations. Of the 12 percent of adults (27 percent of all volunteers) who volunteered five or more hours per week, 78 percent were members.

Membership in religious organizations also seems to lead to a greater cohesiveness among age-groups. Among age-groups, from 68 percent to 82 percent of members contributed. Among nonmembers, the range was from 38 percent to 62 percent. Sixty-eight percent of adults between eighteen and twenty-four years of age who were members of religious organizations contributed compared with 39 percent who were nonmembers. Three-quarters of adults between twenty-five and thirty-four years of age who were members contributed compared with 52 percent of nonmembers. Of adults between thirty-five and sixty-four years of age, 82 percent of members contributed compared with 62 percent of nonmembers. Among adults sixty-five years of age or older, 78 percent of members contributed compared with 54 percent of nonmembers. Members were 45 percent more likely to contribute than nonmembers.

A similar relationship was also found in volunteering. From 45 to 56 percent of members between the ages of eighteen and sixty-four years of age volunteered, and 38 percent of members sixty-five years of age or older volunteered. Among nonmembers, from 28 to 37 percent of adults between the ages of eighteen and sixty-four years of age volunteered, and 26 percent of those sixty-five years of age or older volunteered. Members were 50 percent more likely than nonmembers to volunteer.

Summary and Conclusions

Although a direct causal relationship cannot be established from the two national surveys, the characteristics of members of religious organizations and the activities of religious congregations suggest that what is learned in religious institutions seems to have an influence on giving and volunteering generally. In an average month, volunteers to religious organizations contributed approximately 107 million hours, of which 56 million were devoted to religious ministry and education, and 51 million were devoted to other activities in education, human services and welfare, health, activities for the public benefit, arts and culture, international causes, and environmental quality improvement. The analyses of individual giving and volunteering show that individuals who are members of religious organizations are half again as likely as nonmembers to be both contributors and volunteers.

The findings from these two national surveys suggest that congregations are actively involved in their communities and that members of religious organizations give and volunteer in higher proportions than nonmembers. The findings also suggest that if membership or church attendance at religious institutions declines, giving and volunteering for all charities will decline.

It has been accepted almost as a truism that voluntary associations, particularly religious congregations, provide

Americans with the opportunity to participate directly in their local community and to remind them daily that they live in a society. Alexis de Tocqueville, the first great commentator on American society, asserted that such associations were critically important to preserve democratic traditions and to restrict rampant individualistic materialism. He saw these associations as the local groups in which individuals would constantly be reminded of their public responsibility and to build "the habit and taste" to work for the "good of one's fellow citizens." Without such associations, de Tocqueville warned, the natural development of large bureaucratic structures and a huge centralized government could evolve into a benign dictatorship where individuals were provided their material wants but no longer would be free (de Tocqueville, [1835] 1956, pp. 111–112).

Robert Bellah and his colleagues (Bellah and others, 1985) sought to examine the changes that had taken place since de Tocqueville's time. They found that voluntary associations including religious congregations were more numerous than they were in de Tocqueville's time but that "utilitarian and expressive" individualism was rampant. Commitment had become a "private" rather than a "public" behavior, and voluntary associations were less likely to serve as bridges to the larger "public" community, nation, and world than they were to become places where individuals could escape from those public realms.

Other scholars have also noted the importance of religious congregations in building community cohesion, supporting democratic principles, and preserving the public good (de Tocqueville, [1835] 1956; Moberg, 1984; Reichley, 1985).

A recent review of the literature on motivations for giving and volunteering revealed that social and behavioral scientists have given little systematic attention to the influence of religious belief and involvement upon individual motivations to give, volunteer, or participate in community activities (Hodgkinson, 1990). Some social and behavioral scientists have recognized this lack of attention. Donald Campbell (1975, p. 1120) in his presidential address to the American Psychological Association warned his colleagues that their neglect to study this important area of social and moral tradition "may be contributing to undermining the retention of what may be extremely valuable social-evolutionary inhibitory systems which we do not understand," and called on his colleagues to give far greater attention to the "scientific reasons" for these belief systems that lead people to become "morally committed persons" and to find meaning in their lives.

References

AAFRC Trust for Philanthropy. *Giving USA: The Annual Report on Philanthropy for the Year 1987*. New York: AAFRC Trust for Philanthropy, 1988.

Bellah, R., and others. *Habits of the Heart*. Berkeley: University of California Press, 1985.

Campbell, D. T. "On the Conflict Between Biological and Social Evolution and Between Psychology and Moral Tradition." *American Psychologist*, Dec. 1975, *30*, 1103–1126.

de Tocqueville, A. *Democracy in America*. 2 vols. New York: Viking, 1956.

Hodgkinson, V. A. *Motivations for Giving and Volunteering*. New York: Foundation Center, 1990

Hodgkinson, V. A., and Weitzman, M. S. *Dimensions of the Independent Sector: A Statistical Profile*. Washington, D.C.: INDEPENDENT SECTOR, 1986.

Hodgkinson, V. A., and Weitzman, M. S. *Giving and Volunteering in the United States*. Findings from a national survey conducted by the Gallup Organization. Washington, D.C.: INDEPENDENT SECTOR, 1988.

Hodgkinson, V. A., Weitzman, M. S., and Kirsch, A. D. *From Belief to Commitment: The Activities and Finances of Religious Congregations in the United States*. Findings from a national survey conducted by the Gallup Organization. Washington, D.C.: INDEPENDENT SECTOR, 1988.

Moberg, D. A. *The Church as a Social Institution*. Grand Rapids, Mich.: Baker Books, 1984.

Reichley, A. J. *Religion in American Public Life*. Washington, D.C.: Brookings Institution, 1985.

Chapter 6

William E. McManus

Stewardship and Almsgiving in the Roman Catholic Tradition

"How shall I make a return to the Lord for all the good he has done for me?" (Psalm 116:12) has been popularized by promoters of philanthropy for religious enterprises. It pointedly suggests that the generosity of gifts to religion should approximate God's personal generosity to the donor. To give less than God has given should make a donor feel guilty of ingratitude to the divine benefactor, but to give more than required by normal reciprocity between beneficiary and benefactor will invite God's extraordinary favor upon the recipient of God's largesse. Exploited by for-profit professionals engaged in fund-raising for nonprofit religious organizations, this biblical slogan threatens God's punishment on less-than-generous or negligent donors but promises heavenly rewards to liberal donors, particularly to exceptionally "big givers." Is that "stewardship"?

In the context of the psalm from which this much-used (and abused) quotation is excerpted, it has nothing to do with philanthropy or fund-raising or religious motivation for donations. The psalmist composed a prayer of thanksgiving to God for his recovery from a near-death, critical illness. He wrote: "The cords of death encompassed me; the snares of the nether world seized upon me; I fell into distress and sorrow, and I called upon the name of the Lord, 'O Lord, save my life.'. . . How shall I make a return to the Lord for all the good he has done for me?" (Psalm 116:3–4).

The psalmist's question is rhetorical, purposely unanswerable, his way of saying: Wondrously has God pulled me back from death's door; there is no way for me adequately to thank God for saving my life.

My critique of the psalm need not imply that praying the biblical words in a setting other than its original life-saving scenario is inappropriate. The Bible's words are inspired (here that can be taken doctrinally as meaning God's words or as being literature phrased in revered, sacred words) and, long after their original composition, remain alive and pertinent to the human condition. I should be the last to disparage praying these esteemed words in gratitude for all or any of God's blessings, be they as earthy as winning a state lottery or as heavenly as conversion to a religious way of life.

I will maintain, however, that my comments on the psalm are on target. Exploitive misuse of biblical words to produce philanthropy and donations to religion is wrong regardless of its success in raising large amounts of money for commendable purposes, and all the more so when this misuse seduces contributors into making good donations for the wrong reasons.

In his classic drama *Murder in the Cathedral*, T. S. Eliot has Thomas of Becket confront a temptation to embrace his impending assassination as a glorious martyrdom that will give him an exalted place in heaven, a cathedral on earth in his memory, and the honors of a sainthood in his church. Resisting the temptation, Thomas declares: "This last temptation is the greatest treason: to do the right deed for the wrong reason" (Eliot, 1935, p. 44).

That wicked temptation lurks in much contemporary Roman Catholic fund-raising. The mighty arm of God is stretched almost out of its socket to threaten or to cajole prospective donors. Some Sunday collection envelopes, a customary vehicle for contributions to church, sloganize: "Give to God" over a table of "suggested" donations ranging from the top open ended, for the best givers, to the bottom five dollars, presumably for the worst givers. Other envelopes inquire: "What is your gift to God today?," a question about as tasteless as a hand laundry's paper band around a laundered male shirt asking, "Did you kiss your wife today?"

In the minds of some Roman Catholics this kind of a

heavy-handed appeal has left two deplorably bad impressions: the first, that God, as it were, can be bought and that, like everything else, religion is a service on sale for a fee; and the second, not to pay one's religious dues is to risk God's wrath, punishment, and even expulsion from his sacred quarters. Among senior Catholics these bad impressions linger over from church school classes and Sunday sermons about church law obliging them to give to the church or else be guilty of a sin akin to stealing money from a bank. In a parochial school, students were taught to bring their little children's envelope to Mass every Sunday; the delinquent and negligent were subject to public reprimand on Monday morning.

This brief retrospect, however, would be grossly incomplete and distorted if it did not at least allude to the Roman Catholic church's spectacular success in acquiring enormous amounts of voluntary contributions even though the church's theology of giving, as I see it, was woefully imperfect. For over a little more than a century, U.S. Roman Catholics, though mostly low income, generously gave millions of dollars to finance the construction and operation of thousands of churches and schools and hundreds of hospitals, sanitariums, orphanages, homes for the aged, and cemeteries. Conventional church history would appraise this phenomenon as a deep-seated profession of faith in religious values. And that it was. Religious faith profoundly influenced donors' motives for their extraordinary generosity, but their faith was not detached, nor should it have been, from other values indigenous to an immigrant population. Among these values were ethnicity with which their traditional religious practices were closely associated, an adventurous desire to move their Roman Catholic church into the mainstream of U.S. society, and a dogged determination not to be outclassed by their affluent Protestant neighbors. These pioneer Roman Catholics wanted to retain in their new homeland all the religious values they cherished in their native lands, but to leave behind all the evils they fled by immigrating into the New World. One evil to be entirely rid of was to be dependent upon high-powered government or upon wealthy and powerful benefactors for the financial support of their church institutions. In their new domicile they were willing to pay the price for having their church be independent of any kind of governmental involvement inevitably leading, they believed, to government restrictions and controls. Never before had these immigrants made donations equal to the amounts they gave to their church in their country. But they gave (Dolan, 1985, chap. 5).

This pioneer period, however, also had some episodes that seemed to push God to the side. For almost seventy-five years, trusteeism, a series of bitter power struggles between laity and clergy to own, control, and administer church temporalities, fractured parish communities and dragged laity and clergy into civil courts for settlement of their differences. Trusteeism was at its most bitter when lay trustees, not satisfied with control of church property, demanded authority to appoint and to supervise the clergy. (See Dolan, 1985, index.)

In most pioneer parishes, parishioners rented a church pew for their regular occupancy at parish Masses. In the South, all the choice pews were rented to whites seated up front, while blacks were segregated in the rear. After collecting pew rent became impractical in mobile urban areas, seat payment was substituted, making the rear vestibule of some city churches look like the ancient Jewish temple's portico where Jesus lashed out at the money changers (Mt 21:12–14). This pay-as-you-enter procedure, which I remember from my boyhood, was an unseemly fund raiser, even though the entrance charge was only a dime, children free! In my memory, seat payment was the first crude sign of a trend to make the norm for fund raising an utterly pragmatic test: Does it work; does it bring in some money? That trend began not with any thought or intention to minimize religious motives; it was, I believe, a reaction to a mounting need for more money to finance the church services that parishioners rightfully expected in return for their donations.

After World War II, the U.S. Roman Catholic church launched an unprecedented expansion of its facilities and services to care for several millions of Catholics who, having moved from urban "old neighborhoods" or rural towns to brand-new suburbs or to Sunbelt cities, were clamoring for parish churches in which to worship and for parochial schools in which to educate their baby boom children. Exhilarated by this dramatic growth, religious orders (for example, Jesuits, Sisters of Charity, and so on), anticipating substantially increased membership, constructed additions and new buildings to accommodate young people whom they intended to recruit energetically. (A very disappointing response starting in about 1965 left the orders with many empty or underused "white elephants".)

Confident that the church's financial condition was sound and would improve along with its expansion projects, banks loaned millions at prime rate. Everywhere, church administrators, particularly parish pastors, facing enormous debt and soaring costs for operations, needed money in a hurry and went after it hastily. During this time I heard no one prominent in the church speak about "theology of giving" or "religious motivation" for donations. All administrative attention seemed to be focused on raising a lot of money quickly. Staying solvent allowed no alternative. Consequently, the church's fund raising techniques became almost entirely secularized, being not much different from those used by a myriad of good-cause organizations and agencies in need of quick money for their activities.

Some techniques were dignified and proper; others were vulgar, even crude. Few had an overt religious component other than the religious character of the beneficiary to which all the fund raising was directed.

Two prominent dignified techniques were "professional counsel" and "development programs." Professional counsel opened church offices to fund raising specialists who usually were versatile enough to solicit money for anything from a humane society's animal shelter to a renovated cathedral. Give me a good case, these specialists would say to a prospective client, and our company will appraise its appeal, set a goal for the money it will attract, and set up a program to gather in the funds in both up-front gifts and long-term pledges. Where the "case" and its value fit into the church's eccelesiology was of little or no concern to the professionals, other than to advise rather seductively that contributors readily donate to things they can see and use, like a social hall or gymnasium, but they don't respond as well to appeals for institutional charity and even less to appeals for funds to hike church employees' salaries and benefits. Repeatedly, however, professionals produced far better results than did unassisted local efforts.

"Development" gave professional fund raising a permanent position in church institutions with long-range financial needs and plans. Generally, development officers have had a clear idea of their institution's purposes and values and have geared their fund raising to the institution's goals and objectives. Unlike "counselors," who stage a fund drive over a fixed period of time and then move on, developers are established officers of an institution. They undertake a variety of fund-raising activities, ranging widely through annual dinners, alumni appeals, wills, insurance bequests, approaches to philanthropic organizations, solicitation of donations from wealthy individuals, and the like. Developers usually search for funds anywhere they may be and are little concerned with a benefactor's sources of wealth. Ironically, some benefactors of the church are individuals whose personal allegiance to the church is minimal or who often disagree with official church teaching on social issues. An example is an industrialist who, responding to a developer's solicitation, may donate a million dollars for Catholic Charities but denounce the church for advocating a raise of the minimum wage.

During this boom time from about 1948 to 1968, the most prominent "vulgar" fund-raising technique was legal and illegal gambling that sometimes produced local church income as much as 25 to 50 percent of the revenue from normal contributions. Much of this money went into the finances of parochial schools. The gambling therefore was rationalized as being appropriate because many gamblers at church affairs were nonmembers who in the long run benefited from parochial schools' voluntary support in lieu of taxes the gamblers would have to pay. Many church leaders deplored their involvement in gambling, were embarrassed by its vulgarity, and regretted their dependence upon it but nonetheless felt compelled to tolerate it as a desperate way to remain solvent.

The worst vulgarity was the despicable use of school

children to huckster overpriced candy bars and junk jewelry for the benefit of their parochial school. This "industry," however, was big business at annual conventions of the National Catholic Education Association (which also featured sessions on child abuse and its prevention) and still holds a place despite parochial school parents' well-founded fears of child molestation. "Let the little children come to me" with their candy bars for sale was not an appropriate biblical image of a church school.

In 1965, when the U.S. Roman Catholic bishops went to Rome to participate in the first session of the Second Vatican Council, they left behind an institutional church apparently in good shape. Hopes were high that the council would spark even more enthusiastic devotion to the church's improved ministries and organizations. Finances seemed sound even though the cost of expansion had depleted reserves. There was little fear that Catholics, having moved up the economic ladder, would not be able to pay off indebtedness on their church institutions. A business executive might well have said, "That Roman church is big business, and it's doing well. Buy a church bond if there's one to purchase!"

All this had been accomplished by *nontraditional* (as I will explain shortly) fund raising.

Ten years later, in the mid 1970s, the church went into a tailspin. Hundreds of clergy and nuns quit their ministries; active church membership declined; Catholic school enrollment plummeted; expansion of buildings ground to a halt; some seminary and convent buildings only twenty years old were put up for sale; bitter protests against church teaching on sexual ethics were out in the open; some theologians challenged the validity of long-held doctrines and positions. Only hospitals and cemeteries were holding their own!

Reasons, actual and alleged, for this phenomenon are too many and too complex for even summary treatment in this chapter. Though I'm not sure of it, my opinion is that many Catholics misinterpreted Vatican II as being primarily an emancipation from church rules rather than as a call to personal religious renewal that made more demands upon them than did the rules from which they sought escape. For example, excused from the ancient custom of not eating meat on Friday, Catholics enjoyed their Friday steaks and sausage without giving a thought to the council's challenging admonition that they voluntarily undertake self-denial, mortification, and penance in atonement for their sinfulness. When the council broadened its self-understanding of church to mean the "people of God" and not only a hierarchical organization of professed members, it did not mean that each Catholic, being a person of God, could, on a Sunday morning, build his or her church bedside instead of attending Mass in a parish church. Vatican II's full-blown description of a truly active Catholic should have put church members more in need of the church's services than they were before the council. Many, however, did not hear this message or chose not to hear it.

During the turbulent 1970s and into the 1980s Roman Catholic leadership was so preoccupied with the clergy's and laity's surprising reactions to Vatican II that it gave scant attention to church finances. The National Conference of Catholic Bishops, established in 1966, allocated most of its resources to the pressing business of making the best possible application of Vatican II decisions to the U.S. Roman Catholic church. On the diocesan and parish levels, bishops and pastors were dismayed by drops in church attendance and school enrollment. They often were caught in controversies between those who contended that the church was abandoning its traditions and others who complained that the church was dragging its feet in making Vatican II changes. Understandably, church leaders did not give much more than routine care to finances. That is not to say that they found it easy to hold church income apace with rapidly escalating inflation and greatly enlarged expenditures for lay employee salaries; nonetheless, they rarely made finances the number one item on diocesan and parish agendas. As one pastor put it to me: "Our parish is comfortably broke; every month we pay our bills and wind up with a zero balance; there isn't a penny to spend for improvements or to lay aside in reserve for repairs of aging buildings. Each year we increase our revenue four or five percent but because of inflation, continue to be 'comfortably broke.'"

Fund-raising techniques remained conventional: Sunday envelopes, "special" collections, professionally conducted fund drives, development programs, solicitation of bequests, and as much gambling as the law allowed or tolerated. In the bishops' conference a plan to consolidate an excessive number of national appeals into a reasonably small number, each backed up by sound doctrinal and theological reasoning, collapsed when vested interest organizations, flying a church flag, reneged on allowing their particular identity and "traditional Sunday" to be submerged into the consolidation.[1] It was argued by some that frequent appeals for money would raise more than appealing for it less often, even for persuasive spiritual reasons.

Meanwhile, the National Catholic Stewardship Council,[2] a relatively inconspicuous organization in the Church structure, valiantly tried to encourage the articulation of religious motivation for the vast amount of donations the church needs to maintain and to expand its ministries. Alas, the council's convention programs seem to have been preempted by developers, professionals, and technicians who specialize more in the extraction of money than in advocating the right religious reasons for donating it. However, in this secular wilderness, a few prophets (Derek, n.d.), like the Bible's John the Baptizer, have been crying out "to make way for the Lord" (Mt 3:3) and to return to his gospel of stewardship as the Christian way to raise money for his church. Their prophecies now are receiving more attention.

In our little book about Catholic contributions (Greeley and McManus, 1987), my colleague, Father Andrew Greeley, documents a serious downfall of Catholic church income from 1963 until 1984. (An unpublished document reports a further decline into 1988.) In 1963, U.S. Roman Catholic contributors, sampled scientifically, donated to their church 2.2 percent of their gross income; in 1984, this percentage dropped to 1.2 percent. In round figures this means that a typical contributor with a gross income of $10,000 in 1963 made a $220 donation that year. In 1984, this same Catholic, though now having an income of $30,000 (which adjusted for inflation in 1984, is the same as the $10,000 in 1963) donated $330, an increase of $110 over 1963. Because of inflation, however, church expenses in

1984 were more than triple the cost for the same expenses in 1963. If the donor's contribution had risen at the same pace as church expenses, it would have been $660, three times the amount donated in 1963, and equal to 2.2 percent of the donor's $30,000 gross income in 1984.

The above calculation is a reliable indicator that the church's income, adjusted to inflation, has been and is decreasing at an alarming rate. Other sounds in the alarm are a declining number of active members who usually are steady contributors, diminished donations from contributors who have moved up the economic ladder, Protestant churches' success in maintaining donations at 2.2 percent of gross income while the Catholic church's went down 1.1 percent, the embarrassment being felt by a church that after boldly proclaiming that it would be "exemplary" (National Conference of Catholic Bishops, 1984) in the management of its temporalities does not have the finances to pay school teachers salaries that meet even minimum standards of justice.

Though the National Conference of Catholic Bishops, a coordinating agency for the U.S. Roman Catholic church, has so many departments, committees, and task forces that some of its critics refer to it as a bureaucracy, surprisingly, it does not have a committee on church finance. Moreover, the conference's own financial condition and procedures are far from exemplary. In November 1988, the conference appointed a small committee of bishops[3] to look into the religious dimensions of fund raising, with particular attention to stewardship.

And now, an impatient reader of this chapter might ask, what is the place and role of stewardship in the Roman Catholic tradition? Obviously, stewardship has had no overt place or role in the fund raising I have described thus far in this chapter. Moreover, stewardship was not prominent in church support patterns during the past seventeen centuries. During these centuries, the main sources of church support were taxes levied by governments with which the church was allied and income from rich benefices owned by the church or by wealthy individuals. The extent to which stewardship prevailed during the church's first three centuries is as obscure as is much of the history of that ancient time.

Stewardship, I think, was a sound and sacred ideal emphasized by Jesus Christ, advocated by the Evangelists and St. Paul, practiced by the earliest Christian communities, and preserved in the Bible for most of Christianity's time. In the Roman Catholic church, however, stewardship in its full biblical dimensions has been an unpracticed tradition. Presently, it seems to me, it is a precious gem whose time to be renewed has come.[4]

From twenty-six direct references to steward or stewardship in the Bible, I briefly will draw a profile of the biblical concept of a steward.

A steward is a highly trusted manager of an owner's properties, is expected to enhance their value, must be accountable to the owner for the managed properties, and to the extent of trustworthiness, should participate in the owner's comprehensive direction of management plans.

While retaining ultimate dominion over the universe, God has entrusted stewardship of this marvelous creation to human beings. God's people, made a little less than the angels, are stewards of their environment, of the earth's fabulous resources, and of their personal valuables—mind, heart, body, talents, time, wealth, success, everything!

This idea of biblical stewardship has been made contemporary in the adage "stewardship of time, talent, and treasure." Unfortunately, however, some well-intentioned devotees of stewardship have truncated (Hall, 1985) the biblical idea into stewardship of treasure only and, accordingly, are programing it in how-to manuals as an effective way to increase donations to the church. I have heard pastors boast that "stewardship boosted the parish's income 30 percent a Sunday," as though this were proof positive that stewardship had caught on as a faith experience in the parish. Because the word *stewardship* sounds religious, has a place in the Bible, and is the theme of some of Jesus's most interesting parables (for example, Luke 12:13–21, 35–48; 16:1–13; 19:11–26), it runs the risk of being a buzzword exploited by professionals, developers, and promoters in the hope of having a blessing on their pragmatic practice of trying "anything that raises a buck."

Inevitably, I suppose, treasure, that is, money, will be in the limelight of a church-sponsored stewardship project. Perhaps that will be good. Stewards often have a tendency, after they have donated to the church, to think of the rest of their money as all their own, to be spent as they wish with little or no regard for what their religious faith and values may be saying to them about the holy use of money.[5] Conscientious stewardship of treasure, therefore, may set norms not only for donations to church but also for use of all money in light of religious faith and values.

A homey example may clinch my point—and also conclude this chapter's treatment of stewardship. In a church, three stewards, each earning about $40,000 a year, kneel in prayer to ponder their stewardship. Each acknowledges that his income is ultimately God's money and he is managing it for God. The first steward asks: "God, what should I give to my church in testimony to my gratitude to you for allowing me to manage a rich share of your wealth?" The proverbial "voice of conscience" answers: "Give five," that is, five percent of the gross. That the steward does, confident then that reasonably he can do as he pleases with the balance. The second steward prays longer because he is seeking God's guidance on how to manage his total income in accord with his religious convictions and values applied to his responsibilities as husband, father, employer, citizen of his country, member of his neighborhood community, and active member of the church. His donation to the church will be proportioned to his perceptions of financial needs. The amount of the donation will be correlated with his other stewardship responsibilities. The third steward, like the second, relates his donation to the church to his comprehensive stewardship plan for his whole income, and adds to it a stewardship plan for his talents and leisure time. He therefore volunteers a block of talent and time to community projects and, as needed, to his church.

The third model should be the kind of stewardship fostered by the Roman Catholic church.

Much more than stewardship, almsgiving has a prominent place in Roman Catholic tradition. In this tradition, alms-giving is a religious act, usually motivated either by a sense of obligation to help the poor and needy or by compassion, a feeling of suffering with the poor, or by both motives. In this action, individuals or organizations contribute some of their personal or organizational wealth to those in need because of pervasive poverty in their locality or because of local disasters or catastrophes.

The Bible's Old Testament repeatedly emphasizes God's plan and wish that all his people actually be beneficiaries of the abundant wealth and resources he created for all humankind. Observing that this wealth was being mismanaged (failed stewardship!), with some having far more than they needed while others were depressed into poverty, God, the Old Testament says, instructed his prophets-messengers to inform the affluent about their obligation *in justice to God* to share their riches with the poor. A society of haves and have-nots did not merit divine pleasure. So, the Old Testament's book Leviticus (19:9–10) reveals God's message to Moses: "Speak to the whole community and tell them: when you reap the harvest of your land, you shall not be so thorough that you reap the field to its very edge, nor shall you glean the stray ears of grain. . . . These things you shall leave to the poor and the alien. I, the Lord, am your God." Every seventh year, according to Jewish law, farmers were obliged to let their land "lie untilled and unharvested, that the poor may eat of it and so also for vineyards and fruit groves" (Ex 23:10).

The Bible's book Deuteronomy, its origins being about nine centuries before Christ, is so named because its principal messages are "second law"; that is, amplifications, revisions, and completions of the law promulgated to the Israelites by Moses. Deuteronomy introduced three fresh concepts into almsgiving: (1) setting a norm for donations, called "tithing," that is giving 10 percent of one's wealth or income; (2) gathering alms into the temple both for distribution to the poor and for financing the temple's maintenance and service; and (3) incorporating alms-giving into ritual worship. Down the centuries until the time of Christ, almsgiving in the form of a tithe became a temple membership obligation. As such, it was subject to some abuses; for example, rich or poor, all temple members were expected to pay a tithe and so the burden was heavier on the poor than on the rich; some temple officials exploited the tithing process for personal gain; some temple members cheated on their calculation of income; a few, or maybe many, temple members paid their tithe without any true worship of the God they pretended to adore.

According to Saint Matthew's Gospel, Jesus Christ severely condemned pretentious almsgiving: "Be on guard against performing religious acts for people to see. Otherwise expect no recompense from your heavenly Father. When you give alms, for example, do not blow a horn before you in synagogues and streets like hypocrites looking for applause. You can be sure of this much: they are already repaid. In giving alms, you are not to let your left hand know what your right hand is doing. Keep your deed of mercy secret, and your Father who sees it in secret will repay you"(Mt 6:1–4).

On another occasion, Jesus sharply reprimanded some Scribes and Pharisees who, though some were well-intentioned and probably sincere, were usually self-righteous and self-centered. "You frauds," Jesus said, "you pay tithes on mint and herbs and seeds while neglecting the weightier matters of the law, justice and mercy and good faith. It is these you should have practiced, without neglecting the others" (Mt 23:23).

Though critical of abused tithing, Jesus did not reprove almsgiving. On the contrary, he dramatically described its indispensability in his classic description of God's final judgment of his people. Matthew's Gospel tells the story.

In summary, the gospel story compares God with a king who separates his subjects like a shepherd would divide his flock, sheep to the right, goats to the left. To the right are those who gave alms to poor, neglected, handicapped, dispossessed, afflicted, unfortunate people. Come into my kingdom and enjoy it. To the left, however, are those who refused or neglected to give alms. To these the king declares: You are banished from my kingdom forever. So it will be God's final judgment, said Jesus Christ. There is no more forceful sanction of religious almsgiving.

For twenty centuries, the Roman Catholic church has encouraged almsgiving. St. Paul commended the Macedonian Christians, who were relatively poor people, for their alms to the developing church in Corinth and urged the Corinthians to do the same. During its first three centuries the church so successfully cared for the poor that Constantine the Great, the famous Roman emperor, apparently saw advantages for the empire in coopting the church's charities while granting the church immunity from persecution and militant support of its missionary expansions. Thought to be, at the time, a "holy" alliance, it created, I think, an unholy intermingling (to us the U.S. Supreme Court's favorite word), the pattern of which for centuries has made the church in European nations depend excessively upon government sources for its finances. Somehow, however, the Roman Catholic church, for centuries, has managed to maintain its institutional charities even during periods of persecutions by hostile governments, of devastating internal corruption, and of mass alienation of large groups of members. In the United States, the church, in its early days much dependent upon alms from European nations, consistently has encouraged and practiced almsgiving in parishes, dioceses, and the nation as a whole. After both world wars, the U.S. church sent bountiful alms to both victor and vanquished in Europe.

Because most almsgiving is voluntary, spontaneous, and unrecorded, its actual amount under Roman Catholic auspices is almost impossible to estimate. Whether Catholics' total almsgiving, adjusted to inflation, for the past twenty years has been up or down is uncertain. Surveys of Catholics' "charitable giving" do not pinpoint almsgiving but lump it with donors' self-perceptions of "all they give to the church," for example, stewardship obligations, payments to Catholic schools, donations to organized Catholic Charities, and so forth. The probability, however, is that almsgiving is caught up in the present-day downward trend of charitable giving in the Catholic church.

In one of her syndicated columns, Jane Bryant Quinn, an accomplished economist, observed that while organized charity pleads for families to "Give five," that is, five percent of family gross income, a Gallup poll commissioned by INDEPENDENT

SECTOR shows that in 1987, "only 9 percent of households gave 5 percent or more; one-third gave less than 1 percent, and 29 percent gave nothing" (Hodgkinson and Weitzman, 1988).

Money, however, is not the only kind of alms. As seen in Chapter 5, almost half of all American adults offer their time to a cause. On the average, these volunteers donate five hours a week of their time. That comes to an amazing total of 19.5 billion hours in 1987 — the equal, roughly of ten million full-time employees.

Between 1982 and 1987, 105,000 new service organizations were "born"; their life, I believe, depends mainly on alms, that is, voluntary donations of "time, talent and treasure." This situation suggests a close link between stewardship and alms in the latter's prime pre-Christian concept of being a means at least partially to correct or to mitigate social injustice.

Organized almsgiving in the U.S. Roman Catholic church has not been doing as well as it should. A distressing example is a recent report on the church's nineteen-year-old Campaign for Human Development, an almsgiving project for the benefit of "the poor who want to help themselves," which to the great embarrassment of church leaders, revealed that from 1970 to 1986 almsgiving to the campaign increased only $2.2 million, from $6.2 million in 1970 to $8.4 million in 1986, a miserable increase of only 14 percent, actually a *decrease* of $4 million adjusted to inflation by the Consumer Price Index, or a 25 percent decrease. To their credit, the U.S. Roman Catholic bishops, who sponsor the campaign, did not attempt to conceal or whitewash the bad record; instead, they issued a comprehensive account of how bad it was by every index of what it should be, directed a complete overhaul of its procedures, and vowed to stay with it because of its high importance to the church.

On the parish level, the difference between stewardship and almsgiving often is badly blurred to the detriment of both. So too are the operative virtues for stewardship and almsgiving; for the former, it is justice; for the latter, charity. Confusion arises when contributors presume that their stewardship obligations, that is, what they *owe* the church for its ministries, can be satisfied by tossing a freehanded alms into a collection basket without giving a thought to whether the amount of the contribution is payment of a fair (that is, just) share of parish expenses. People who contribute nothing beyond this fair share are not giving alms at all. On the other hand, a devout and zealous almsgiver, donating handsomely to every good cause the parish church announces, may totally neglect obligations in justice to support the church itself. In my judgment, parishioners should be given ample guidance on how to assess themselves for a fair share of church expenses and should be expected to pay their assessments in the practice of justice. Almsgiving, on the other hand, should be left to each individual's convictions about charity in general and in particular. Simply put, the adage should be: Pay what you owe and give what you can. The first is for stewardship, and the second is for almsgiving.

For the future, as indeed in the past too, Roman Catholics and all Christians who take the gospel to heart, will have to be serious about Jesus's warning that they cannot serve both God and mammon. God they know all about and want to serve, but mammon, an insidious wicked evil force active in wealth, mainly in money, they know less about and are easily misled and seduced. But mammon has a way of seizing control of individuals not on guard against it. When mammon gains control, God is forced out; no two ways—one must serve either God or mammon.

For many Catholics, stewardship and almsgiving in their traditional ways will express a devout service of God and a resistance to mammon.

A postscript. INDEPENDENT SECTOR, distinguished for its direction and sponsorship of research on voluntary giving, has asked me to propose research that, had it been conducted, would have enriched this chapter. Specifically, I would designate the following research areas:

1. Roman Catholic theology of stewardship and almsgiving
2. Successful religious motivations of voluntary donations to religion and to charity
3. Practical models for estimating the total stewardship resources in a parish or similar local church unit

4. Ways to estimate the cash value of alms donated in the form of volunteer services
5. Models of organizational sponsorship of one-to-one charity
6. Research on tax credit rather than tax deduction for desig-nated forms of volunteer giving, for example, care of victims of AIDS

Descriptions of these research areas are beyond the scope of this chapter. They would, however, be related to traditional stewardship and almsgiving.

Notes

1. "Second collections" during Sunday Masses, normally about one a month, irritate many clergy (compelled to "make the pitch") and laity (feeling like a "captive audi-ence"), who, I think, would prefer to have the parish church itself make contributions to worthy causes. That, of course, would require larger contributions to the parish so that it could afford to make charitable donations on behalf of the whole congregation.
2. National Catholic Stewardship Council, 1 Columbia Place, Albany, N.Y. 12207.
3. The committee of five is chaired by Archbishop Thomas Murphy, Co-Adjustor Archbishop of Seattle, Washington. I am a consultant.
4. Douglas John Hall's *The Steward, A Biblical Symbol Come of Age* (1985) is by far the most enlightening book, now in its fourth printing, on the biblical roots of stewardship in its full traditional and contemporary meaning.
5. John C. Haughey's extraordinary book *The Holy Use of Money* (1986) is a cogent, profound, and brilliant exegesis of and commentary on the Bible's teaching on stewardship, alms-giving, and related issues.

References

Derek, R. H. *The Spiritual Meaning of Stewardship of Time, Talent, and Treasure.* Albany, N.Y.: National Catholic Stewardship Council, n.d.

Dolan, J. P. *The American Catholic Experience.* New York: Doubleday, 1985.

Eliot, T. S. *Murder in the Cathedral.* San Diego, Calif.: Harcourt Brace Jovanovich, 1935.

Greeley, A., and McManus, W. *Catholic Contributions: Sociology and Policy.* Chicago: Thomas More Press, 1987.

Hall, D. J. *The Steward, A Biblical Symbol Come of Age.* New York: National Council of Churches of Christ in the U.S.A., 1985.

Haughey, J. C. *The Holy Use of Money: Personal Finances in Light of Christian Faith.* New York: Doubleday, 1986.

Hodgkinson, V. A., and Weitzman, M. S. *Giving and Volunteering in the United States.* Findings from a national survey conducted by the Gallup Organization. Washington, D.C.: INDEPENDENT SECTOR, 1988.

National Conference of Catholic Bishops. *Economic Justice for All.* Washington, D.C.: National Conference of Catholic Bishops, 1984, p. 174.

Yankelovich, Skelly, & White, Inc. *The Charitable Behavior of Americans.* Washington, D.C.: INDEPENDENT SECTOR, 1986.

Chapter 7

Mordechai Rimor
Gary A. Tobin

Jewish Giving Patterns to Jewish and Non-Jewish Philanthropy

In this chapter, we analyze giving patterns in the Jewish community to both Jewish and non-Jewish philanthropies.* Prior works
(for example, Israel, 1987; Rappeport and Tobin, 1987; Tobin,
1987b; Tobin and Fishman, 1988a, 1988b; Tobin and Sassler,
1988) have shown that Jewish philanthropic behavior within the
Jewish community is high. We further ask: To what extent do Jews
contribute to non-Jewish philanthropies? Are the patterns of
giving of Jews to Jewish philanthropies similar to giving to non-
Jewish philanthropies? And is higher Jewish religious identity
associated with giving to non-Jewish philanthropies?

The Jewish tradition of giving is a strong one; *tzedakah* is
an integral part of Jewish culture and religious identity. In the
United States, a vast fund-raising network has been developed to
assist in the support of Jewish organizations and institutions,
individual Jews in need, and the State of Israel and other Jewish
communities around the world. Popular impressions often refer
to the Jewish fund-raising system as a model of efficient and
effective organizational planning in the philanthropic realm.

Jewish philanthropy, defined as giving to Jewish organizations, institutions, agencies, and individuals, is a critical

* We wish to thank Drs. Sylvia Barack Fishman and Lawrence Sternberg for
their helpful comments on prior versions of this chapter. A shorter version of
the chapter was presented at the Forum on Philanthropy and the Religious
Tradition, INDEPENDENT SECTOR, Washington, D.C., March 1989.

component in ensuring a vibrant Jewish community. The organizational and institutional structure that binds the Jewish community together, as well as the financial and political support of Israel and other Jewish communities, rests in the ability of Jewish fund-raising organizations to provide revenue. In many ways, patterns of philanthropy mirror the relative health of the contemporary Jewish community in the United States. A weakened tradition of *tzedakah* would reveal a weakened sense of Jewish identity and, therefore, a less vibrant Jewish community in general.

The Jewish tradition of *tzedakah* also requires that Jewish patterns of giving be extended beyond the religious boundaries of Jews alone. At least according to the biblical traditions of Jewish giving, Jews are required to give to both Jewish and non-Jewish needs. Therefore, this study examines the relationships that exist between patterns of giving to Jewish and non-Jewish philanthropies.

In previous studies (for example, Rimor and Tobin, 1988), it has been demonstrated that a stronger sense of religious identity does indeed increase greater participation in both giving time and monetary contributions to Jewish philanthropies. Ritual observance, synagogue attendance, organization and synagogue membership, and support for Israel, to name a few of the religious identity indices, are associated with increased contributions and volunteer time to Jewish organizations. Logically, one would expect that similar association would also be found between Jewish identity and contributions to non-Jewish organizations. The chapter examines this hypothesis as well.

It must be noted that we are examining a set of relationships in behavioral areas, such as giving to Jewish philanthropies within the Jewish community, giving to non-Jewish philanthropies, voluntarism, and religious identity, which all may belong to the same hypothetical construct. In other words, various philanthropic behaviors and voluntarism may belong to the area of religious identity. The differentiation that is posed may be more artificial than real, part of a tautology that is not easily dissected. Nevertheless, our aim is to present an interactive model that explores the relationship between giving to

Jewish and non-Jewish philanthropies and the association between religious identity and philanthropic behavior.

While an existing substantial general literature discusses philanthropy in economic or, more specifically, in mathematical or organizational terms (see, for example, Andrews, 1950; Olson, 1968; Phelps, 1975), as well as in psychological terms (for example, Milgram, 1970; Mussen and Eisenberg-Berg, 1977), it is not specific enough for our purposes. Patterns of philanthropy are usually not discussed. Social scientists who have explored the philanthropic behavior of the general American population (Andrews, 1950; Hodgkinson and Weitzman, 1986; Yankelovich, Skelly, & White, Inc., 1986) did not focus specifically on the Jewish community.

The social science literature that discusses Jewish patterns of philanthropy is quite limited. Social scientists who have collected data describing Jewish philanthropy in Jewish communities (for example, Cohen, 1978, 1980, 1983; Ritterband and Cohen, 1979; Sklare, 1962; Tobin, 1987b) have focused almost exclusively on one aspect of the issue—giving to Jewish philanthropies. A large literature has been written about Jewish identity (for example, Himmelfarb, 1975), but it has dealt primarily with religious behaviors. Given some of the conventional wisdom about the success of Jewish philanthropy in the United States and given the economic success of Jews in the United States, one might have anticipated a greater analytical background for Jewish philanthropy. However, it is rare to find an empirical analysis on why Jews give, to which philanthropies, and the relationship of religious identity to philanthropic behavior.

Recently, some analyses have been completed (for example, Rappeport and Tobin, 1987; Silberstein, Ritterband, Rabinowitz, and Kosmin, 1987; Tobin, 1987b). These works compared philanthropic behavior in a number of Jewish communities. Certain demographic factors, such as age, and religious identity variables, such as ritual observance, are associated with higher rates of philanthropic behavior. Rimor and Tobin (1988) investigated the combined effects of a wide spectrum of religious and civil Jewish identity on giving to Jewish philanthropies in the Jewish community of Morris and Essex counties in New Jersey. It was shown that higher giving behavior for Jewish philanthropies is strongly related to high religious identity.

Data from other Jewish communities, including Baltimore; Rochester, N.Y.; Worcester, Mass.; Washington, D.C.; and San Francisco, demonstrate the high association between strong Jewish identity and increased giving to Jewish philanthropies (Tobin, 1984, 1986; Tobin and Fishman, 1988a, 1988b; Tobin and Sassler, 1988).

The recent studies of philanthropy in a number of Jewish communities explored patterns of giving to Jewish philanthropies, as well as giving to non-Jewish philanthropies. However, the connection between the two has never been thoroughly analyzed. These studies examined the proportion of Jews who contributed to Jewish philanthropies, how much they contributed to Jewish philanthropies, and the influences of various demographic and attitudinal factors on these patterns. Similar, though less-detailed, analyses were completed for non-Jewish philanthropies. The interaction between the two, between voluntarism to Jewish and non-Jewish purposes, as well as between Jewish identity and giving, was absent in each of these studies and is presented in case study form in this chapter.

Methodology

Data gathered from a demographic and behavioral survey of the Jewish community of Morris and Essex counties, New Jersey, in 1986 (Rappeport and Tobin, 1987; Tobin, 1987b), sponsored by the United Jewish Federation of MetroWest, are used as a case study for our investigation. The study randomly sampled 1,655 households (representing more than 45,000 households) via an in-depth telephone survey (181 questions) and covered a wide range of issues relating to Jewish demography, religious identity, and communal behaviors. More than 20 questions focused on issues of philanthropic behavior and voluntarism. Morris and Essex counties will be referred to in the remainder of this paper as MetroWest.

We selected the MetroWest study for our analysis for a number of reasons. This community study was the first to devote an extensive section of its survey instrument to questions concerning philanthropy. Subsequently, communities such as Worcester, Mass.; Rochester, N.Y.; San Francisco; and Dallas have built upon the questions initially formulated in MetroWest. The survey included questions on both giving frequencies and motives.

Second, while we do not contend that Morris and Essex counties reflect the general demography or religious behavior of the American Jewish community as a whole, this geographic area provides a useful case study. The philanthropic patterns revealed in the MetroWest study fall within the middle range of the frequency distributions of many Jewish communities around the United States. While it is not a "model" Jewish community, it is certainly a community that rarely deviates from overall inter-metropolitan patterns that appear when one examines a broad range of Jewish communities. In the absence of a national Jewish population study, community data provide the most thorough data base available. Therefore, analyses such as the one contained in this case study would very likely yield similar results in some other data sets.

The following questions from the MetroWest survey that relate to philanthropy and voluntarism were used in this analysis:

- Do you or any member of your household make outright contributions or gifts to Jewish philanthropies or charities?
- Total contribution of your household in this year to all Jewish philanthropies (in ranges of dollars)
- Did your household make a contribution to MetroWest Federation's United Jewish Appeal this year?
- Total contribution (in ranges of dollars)
- Did your household make a gift to the Women's Division last year?
- Total contribution (in ranges of dollars)
- Contributions to Jewish campaigns besides the Federation

- Does your household contribute to any non-Jewish philanthropies?
- Total contribution (in ranges of dollars)
- Names of all non-Jewish philanthropies to which the household contributes
- General philosophy of giving
- How many hours per month do you volunteer on behalf of Jewish organizations?
- How many hours per month does your spouse volunteer on behalf of Jewish organizations?
- How many hours per month do you volunteer on behalf of non-Jewish organizations?
- How many hours per month does your spouse volunteer on behalf of non-Jewish organizations?

In addition, questions that deal with Jewish identity were analyzed. They pertain to a range of eleven religious practices: lighting Shabbat candles, participating in a Passover seder, staying home from work or school or altering normal activities on the High Holidays, fasting on Yom Kippur, not having a Christmas tree, buying only Kosher meat for home use, not driving or riding on the Sabbath, having two sets of dishes for purposes of keeping Kosher, reciting the Kiddush on Friday night, building a Sukkah, putting on Tefillin daily. They pertain to synagogue attendance: a seven-point scale measuring attendance at Jewish services, ranging from never, never except for weddings and bar mitzvahs, only during High Holidays, a few times a year, a few times a month, weekly, to several times a week or more. They pertain also to synagogue and organization membership (yes/no), religious identification (Orthodox, Conservative, Reform, or "just Jewish"), visiting Israel (yes/no), and having Jewish friends (how many of your three best friends are Jewish—from none to all).

Because of the large number of cases involved in the analyses, the level of significance chosen for rejecting the null hypothesis in the cross-tabulations and the associational (correlations, regressions and factor analysis) analyses was $p < 0.001$.

Two types of data extraction were used: descriptive and correlational. The descriptive analyses are comprised of frequency distributions (mainly in figures) and cross-tabulations (in tables). The frequency distributions, in percentages, present general trends in the population; therefore, no tests for significance were computed. However, a sound rule of thumb for testing significant difference between subpopulations' percentages in the figures and cross-tabulations is an average difference of 6 percent or more. For the cross-tabulations (2×2 tables), we used the chi-square statistics with the appropriate level of significance. The correlational analyses are comprised of zero-order correlation coefficients, presented in the text or the tables with their ns and significant level, multiple regression analyses, and factor analysis (Principal Components, Varimax Rotation).

The data are presented in six areas. First, we briefly examine the relationship between background and Jewish identity variables and giving to Jewish philanthropies. Second, we discuss the total proportion of the Jewish population that contributes to Jewish philanthropies and to non-Jewish philanthropies, the levels of contribution, and their association. Third, we explore the relationship between contributing to Jewish and non-Jewish philanthropies and voluntarism to Jewish and non-Jewish philanthropies. Fourth, we discuss the relationship between the contribution to Jewish and non-Jewish campaigns. This is followed by an analysis of which variables affect giving to non-Jewish philanthropies and Jewish identity. Finally, we briefly discuss explicit motivation for giving.

Demographic Variables, Religious Identity, and Giving to Jewish Philanthropies

Following is a preliminary examination of demographic variables, religious identity variables, and philanthropic behaviors within the Jewish community in MetroWest. Previous studies indicated that income, age, family composition, length of residency, and generation are correlated with giving patterns. Higher income households, households with two middle-aged parents and children, those who have lived in the community for ten years or more, and first- and second-generation Jews were the most likely to give something to a Jewish philanthropy and most likely to be the largest contributors as well. Similar findings were, as expected, repeated in the MetroWest study (see also Rimor and Tobin, 1988; Tobin, 1987b) and are presented in Table 7.1.

Table 7.1 indicates that most Jews (77 percent) contribute something to a Jewish philanthropy. A contribution is signified by a gift of at least one dollar. Examination by income, age, family structure, or length of residency indicates that the vast majority of Jews in each cohort contribute at least one dollar to a Jewish philanthropy. This includes all philanthropies, including organizations, synagogues, and temples, Federation or United Jewish Appeal, or any other Jewish-oriented philanthropy. It excludes dues to synagogues, Jewish community centers, Jewish day schools, or others.

The table shows that making some contribution to a Jewish philanthropy is highly and linearly associated with income. The correlation is 0.51 and is highly significant ($p < .00001$). Lower-income households are less likely than higher-income households to contribute to a Jewish philanthropy. Virtually every household comprising the "highest income" bracket, those over $150,000 per year, contributes to a Jewish philanthropy (95 percent). It should be pointed out that lower incomes associate highly with age: people over the age of sixty-five on fixed incomes and people under the age of twenty-five, who often are still students or part-time workers, comprise most of these categories.

When amount of contribution is considered (see Figure 7.2), the vast majority of Jews in the MetroWest area give a few hundred dollars per year total to all Jewish philanthropies. More than 60 percent of the households give less than $250 per year. Most Jews are giving less than 1 percent of their annual income to Jewish philanthropies. Most total gifts are quite low (considering potential) in terms of the actual dollar amounts contributed, measured either by the size of the gift or by percentage of income.

Age is related curvilinearly to giving, probably because of

Table 7.1. Contribution to Jewish Philanthropy and
Basic Social and Jewish Background Variables.

	Contribution	No Contribution
Income		
Less than $30,000	65	35
$30,000–40,000	71	29
$40,000–50,000	78	22
$50,000–75,000	78	22
$75,000–100,000	87	13
$100,000–150,000	88	12
Over $150,000	95	5
Age		
18–24	51	49
25–34	69	31
35–44	79	21
45–54	83	17
55–64	91	9
65–74	91	9
75 +	76	24
Family Structure		
Single	60	40
Widowed/Divorced/Separated	76	24
Conventional	81	19
Year Moved to Present Residence		
Life	68	32
Before 1970	88	12
1970–1979	81	19
After 1980	60	40
Synagogue Attendance		
Never to few times a year	72	28
Twice a month to every day	93	7
Organizational Membership		
No	69	31
Yes	91	7
Synagogue Membership		
No	70	30
Yes	89	11
Visit Israel		
No	74	26
Yes	93	7
Overall	77	23

income level and life cycle. Those who are younger, single, and most mobile are least likely to make a contribution to a Jewish philanthropy. Yet it is also true that those younger people who do not currently give are nevertheless likely to contribute as they marry, have children, and reach higher income levels. The attitudinal data from the MetroWest study indicate, however, that life cycle alone does not account for differences by age-group or generation. The data indicate that there has been a shift for younger Jews in their general willingness to support Jewish organizations and institutions. Lack of support for Israel (attitudinally) is higher among younger Jews, for example, and may translate in the future into lower levels of participation in Jewish philanthropy. Data from other communities show that generation also relates inversely to giving to Jewish philanthropies (Ritterband and Silberstein, 1988). Therefore, while life cycle plays a major role, it should not be assumed that it solely determines giving patterns.

Table 7.1 shows that conventional family structure and length of residency affect patterns of philanthropy. Specifically, greater length of residency, either in the community or at the same address within the community, has positive effects on patterns of philanthropy. Mobility is highly associated with age and marital status; that is, younger single people tend to move more often, and this is negatively associated with giving patterns. These factors account partially for the negative effect mobility plays upon patterns of Jewish philanthropy. Relocation causes dislocation between the individual or family and the Jewish communal structure. Some time apparently transpires before someone who moves reconnects with the Jewish community. Therefore, the lag time may be as much as three years or even more before the relocated individual contributes again to a Jewish philanthropy.

Table 7.1 also shows that religious identity and involvement in Jewish organizations also have a positive effect on giving. Synagogue attendance, synagogue membership, and organizational membership are closely related to giving. The special status of Israel in giving behavior should also be noted; visiting Israel is tied strongly to giving to Jewish philanthropies.

These four religious identity related variables were found in our previous work to be the best predictors of contribution to Jewish philanthropies from a wide range of behaviors that express ethnic religious identity (Rimor and Tobin, 1988).

Overall Giving to Jewish and Non-Jewish Philanthropies

About three out of every four Jewish households make a contribution to a Jewish philanthropy. The proportion given to non-Jewish philanthropies is almost identical, as shown in Figure 7.1.

In most communities, "Jews are slightly more likely to make some kind of contribution to a non-Jewish philanthropy than to a Jewish philanthropy" (Tobin, 1987a, p. 21). In Metro-

Figure 7.1. Percentage of Respondents Contributing to Jewish and Non-Jewish Philanthropies.

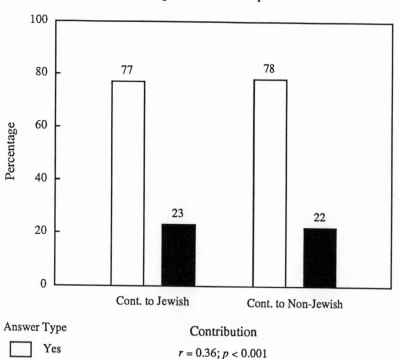

Answer Type

☐ Yes

■ No

Contribution

$r = 0.36; p < 0.001$

Table 7.2. Contributing to Jewish and Non-Jewish Philanthropies.

		Contributing to Non-Jewish Philanthropies		
		Yes	No	
Contributing to	Yes	86%	14%	77%
Jewish Philanthropies	No	50%	50%	23%
		78%	22%	100%

χ^2, $p < 0.001$

West, the difference is insignificant and is only slightly significant in most other areas. It seems that the primary reason for the difference being manifest at all has to do with access to Jewish households via telephone and mail. Because Jews are so mobile, many Jewish households are not currently on any Jewish organizational list. Therefore, a direct solicitation by telephone or mail is impossible. On the other hand, the Jewish household can be targeted by non-Jewish philanthropies on a random basis, via telephone or mail, in a wide number of appeals. Thus, the propensity to give at least a small gift to a non-Jewish philanthropy is greatly increased simply by the relative access of non-Jewish philanthropies to all Jewish households.

The correlation between giving to Jewish and to non-Jewish philanthropies is significant: 0.36 ($p < 0.001$). It shows clearly that Jews who give to Jewish philanthropies tend to give to non-Jewish philanthropies as well. One may argue that this relationship is an artifact caused by background variables such as income level, age, or length of residency. However, when these seemingly confounding background variables are controlled, the partial correlation is still significant, $r = 0.27$ ($p < 0.001$). A significant relationship between giving to Jewish philanthropies and giving to non-Jewish philanthropies exists far and above socioeconomic factors. This relationship is seen clearly in Table 7.2.

While 86 percent of those who contribute to Jewish philanthropies contribute to non-Jewish philanthropies as well, the proportion of contribution to non-Jewish philanthropies among noncontributors to Jewish philanthropies is exactly half. Given this strong association between giving to Jewish and to non-Jewish philanthropies, it seems that the target population for fund-raising to non-Jewish philanthropies is similar to the target population for fund-raising to Jewish philanthropies (see also Kosmin, 1988, p. 18).

The amounts contributed to Jewish and non-Jewish philanthropies, however, are substantially different. The data are presented in Figure 7.2. In general, Jews are much more likely to make contributions of $500 or more per year to Jewish philanthropies than to non-Jewish philanthropies (26 percent versus 12 percent). The reverse holds for contributions of less than $100 per year: 46 percent give to Jewish philanthropies and 64 percent give to non-Jewish philanthropies.

Nevertheless, contributions to both Jewish and non-Jewish philanthropies alike are generally under $500 per year: 74 percent give to Jewish philanthropies versus 88 percent who give to non-Jewish philanthropies. Of course, some of these totals are artificially depressed because they exclude synagogue dues, for example, which generally range from $500 to $1,000 per year. Even including synagogue dues, however, most Jews are contributing only a few hundred dollars total to all Jewish philanthropies combined.

The relationship between contributing to Jewish and non-Jewish philanthropies is demonstrated again when amount is examined: a highly significant correlation of 0.59. This strong correlation is not an artifact resulting from background variables such as income level, where a highly significant correlation remains — partial $r = 0.36$ ($p \leq 0.001$) — when income level, age, and length of residency are controlled.

We also estimated the median gift to both Jewish and non-Jewish philanthropies. The data indicate that the median annual household gift to Jewish philanthropies is $175 and to non-Jewish philanthropies is $75. Considering that the median income level of the Jewish household in MetroWest is $51,000, the median size donation to Jewish and non-Jewish philanthropies is less than 1 percent of the median annual income.

Figure 7.2. Amount Contributed to Jewish and Non-Jewish Philanthropies.

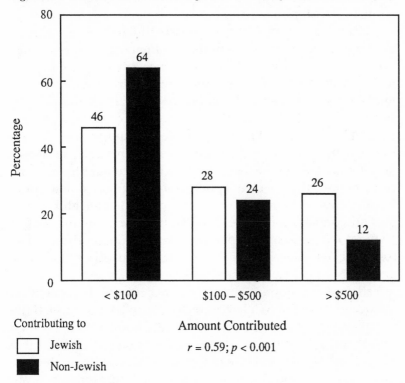

The median gift value should, however, be cautiously perceived because of the reason outlined below.

Contributions were queried in terms of increments of up to $10,000 or more per year. Therefore, a contribution of $50,000, $100,000, or $1 million from a household would not be differentiated from a contribution of $11,000, for example. Thus it is not possible to estimate accurately what percentage of the total giving dollar is going to either Jewish or non-Jewish philanthropies. The above median gift value may be perceived as a "minimal" estimate. Consequently, we did not estimate the total gift amounts to Jewish and non-Jewish philanthropies on the basis of the projected frequencies. We may assume that, proportionately, since the larger number of bigger gifts are going to Jewish philanthropies, the comparable proportions of the largest gifts are going to Jewish philanthropies as well. Therefore, and on the basis of the minimal median gift estimation, we would assume that at least two-thirds (perhaps even more) of the philanthropic dollar coming from Jewish households is going to Jewish philanthropies (see also Kosmin, 1988, p. 17).

The data from Figure 7.1, Table 7.2, and Figure 7.2 (and subsequent data concerning individual campaigns, as shown below) indicate that the proclivity to give correlates highly. One could deduce that in a fixed pool of philanthropic dollars, non-Jewish philanthropies are competing with Jewish philanthropies for contributions. One could argue as well that the pool of giving dollars expands depending on both the motivating factors and agencies involved. The latter illustrates that philanthropists give to a wide variety of causes, both Jewish and non-Jewish, and the amount given is not necessarily dependent on the decision to give to a Jewish versus a non-Jewish cause. If the donation pool, that is, the amount given, is somewhat fixed, then non-Jewish philanthropies have serious competition from Jewish philanthropies. If the pool expands, depending on the case made and the motivation that is provided, the amounts given tend to reinforce one another rather than to be competitive. In either case, giving to any set of philanthropies correlates highly with giving to other philanthropies.

Philanthropy and Voluntarism

Patterns of philanthropy and voluntarism are generally thought of as being theoretically connected. Those who contribute their money are also more inclined, it is believed, to contribute their time. Indeed, the literature on voluntarism is often connected to the literature on philanthropy (for example, Layton, 1987). Certain voluntary patterns are expected to be associated empirically with philanthropic behavior. These assumptions were tested for the Jewish population in the MetroWest area.

Previous work (Rimor and Tobin, 1988), the above data,

and data presented below have indicated that philanthropic behavior is basically self-strengthening: The more one gives to one Jewish philanthropy, the more likely one is to give to another Jewish philanthropy and to non-Jewish philanthropies as well. Here we explore whether the same reinforcing effect also holds true for voluntary behavior.

Two questions are therefore posed. First, do households that volunteer time for Jewish purposes tend to volunteer time for non-Jewish purposes as well? Second, are either the frequency or amounts contributed to Jewish or non-Jewish philanthropies also associated with voluntary behavior to Jewish or non-Jewish tasks? The data necessary to address the first issue are presented in Figure 7.3.

Figure 7.3. Volunteering Any Time for Jewish and Non-Jewish Purposes: Households in Which at Least One Member Volunteers.

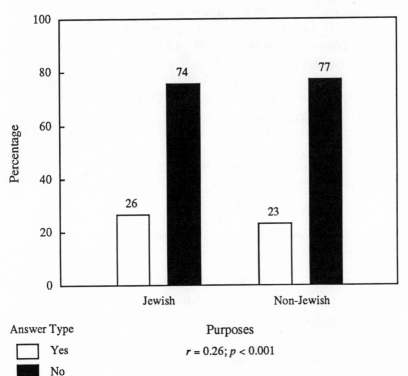

Answer Type   Purposes
☐ Yes $r = 0.26; p < 0.001$
■ No

The figure shows that unlike contribution of dollars, most of the households do not volunteer any time for any purpose. Voluntarism, a highly committed and involved behavior, is much lower than contribution. Figure 7.3 shows that only about a quarter of the households volunteer any time for either Jewish or non-Jewish purposes. Even fewer households, 8 percent each, volunteer six hours or more for either Jewish or non-Jewish purposes (not shown in the figure). However, the correlation of volunteer time for Jewish purposes with volunteer time for non-Jewish purposes is moderately significant ($r = 0.26$, $p < 0.001$): The more a household volunteers time for Jewish purposes, the more it tends to volunteer time for non-Jewish purposes. Interestingly, we also found that this relationship holds within a household; the more one spouse volunteers time for Jewish or non-Jewish purposes, the more the other spouse tends to volunteer: $r = 0.34$ ($p < 0.001$). Volunteering time may thus be thought of as both a household syndrome and an individual trait. The relationship between volunteering time to Jewish and non-Jewish philanthropies is detailed in Table 7.3.

Table 7.3 shows that of those who do volunteer time for Jewish purposes, 35 percent volunteer for non-Jewish purposes as well. Of those who do not volunteer time for Jewish purposes, only 16 percent give any time for non-Jewish purposes. The first question in this section is answered, then, with an unqualified yes.

The second question investigates the expected relationship between contribution and voluntarism. Correlations

Table 7.3. Volunteering Any Time to Jewish and Non-Jewish Causes.

| | | Volunteering to Non-Jewish Causes | | |
		Yes	No	
Volunteering to	Yes	35%	65%	26%
Jewish Causes	No	16%	84%	74%
		23%	77%	100%

χ^2, $p < 0.001$

Table 7.4. Pearson Correlation of Volunteering to Jewish and Non-Jewish Causes with Contributing to Jewish and Non-Jewish Philanthropies.

	Contributing	
Volunteering	Contributing to Jewish	Contributing to non-Jewish
Volunteering to Jewish	0.20	ns
Volunteering to non-Jewish	ns	0.17

$p < 0.001$

between household volunteering for Jewish and for non-Jewish causes were calculated and checked against household contributions to Jewish and non-Jewish philanthropies. The results are presented in the correlation matrix in Table 7.4.

Voluntarism does not correlate highly with philanthropic behavior. Although two correlations are positive, they are low. Their significance is largely due to the large number of cases and seems not to be substantial. The other two are nonsignificant. The correlation between voluntarism for Jewish causes and contributions to Jewish philanthropies is less than moderate (0.20). Similar low correlation (0.17) exists within the non-Jewish realm. At the same time, the correlations between contributions to Jewish philanthropies and voluntarism for non-Jewish causes and between voluntarism for Jewish causes and contributions to non-Jewish philanthropies are null. These nonsignificant correlations contrast strongly with the significant relationships presented above between contributions to Jewish and non-Jewish philanthropies ($r = 0.36$), and between voluntarism for Jewish causes and voluntarism for non-Jewish causes ($r = 0.26$).

These results indicate that the reinforcing effects within philanthropic behavior and within voluntarism behavior do not generalize, or generalize very slightly, across those two behaviors. More exactly, while they generalize slightly within the Jewish and non-Jewish realms, they do not generalize at all across the Jewish and non-Jewish realms. This may indicate, in spite of common belief (for example, Kosmin, 1988, p. 18), that voluntarism does not belong directly in the behavioral "bundle" of philanthropic behavior. Thus, the answer to the second question posed at the beginning of this section is a qualified no.

One may conclude that major contributions can be achieved without high levels of involvement as measured by volunteer time. Building contributing behavior need not focus mainly on increasing volunteer efforts. Certainly, volunteers are necessary for a wide variety of organizational and institutional needs. And it is clear that for some proportion of the population the association between voluntarism and contribution exists (for example, women's volunteering and contribution to the Federation's Women Division; see Rimor and Tobin, 1988). But the overall correlation is low, suggesting that voluntarism and philanthropy tap different traits. It seems that other means of promotion for some kinds of involvement may be more successful than others to integrate individuals into both volunteer and contributing tracks.

Individual Campaigns

The next area of concern involves the analysis of contribution patterns to the various campaigns. What are the Jewish and non-Jewish campaigns to which Jews contribute? In addition to annual giving to the Federation, is a household likely to give to other campaigns? Does a contribution to one non-Jewish campaign lead to gifts to other non-Jewish campaigns? Finally, if either of these two patterns are reinforcing, are they also mutually reinforcing (as the overall prior data indicate)? That is, does giving to campaigns within the Jewish community also lead Jews to give to campaigns within the non-Jewish community? Figure 7.4 presents the Jewish campaigns to which Jews give.

Figure 7.4 shows those Jewish campaigns to which Jews give, and as expected, the Federation drew the greatest proportion, 83 percent. The Israel Emergency Fund accounted for 40 percent, and the Israel Building Fund accounted for 36 percent of those who gave to special campaigns. Other special campaigns account for between about 15 and 25 percent of special gifts. These projects are mutually reinforcing. The matrix of correlations shows positive and significant intercorrelations

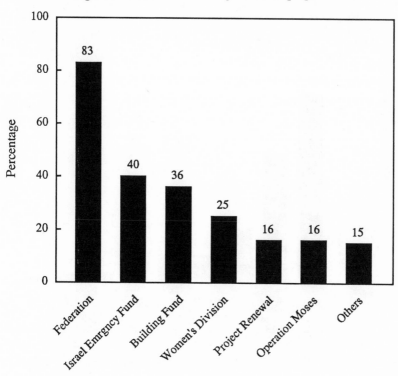

Figure 7.4. Contributions to Jewish Campaigns.

Campaigns

Range of Intercorrelations: 0.11 – 0.59; mean = 0.29

ranging from 0.11 to 0.59, with a mean correlation of 0.29. The more a Jewish household gives to the Federation or to a Jewish campaign, the more it will give to another Jewish campaign.

Figure 7.5 presents the non-Jewish campaigns to which Jews give. Among the non-Jewish campaigns to which Jews give, health-related philanthropies drew the most gifts. The United Way was second, with more than a third of those contributing to campaigns making a contribution to the United Way. Other

Figure 7.5. Contributions to Non-Jewish Campaigns.

Campaigns

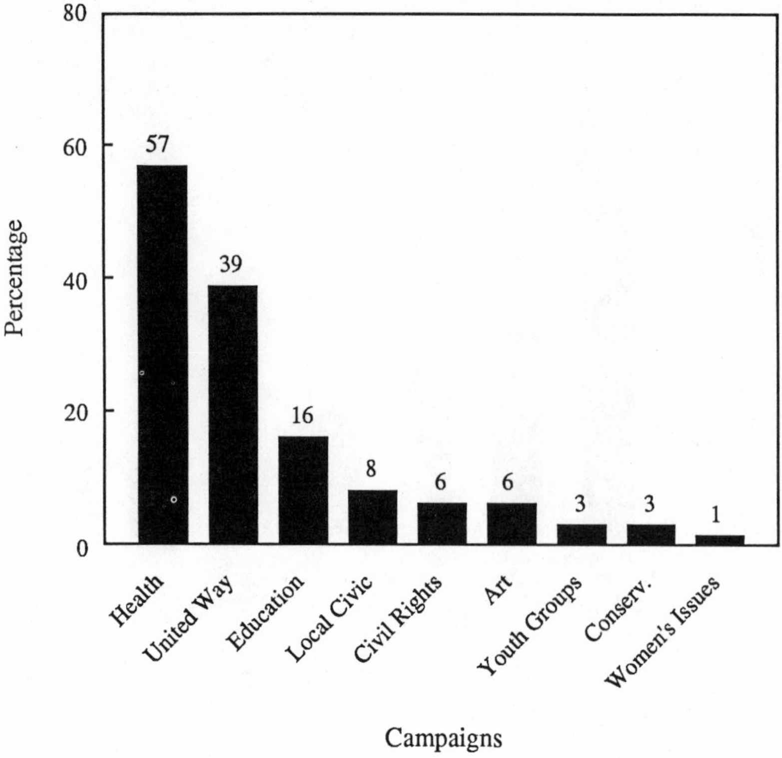

Range of Intercorrelations: 0.00 – 0.20; mean = 0.06

campaigns in the non-Jewish community draw very small proportions of the contributions.

Interestingly, unlike the finding for the Jewish campaigns,
the matrix of intercorrelations for the non-Jewish campaigns
does not show a clear reinforcing effect. The mean correlation is
null. Jewish households tend to give to non-Jewish campaigns
one campaign at a time, that is, in a more random fashion; the
non-Jewish campaigns are not mutually reinforcing as the Jewish campaigns are.

The relationship between giving to Jewish campaigns and
to non-Jewish campaigns was found to be less than moderate —
0.16 (its significance — $p < 0.001$ — is due primarily to the large

number of cases). The strong relationship discussed earlier between giving to Jewish and non-Jewish philanthropies is attenuated when individual campaigns are measured; the reason lies probably in the random fashion in which Jews give to non-Jewish campaigns. Giving to one individual Jewish campaign does not necessarily entail giving to other individual non-Jewish campaigns.

Variables That Affect Giving to Non-Jewish Philanthropies

In earlier works, we have documented that religious identity, whether expressed by ritual observance or participation in communal activities, was highly correlated with giving to Jewish philanthropies. Synagogue attendance, synagogue membership, organizational membership, and visiting Israel were found (through regression analysis) to be the most important variables associated with making a contribution to a Jewish philanthropy and the amount contributed to Jewish philanthropies. Philanthropic behavior itself was found (through factor analysis) to be a bundle of variables that constitutes a component of Jewish identity (Rimor and Tobin, 1988).

Similar questions are posed here for contribution patterns to non-Jewish philanthropies. How does Jewish identity relate to contributions to non-Jewish philanthropies? The following data are the results of two regression analyses in which the dependent variables are contribution and the amounts contributed to non-Jewish philanthropies, respectively, and the independent variables are synagogue and organizational membership, synagogue attendance, visiting Israel, and contributions to Jewish philanthropies. See Table 7.5.

While religious identity (expressed by synagogue attendance and membership), visiting Israel, and communal involvement (expressed by organizational membership) significantly influence contributions to non-Jewish philanthropies, the key variable is contributions to Jewish philanthropies. Philanthropic behavior itself is the reinforcing factor, more so than other factors. The standardized betas of contribution and amount contributed to Jewish philanthropies (0.32 and 0.50, respectively) are much higher than those of the other variables. The results may indicate that philanthropic patterns, in both Jewish and non-Jewish realms, are related to the structure of Jewish identity. In our prior analyses (Rimor and Tobin, 1988), we investigated the relevant variables that constitute Jewish identity as expressed in various religious, philanthropic, and communal behaviors. Giving, mainly to Jewish philanthropies, ap-

Table 7.5. Summary of Forward Regression of Jewish Identity with Contribution and Amount Contributed to Jewish Philanthropies.

	Dependent Variable Contribution to non-Jewish philanthropies	
	Standardized B Coefficient	t-test p < 0.001
Contribution to Jewish philanthropies	0.32	*
Organizational membership	0.09	*
Visiting Israel	0.03	*
Synagogue attendance	0.05	*
Synagogue membership	0.05	*
	intercept (B = 0.59)	*
	multiple r = 0.36	
	Dependent Variable Amount contributed to non-Jewish philanthropies	
	Standardized B Coefficients	t-test p < 0.001
Amount contributed to non-Jewish philanthropies	0.50	*
Organizational membership	0.03	*
Synagogue membership	0.02	*
Visiting Israel	0.01	*
Synagogue attendance	0.01	*
	intercept (B = 1.10)	*
	multiple r = 0.49	

Table 7.6. Factors of Jewish Identity and Contribution.

	Factor 1	Factor 2	Factor 3
{eigenvalue}	3.4	1.5	1.3
Religious practices	0.79		
Synagogue attendance	0.77		
Synagogue membership	0.70		
Religious identification	0.70		
Organizational membership	0.53		
Volunteering to Jewish causes	0.49		
Visiting Israel	0.36		
Amount contributed to non-Jewish philanthropies		0.83	
Amount contributed to Jewish philanthropies		0.76	
Volunteering to non-Jewish causes		0.49	
Contributing to non-Jewish philanthropies			0.81
Contributing to Jewish philanthropies			0.68
% Variance	29	13	11
	Religious	Amount contributed	Contribution
Total Variance		52%	

peared as a factor in Jewish identity. Here we wanted to reexplore the likelihood that philanthropic behavior would become a "factor" in the construct of Jewish identity and to check to see whether Jewish identity includes philanthropic behavior in both Jewish and non-Jewish realms. Table 7.6 presents the results of a factor analysis (Principal Components, Varimax Rotation) performed on the variables that express Jewish identity together with the philanthropic variables.

Table 7.6 shows that contributions to both Jewish and non-Jewish philanthropies constitute a factor in Jewish identity (factor 3). The religious factor in Jewish identity, as expected, is the dominant one, including all religious behaviors, whether expressed by ritual observance or Jewish communal activities (factor 1). Volunteering behavior in the Jewish realm was associated with the religious factor and not with contributing factors. This may be due to higher participation in temple and synagogue life. However, voluntarism for non-Jewish causes is associated with contributing behavior (factor 2). This is probably due to the relatively low relationship that was found between contribution patterns and voluntarism.

Defining contribution as an integral part of Jewish identity widens and enriches the definition of Jewish religious and communal identity. Helping others, as expressed in terms of philanthropic behavior, is deeply rooted in Judaic values. Helping all others, Jew and gentile alike, is one of the maxims of Judaism and is well summarized in the biblical Hebrew term *tzedakah*, whose root in Hebrew originates literally from the notion of "justice." Giving to both Jewish and non-Jewish philanthropies as a measure of Jewish identity reinforces the concept of *tzedakah* as an integral part of Jewish behavior.

Why Do Jews Give?

As a final note, we examined the question of why people say they contribute. In the prior sections of this chapter, we examined philanthropic behavior by looking at their interrelations and at the association of the indices of Jewish identity with philanthropy. These interrelations and indices of Jewish identity may represent some unconscious motivations of the giver. Therefore, it is important to examine the respondent's own verbal replies to the following question: "Please try to describe for me your overall philosophy regarding your donations to various organizations." The results are presented in Table 7.7.

Table 7.7 shows that answers varied greatly; they were not easy to categorize. More than a third of the answers were classified as not applicable or no reason, supporting the notion that it was difficult for people to articulate their reasons for giving, even though these are the same individuals who are classified as givers. However, there was enough of a general trend in the responses to allow some content analysis. The table shows that most individuals state that they contribute for what can be classified as general altruistic reasons, such as "trying to help

Table 7.7. Reasons for Giving.

Reasons	Percentage
General altruism	33
Jewish causes and *tzedakah*	14
Specific organizations	8
Disease cure	7
Personal reasons	4
Not applicable and no reason	34

others" or "to help the needy," even though they may not specify religious or organizational purposes. Such reasons are supportive of our finding that philanthropic behavior—giving to Jewish and non-Jewish philanthropies—reflects a general sense of *tzedakah* and commitment to giving. This is further supported by the second most common answers, a set of answers such as "anything to help Jews," "to maintain Judaism," "obligation to give," or "*tzedakah*." These reasons are tied more specifically to religious purposes within the Jewish community, but they still reflect a general involvement in philanthropic behavior as a "just" endeavor. Other reasons for giving were related to the purposes of specific organizations, the desire to fight particular diseases, and a whole host of personal reasons that included "because it makes me feel better" or "because I want to help" and so on.

These results may reflect, in an intuitive fashion, the higher-order results presented through the regression analysis. The five variables that explain philanthropic behavior, in terms of both frequency and amount, were related to both generalized giving patterns and religious and communally expressed Judaism. The generalized pattern of giving outweighed the religious and communal identity variables. These same results are found in the stated reasons for giving. "Altruistic reasons," which relate more to generalized patterns of giving, were listed first, and these outnumbered the strictly religious reasons. A strong commitment to traditional Jewish values and life, as expressed by synagogue attendance, for example, does play a role in giving, but it is generalized far beyond specific religious boundaries within the Jewish community toward the general non-Jewish community as well.

Summary and Conclusions

The main results may be summarized as follows:

- Giving to Jewish philanthropies is strongly related to socioeconomic variables and to major religious identity behaviors.
- More than three-fourths of Jewish households give to Jewish and to non-Jewish philanthropies.
- Giving to Jewish philanthropies and the amount given to Jewish philanthropies are strongly related to giving to non-Jewish philanthropies and to the amount given to non-Jewish philanthropies.
- The median annual gift to non-Jewish philanthropies is $75, which is less than 1 percent of the median annual household income and about a third of the amount given to Jewish philanthropies.
- Less than a third of Jewish households volunteer time for Jewish and for non-Jewish causes.
- Voluntarism for Jewish causes is associated with voluntarism for non-Jewish causes. This behavior, however, is not generalized to contributions to non-Jewish philanthropies and is only slightly generalized for contributions to Jewish philanthropies.
- There is a reinforcing effect of giving to Jewish fund-raising campaigns. This is not true for non-Jewish campaigns.
- Similar religious identity behaviors are associated with giving to Jewish and to non-Jewish philanthropies.
- Contributing to Jewish and to non-Jewish philanthropies, a generalized, altruistically motivated behavior, is a factor in Jewish religious identity.

This analysis indicates that Jews as a group have become well integrated into the fabric of American society. Their philanthropic behavior, while targeted in the Jewish community, extends far beyond it. Jews are as likely to give to non-Jewish as to Jewish philanthropies, even if the dollar amounts are more likely to be higher in the Jewish community. Jews have become active participants in both their secular and nonsecular worlds.

Philanthropic behavior of any kind is mutually reinforcing. Those who tend to give, tend to give in multiple outlets, while those who are nongivers tend to be nongivers in all outlets. Tracking someone into the giving system through any one mechanism suggests that this person is a likely candidate for contributions to a multiplicity of philanthropies. Since the primary reason for giving is a general commitment to helping others, this general altruism can be built upon for a wide variety of philanthropies, within both the Jewish and non-Jewish communities.

On the other hand, patterns of voluntarism are not highly associated with contribution patterns. This is true for both the propensity to give at all and the amount given. A multiplicity of tracks for increasing giving behavior in terms of dollar amounts is obviously indicated. One may be somewhat detached from a certain philanthropic institution and still be called upon to make a large contribution. On the other hand, the data may indicate that certain levels of participation are more effective than others. It may not be that the amount of voluntarism as reflected in the number of hours is the key variable, but rather the type of voluntarism and the nature of the association with the organization. Tracking people into heavier board or committee involvement, for example, may be less effective than other forms of contact and participation.

Finally, religious identity reinforces philanthropic behavior, both to the specific religious group and to the general society as a whole. Philanthropic behavior itself is an expression of religious identity, and therefore this set of mutually reinforcing variables finds increased giving and increased religious participation, whether defined by ritual observance or communal activity, as key elements in an overall set of identity patterns (see Cohen, 1988, for an interactive analysis of Jewish involvement). Increasing an individual's religious participation increases his or her philanthropic behavior and vice versa. Institutional and organizational programs and activities that reinforce

Jewish identity will ultimately benefit both Jewish and non-Jewish philanthropies alike. Making better Jews makes better givers, and making better givers makes better Jews. And both of these reinforce patterns of philanthropy to the non-Jewish community as well.

References

Andrews, F. M. *Philanthropic Giving*. New York: Russell Sage Foundation, 1950.

Cohen, S. M. "Will Jews Keep Giving? Prospects for the Jewish Charitable Community." *Journal of Jewish Communal Service*, 1978, *55*, 1.

Cohen, S. M. "Trends in Jewish Philanthropy." *American Jewish Yearbook*, 1980, p. 80.

Cohen, S. M. *American Modernity and Jewish Identity*. New York: Tavistock, 1983.

Cohen, S. M. *American Assimilation or Jewish Revival?* Bloomington: Indiana University Press, 1988.

Himmelfarb, H. S. "Measuring Religious Involvement." *Social Forces*, 1975, *53*, 606–618.

Hodgkinson, V. A., and Weitzman, M. A. *The Charitable Behavior of Americans*. Washington, D.C.: INDEPENDENT SECTOR, 1986.

Israel, S. *Boston's Jewish Community: The 1985 CJP Demographic Study*. Boston: The Combined Jewish Philanthropies of Greater Boston, 1987.

Kosmin, B. "The Dimensions of Contemporary American Jewish Philanthropy." In *Jewish Philanthropy in Contemporary America*, prepublication papers, printed by the North American Jewish Data Bank and the Council of Jewish Federations, Information Series No. 2. New York: Center for Jewish Studies, Graduate School and University Center, City University of New York, 1988.

Layton, D. N. *Philanthropy and Voluntarism: An Annotated Bibliography*. New York: Foundation Center, 1987.

Milgram, S. "The Experience of Living in Cities." *Science*, 1970, *167*, 1461–1468.

Mussen, P., and Eisenberg-Berg, N. *Roots of Caring, Sharing and Helping: The Development of Prosocial Behavior in Children.* New York: W. H. Freeman, 1977.

Olson, M. *The Logic of Collective Action: Public Goods and the Theory of Groups.* New York: Schoken, 1968.

Phelps, E. S. (ed.). *Altruism, Morality and Economic Theory.* New York: Russell Sage Foundation, 1975.

Rappeport, M., and Tobin, G. *A Population Study of the Jewish Community of MetroWest New Jersey.* Newark, N.J.: United Jewish Federation of MetroWest, 1987.

Rimor, M. and Tobin, G. "Is a Good Jew a Contributing Jew: The Relationship Between Jewish Identity and Philanthropic Behavior." Paper presented at the Conference on Jewish Philanthropy, Graduate School and University Center, City University of New York, June 15–16, 1988.

Ritterband, P., and Cohen, S. M. "Will the Well Run Dry? The Future of Jewish Giving in America." *Response,* 1979, 23.

Ritterband, P., and Silberstein, R. "Generation, Age, and Income Variability." In *Jewish Philanthropy in Contemporary America,* pre-publication papers, printed by the North American Jewish Data Bank and the Council of Jewish Federations, Information Series No. 2. New York: Center for Jewish Studies, Graduate School and University Center, City University of New York, 1988.

Silberstein, R., Ritterband, P., Rabinowitz, J., and Kosmin, B. *Giving to Jewish Causes: A Preliminary Reconnaissance,* printed by the North American Jewish Data Bank and the Council of Jewish Federations, Reprint Series No. 2. New York: Center for Jewish Studies, Graduate School and University Center, City University of New York, 1987.

Sklare, M. "The Future of Jewish Giving." *Commentary,* Nov. 1962, p. 423.

Tobin, G. *An Analysis of the Fund Raising Campaign of the United Jewish Appeal Federation of Greater Washington.* Washington, D.C.: United Jewish Appeal Federation of Greater Washington, D.C., 1984.

Tobin, G. *Analysis of the Fund Raising Campaign of the Associated*

Jewish Charities and Welfare Fund of Baltimore. Baltimore, Md.: Associated Jewish Charities & Welfare Fund, 1986.

Tobin, G. "We Are One, We Are Many: Reaching Potential Givers." Paper presented at the International Leadership Reunion of the United Jewish Appeal and Keren Hayesod, New York, 1987a.

Tobin, G. *Patterns of Philanthropy in the MetroWest New Jersey Jewish Community*. Newark, N.J.: United Jewish Federation of Metro-West, 1987b.

Tobin, G., and Fishman, S. *Analysis of the Fund Raising Campaign of the Jewish Community Federation of Rochester*. Rochester, N.Y.: Jewish Community Federation of Rochester, NY, 1988a.

Tobin, G., and Fishman, S. *Analysis of the Fund Raising Campaign of the Worcester Jewish Federation*. Worcester, Mass.: Worcester Jewish Federation, 1988b.

Tobin, G., and Sassler, S. *Analysis of the Fund Raising Campaign of the Bay Area Jewish Community*. San Francisco: Jewish Federation of the Greater East Bay, Jewish Community Federation of San Francisco, and Jewish Federation of Greater San Jose, 1988.

Yankelovich, Skelly, & White, Inc. *The Charitable Behavior of Americans*. Washington, D.C.: INDEPENDENT SECTOR, 1986.

Chapter 8

James R. Wood

Liberal Protestant Social Action in a Period of Decline

All U.S. churches encourage acts of human kindness, and most mobilize their members to give time and money to help people outside their own social circles. Churches are particularly effective at such mobilization because they instill philanthropic values and present information and opportunities for philanthropic activities in face-to-face settings such as worship services and Sunday school classes. The liberal mainline churches in the United States share with other churches in a vast mobilization of voluntary time and money in activities caring for individuals such as the poor, the sick, and the elderly. *In addition,* the liberal churches have played an important role in implementing socially liberal policies, that is, policies designed to change the structure of society so that, for example, income and also opportunities for individual achievement are more widely distributed throughout society. The liberal social agenda further includes sharp criticism of the U.S. government's role as promoter of U.S. business interests abroad. This additional role—mobilizing individuals and groups to press for the acceptance and implementation of a liberal social agenda—may be these churches' greatest contribution to human welfare.

This chapter looks at liberal Protestantism—the sources of its liberal social agenda, its distinctive role in U.S. society, and the potential impact of declining membership on that role.

Theological Roots of Liberalism

Ultimately, the liberal churches owe the character of their social and political agenda to the Hebrew prophets. Ahlstrom, however, traces roots of the strong movement for humanitarian reform in the United States during the first half of the nineteenth century to "the Puritan's basic confidence that the world could be constrained and reformed in accordance with God's revealed will" (1972, p. 637). Also nurturing the movement were a national sense of millennial expectation—a sense heightened by revivalism—and arising from the second Great Awakening, "the evangelical vision of a great Christian republic stretching westward beyond the Appalachians as a beacon and example for the whole world" (1972, p. 637). The enlightened rationalism espoused by the nation's Founding Fathers was another source of optimism and the expectation of progress. All of these elements were to inform the Social Gospel movement a century later. That movement, in the late nineteenth and early twentieth centuries, is the more immediate source of social liberalism in American religion. Central to the Social Gospel movement was a specific interpretation of the biblical notion of a Kingdom of God. A principal figure in the movement, Walter Rauschenbusch, in *The Righteousness of the Kingdom* ([c. 1900] 1968, p. 81), stresses that Jesus's idea of the Kingdom of God is firmly rooted in the history and culture of the Hebrew people: "This was the essence of the Messianic hope: the theocratic idea was at last to have its perfect realization in a Kingdom of God on earth, with the Messiah as its head, Israel as its dwelling-place and organ, and all the world as the sphere of its manifestation."

According to Rauschenbusch, Jesus accepted the idea of the Kingdom of God and attempted to develop it "in the same direction in which the spirit of God had been slowly leading the prophets" (1968, p. 82). Jesus regarded the spiritual nature, the religious and moral nature, of men and women as the formative force in the life of society. He initiated his Kingdom on earth by establishing a community of spiritual persons, in inward communion with God and in outward obedience to God.

"This was the living germ of the Kingdom. . . . By the power of the spirit dwelling in it, it was to overcome the spirit dominant in the world and thus penetrate and transform the world. In place of cruel customs it was to establish merciful customs. It was to push up steadily the average standard of right, making it approximate to the absolute standard of God" (1968, pp. 86–87).

Jesus, thought Rauschenbusch, was fully aware of the importance of the social context in which individuals develop and act as responsible individuals. "It is not enough to christianize individuals; we must christianize societies, organizations, nations, for they too have a life of their own which may be made better or worse. Christ addressed Capernaum and Bethsaida as responsible personalities. He lamented over Jerusalem as a whole" (1968, pp. 102–103).

Rauschenbusch, trained in sociology as well as in German higher criticism and in theology, based his crusade for social justice on the Judeo-Christian emphasis on the value of the individual personality. Rauschenbusch held that ordinary people can participate in establishing the Kingdom of God on earth. Jesus appeared the first time in "the fullness of the time." And so with the second time. "When that will be depends largely on us. In all the dealings of God with [humanity] the human factor is the variable quantity." Within certain limits God allows us free action, and the fulfillment of God's counsel is hastened or retarded according to our obedience (p. 108).

There are certain forces that are antagonistic to Christ and must be weakened if he is to reign; there is work still to be done in the world to make it acceptable for the Lord. And we do not have to wait for his coming to have power to tackle these things because we already have the means of power he approved — the flashing sword of truth and "the persevering faith that can cart a mountain away in wheelbarrow loads" (Rauschenbusch, 1968, p. 108). These provide power enough to win stubborn hearts, uncover social lies, and right injustice. Hence Rauschenbusch envisions the possibility of steady progress toward a society ruled by Judeo-Christian values. The Social Gospel movement was driven by hundreds of Christians who, believing with Rauschenbusch that the Christ will not return to force a kingdom upon us in violation of our autonomy as persons, were determined to try to foster those social structures that facilitate the voluntary acceptance of the values that Jesus proclaimed.

The development of cooperative relationships among several denominations both sustained this liberal theology and provided a vehicle for formulation and implementation of the social policies that sprang from it. The formation of the Federal Council of Churches in 1908 provided an organizational base that encouraged the implementation of the principles of the Social Gospel movement, officially espoused the need for a new social order, and championed the rights of laboring people (Ahlstrom, 1972, pp. 802–804). A study of the role of the National Council of Churches (successor to the Federal Council of Churches) in mobilizing denominational participation in the 1960s civil rights movement showed that the denominations historically associated with ecumenicism were most involved in the civil rights movement. The study also demonstrated that the ecumenical structure in many cases overcame the conservative tendencies resulting from a Southern resource base (Wood, 1972).

The Distinctive Role of the Liberal Mainline Churches in U.S. Society

The denominations classified here as liberal mainline denominations are the American Baptist Churches in the U.S.A., the Christian Church (Disciples of Christ), the Episcopal Church, Presbyterian Church (USA), United Church of Christ, and the United Methodist Church. All of them (or their predecessors) were among the founding members of the National Council of Churches of Christ in the United States of America. A national survey of religious congregations (Hodgkinson, Weitzman, and Kirsch, 1988) provides evidence for the differences in the political and social agendas of liberal and conservative churches. Informants for each congregation were asked to rate the church on a ten-point scale from very liberal (1) to very conservative (10). Undoubtedly most of those characterized as liberal (13.7 percent of congregations) are in the liberal mainline denominations and most of those characterized as very conservative (18.1 percent of congregations) are not. The survey asked whether congregations were engaged in each of thirty-six activities of social and political significance. More "liberal" than "very conservative" congregations are involved in each of thirty-five of these activities. (The one exception is right-to-life activities.) Liberal churches led the way in civil rights and social justice, community development, nuclear war/disarmament, and in programs for battered women, migrants/refugees, and housing/shelters for the homeless.

There were sharp differences between liberal and conservative churches in those activities most supportive of social change and in those that potentially challenged national policies. For example, only about 5 percent fewer very conservative than liberal churches provided recreation, camping, or other youth programs. However, the difference in civil rights and social justice activities was almost 35 percent; the difference in peace, security, economic development, and technical assistance was more than 24 percent; and the difference in nuclear war and disarmament was more than 47 percent. Clearly, the money and time members of liberal churches give their churches support different activities than those in conservative churches. The survey also showed that liberal congregations allowed more use of their buildings by outside groups (Hodgkinson, Weitzman, and Kirsch, 1988).

The inferences about differences in liberal and conservative churches drawn from this survey are bolstered by examination of the actions taken at recent national meetings of major Protestant denominations. The liberal churches champion the rights of the poor and minorities and are sharply critical of U.S. foreign policy. For example, Presbyterian Church (USA) in 1988 increased the limits of its grants to community groups that were building low- and middle-income housing, citing "economic conditions and cuts in federal spending [that] have caused widespread suffering to urban Americans" (Office of the General Assembly, 1988, p. 1030). Also, citing continued discrimination against a wide variety of racial and ethnic groups in the United States, the denomination restated its "abhorrence of and opposition to racism" and mandated a study that would "identify specific strategies in which congregations, presbyteries, and synods may oppose racism and ameliorate the problems created by the current racial climate" (p. 976). The General Assembly also "urge[d] members of its congregations to communicate with their senators and representatives to enact appropriate legislation to impose immediate and compulsory comprehensive sanctions against the government of South Africa" (p. 1027) and adopted as a denomination-wide personnel policy a "right to work for persons with AIDS and other life-threatening illnesses" (p. 986).

Resolutions of the 1987 General Assembly of the Christian Church (Disciples of Christ) encourage "congregations to provide informed counseling and support for women and men concerned with wanted or unwanted, planned or unplanned pregnancies" (Office of the General Minister and President, 1988, p. 270); request "the U.S. government to lift the trade embargo and to normalize relations with Vietnam" (p. 276); oppose the "U.S. government's legislative and covert support of the Contra war against the people of Nicaragua and actively urge the Congress of the United States to deny all funds to the Contras and actively seek a peaceful solution to all of the problems of Central America in concert with those nations which are urgently requesting our peaceful cooperation" (p. 278); request "the General Minister and President of the Christian Church (Disciples of Christ) to convey the General Assembly's opposition to the Strategic Defense Initiative (SDI) to the President of the United States, to the Secretary of Defense, to the Secretary of State, and to leaders of Congress of both political parties" (p. 283); endorse "the concept of a U.S. Peace Tax Fund, a fund that would provide a legal alternative for those tax-paying citizens who, on ground of conscience, object to paying for war and human destruction" (p. 304); denounce racist and anti-Semitic groups (p. 309); and call upon "the governments of the United States and Canada to promote in international forums a major emergency response to deal with effects of sanctions in Southern Africa" (p. 317). The assembly also called on the Department of Church in Society to monitor a proposed INS "rule regarding political asylum in the United States" to assure "due process and fundamental fairness to all asylum seekers" (p. 344); affirmed the peace plan for Central America signed by the presidents of five Central American nations (p. 345); and endorsed the voluntary repatriation of Salvadoran refugees (p. 347); reaffirmed its call to churches to "work against injustice and denial of public service in the communities where it lives" and the church's advocacy for "research, education, increased treatment services, and disease prevention" related to AIDS (p. 346).

The 1988 Southern Baptist Convention addressed social issues by "deploring homosexuality as a perversion of divine standards and as a violation of nature and natural affections" (Executive Committee, Southern Baptist Convention, 1988, p. 71); calling on "all Southern Baptists to take an active stand in support of the sanctity of human life" (p. 73); encouraging "the United States to cease to assist these industries [alcohol and tobacco] via trade talks" (p. 73); urging "Baptists agencies and institutions to refuse direct federal assistance, and . . . encourag[ing] those agencies and institutions receiving only indirect assistance to seek legal counsel about seeking exemptions under the Civil Rights Restoration Act where necessary to protect their free exercise of religion (p. 74); observing that some "tax subsidy proposals for child care discriminate against families who choose home child care by taxing all families to subsidize government-approved day-care facilities," affirming "that the principal responsibility of child care is a family responsibility," and expressing concern about "the need for child-care services in those regions where such services may not be available in adequate supply, especially for parents living in poverty, many of whom are single parents" (p. 75); abhorring "the tendency to bypass parental consent involving birth control and abortion," deploring school clinics that "have as any part of their function the provision of contraceptive counseling, medications, or devices" (p. 76); and expressing concern about "The U.S./U.S.S.R. Agreement on Education signed at the 1985 Geneva Summit by the United States and the Soviet Union [calling for] the exchange of curricula and teaching materials for elementary and secondary school children" because "The authority of God and his teaching are ignored or disavowed in wide areas of modern life in officially atheistic nations that promote the state as the ultimate source of human rights and duties" (p. 79).

Not only does the agenda embodied in the resolutions of the liberal churches differ from that of the Southern Baptist Convention, but the process of choosing the people who consider the resolutions and the process of deliberating over their passage differs dramatically. Delegates to the United Methodist Church's General Conference are elected by representatives at state-level conferences where there is genuine debate over the issues. At the General Conference itself, a deliberative process allows the petitions to be debated in relatively small representative committees that recommend action to the larger body. In contrast, Southern Baptist Convention "messengers" are selected by local congregations. There can be one messenger for each church that contributes to the denomination's work plus one "additional messenger from each church for every two hundred and fifty (250) members; or for each $250 paid to the work of the convention during the fiscal year preceding the annual meeting. . . . But no church may appoint more than ten (10)" (Executive Committee, Southern Baptist Convention, 1988, p. 6). The 1988 Southern Baptist Convention conducted business with 29,446 messengers (almost one-fourth of whom came from Texas; the meeting was in San Antonio). By comparison, the 1988 United Methodist General Conference had 996 delegates.

The representative selection procedures for national meetings and the deliberative consensus formation processes typical of the mainline denominations are an important contribution to informed public opinion in U.S. society. Voluntary associations in which individuals can debate the critical issues face-to-face encourage individuals to act out their selfless values rather than their selfish interests and provide a bulwark against the manipulation of the public by computer-generated direct mail and mass media campaigns for a particular group's vested interest in ideology, money, or power.

Amitai Etzioni's theory of the "active" society pays special attention to the process of consensus formation — the process by which perspectives of society's members are conveyed upward to the national leadership. A healthy society is one in which the relationship between citizens and national leaders is mediated by a large network of groups and organizations where multiple perspectives are reduced toward consensus. The effect of any direct appeal by national leaders or by mass media campaigns to individual citizens is determined largely by the multiple membership of the citizens in groups and organizations. This mediation protects against mass emotional manipulation. In this view national policy properly starts with the citizens, who are encouraged to express their values at a level where they can engage in face-to-face debate with those who may have differing views. These debates tend to reduce differences and move toward consensus or at least a narrowed set of alternatives as they are conveyed to national leaders of the executive and legislative branches of the government. These national leaders should form policy on the basis of the consensus or narrowed alternative; the same network of groups and interpersonal relationships that shaped the consensus on the way up will influence the acceptance of leaders' policies as they seek grass-roots support.

The more deliberative consensus formation process in the liberal mainline churches, contrasted to the Southern Baptist Convention, is reflected in the following denominational positions on abortion, perhaps the most volatile issue facing U.S. society today. The 1988 Southern Baptist Convention passed the following resolution:

> WHEREAS, The trustees of the Christian Life Commission have adopted a firm policy opposing abortion except to prevent the death of the mother, which policy states, in part, that "Human life, from fertilization until natural death, is sacred and should be protected not destroyed"; and
> The trustees of the Sunday School Board have adopted a plan to publish annual, dated lessons opposing abortion on Sanctity of Human Life Sunday.
> We . . . express our appreciation to [these] trustees . . . and the Sunday School Board; and
> Be it finally RESOLVED, That we call upon all

Southern Baptists to take an active stand in support
of the sanctity of human life [Executive Committee,
Southern Baptist Convention, 1988, p. 73].

As background for interpreting this resolution, note that
the 1988 Southern Baptist Convention *Annual* contains a minority report of the Christian Life Trustees that faults a new staff
member for, among other things, not having a conviction on
when human life begins and not being willing to say that he
would support legislation that would guarantee the right to life
to potentially handicapped children. The staff member subsequently left the position.

Contrast with the Southern Baptist resolution one passed
by the 1988 General Assembly of the Presbyterian Church
(USA).

That the Moderator. . .
select a Task Force to conduct a study to be completed within two years. . . designed to give forum
to each different theological position in debate of
the issues related to problem pregnancies and
abortion, and that the members of the commission
represent the broadest spectrum of theological
positions within the church. . . .

That the above study and other statements of past
General Assemblies be used to formulate a new
policy statement. . . concerning the issues related
to problem pregnancies, including male responsibility and accountability, and abortion that speak
within the theological, Scriptural, moral and ethical disciplines of the church. [Office of the General
Assembly, 1988, pp. 1015–1016]

A comparison of the largest Protestant denomination,
the 14 million member Southern Baptist Convention—a conservative body—with the second largest, the 9 million member
United Methodist Church—a liberal body—will both demon-

strate the vast philanthropic contribution of conservative churches and highlight the additional role played by liberal churches.

Total gifts to Southern Baptist churches in 1987 were more than $4 billion ($4,008,914,325). The comparable figure for United Methodist churches was $2,573,518,686. Most of this money was spent in providing for the ministry of local congregations. For "benevolences" beyond the local congregation, Southern Baptist churches gave $662,691,289 (16 percent of their total gifts), and United Methodist churches gave $312,508,686 (12 percent of total gifts). This money funded a wide range of health, education, and human welfare activities. The Cooperative Program funds available for distribution by Southern Baptist denominational officials were $130,345,184. The money was distributed to twenty-two denominational units, including six seminaries. Two of the units, the Christian Life Commission and the Public Affairs Committee, include social and political issues within their missions. In 1987, 1.3 percent of the Cooperative Program funds was given to these agencies. In 1987, the United Methodist Church "apportioned" to twelve general agencies a total of $59,830,795. Six percent of this money went to three agencies with specific social and political missions: the Board of Church and Society, the Commission on Religion and Race, and the Commission on the Status and Role of Women.

Though the liberal and social agenda of the United Methodist Church is spread throughout its agencies, as noted above, some of them have a specific focus on societal issues. The emphases of the Board of Church and Society may be inferred from this list of all the grants of more than $1,000 made in 1987 to organizations not formally part of the United Methodist Church:

Agricultural Mission, Inc.
Arrowhead Council of Churches
Black Women's Leadership and Economic Development
  Project
Catholic Family Service, Inc.
Church Women United
Churches' Committee for Voter Registration/Education

East Coast Farm Worker Support Network
IMPACT
Interfaith Action for Economic Justice
Korean Family Relations and Legal Advice Clinic
National Black Women's Health Project
National Coalition for Public Education and Religious
    Liberty
National Conference of Black Lawyers
National Council of Churches of Christ
National Farm Workers Ministry
National Interreligious Service Board of Conscientious
    Objectors
National Interreligious Task Force on Criminal Justice
New Mexico Research Education Enrichment Foundation
Project Caris
Religious Network for Equality for Women
School District No. 9-Browning, MT-Chemical Depen-
    dency Intervention
Washington Office on Haiti

This board spent a total of $76,429 on outside grants in 1987. Note that many of the causes are not controversial. A balance of concerns is also reflected in the smaller gifts. For example, there is a gift to the National Abortion Rights Action League, and there is also a gift to an alternative teenage pregnancy home. However, though most of the money is given to noncontroversial causes, a substantial amount is given to causes (for example, opposing U.S. policies in Central America) that reflect the liberal social agenda that is a long-standing tradition of the church.

This comparison with the liberal mainline churches should in no way devalue the tremendous philanthropic contribution of the Southern Baptist Convention and other conservative churches. The point is to highlight the *additional* role played by liberal churches— pressing a liberal social agenda for the United States. The philanthropic importance of shaping social policies of the U.S. government is underscored by the facts that the total benevolences of the United Methodist Church and the Southern Baptist Convention would barely equal the projected cost of two Stealth bombers, that all the giving to all the religious bodies in the United States in a year amounts to less than the federal government spends on health care, and that the federal expenditure on Social Security is more than two-and-a-half times (and the national defense budget more than three times) the amount contributed to all charitable causes in the United States.

The Decline of the Liberal Mainlines

Before considering the impact of decline on the societal role of the mainlines, it is necessary to assess the decline. In 1972 Dean Kelley, in his book *Why Conservative Churches Are Growing*, predicted that the liberal mainline denominations in the United States would cease to be a vital influence in the nation. In a recent *Time* magazine article, Richard Ostling (1989) describes the unprecedented decline of the mainline denominations. Since 1965 the liberal mainline denominations have certainly shrunk in size: the United Church of Christ by 20 percent, the Presbyterian Church by 25 percent, the Episcopal Church by 28 percent, the Christian Church (Disciples of Christ) by 43 percent, and the United Methodist Church by 18 percent.

Following are growth rates of selected denominations from 1960 to 1986 (sources are Jacquet, 1988; Barrett, 1989):

Christian Church (Disciples)	– 39%
Presbyterian Church (USA)	– 28%
United Church of Christ	– 25%
Episcopal Church	– 23%
United Methodist Church	– 14%
Lutheran Church in America	– 5%
American Lutheran Church	3%
Lutheran Church (Missouri Synod)	10%
Southern Baptist Convention	50%
Roman Catholic	26%
North American Baptist Conference	– 17%
Free Methodist	29%

Salvation Army	70%
Church of the Nazarene	73%
Jehovah's Witnesses	201%
Church of Jesus Christ of Latter-day Saints	160%
Seventh-day Adventists	110%
Jews	33%
Muslims	1512%

Here are some statistics and estimates of growth rates for 1986 to 1987 (sources are Jacquet, 1988; Barrett, 1989):

United Methodist Church	– 0.8%
Southern Baptist Convention	0.7%
Muslims	0.3%
Jews	0.4%
Atheists	4.0%
New religionists	5.0%
Nonreligionists	9.0%

The overall picture of decline of the liberal mainline churches is reinforced by data from public opinion polls. For example, a 1988 Gallup poll on religious preferences showed that the "Methodist" category had the largest drop from child-hood denomination to denomination of current identification. The category with the largest increase was "Nonaffiliated" and the second largest increase was among the smaller fundamentalist and pentecostal groups (Princeton Religious Research Center, 1989a). A series of Gallup polls on religious preference show that Protestants as a category have declined from a high of 70 percent (in 1962) to a low of 56 percent in 1988 (matched in 1983). At the same time, the "None" category has increased from a low of 2 percent in 1952 (matched in 1962 and 1967) to a high of 10 percent in 1988. The "Other" (than Protestant, Catholic, Jewish, None) category increased from a low of 1 percent in 1947 (and most recently in 1977 and 1978) to 4 percent in 1988 (the all-time high was 5 percent in 1974). With 2 percent of the population, Mormons now equal Jewish in preferences (Princeton Religious Research Center, 1989b). Where long-term comparisons are possible within Protestantism, we see that Baptists (including the American Baptists, who are liberal mainline, but predominantly Southern Baptists and other Baptists) have retained virtually the same percentage of preferences (around 20 percent) sine the late 1960s. Methodists (the vast majority related to the mainline United Methodist Church) dropped from 14 to 9 percent and are back to 10 percent. Presbyterians dropped from 6 to 2 percent and are back to 4 percent. Episcopalians dropped from 3 to 2 percent. And Lutherans dropped from 7 to 5 percent and are back to 6 percent (Princeton Religious Research Center, 1989c).

Depending on whether we consider preferences or membership figures, the decline of the liberal churches is either slowing or possibly reversing. Clearly, however, they have declined, both in absolute terms and in relation to other religious bodies.

The Impact of Decline

More important than the declining membership of the liberal mainline denominations is the conservative challenge to their influence in shaping the U.S. social agenda. The liberal churches no longer hold a secure place as the shapers of public policy. Discussing the liberal decline, Ostling (1989) assumes a concomitant loss of influence on society and sees in this decline serious implications for the nation's political and social future. However, there is little evidence that the conservatives are gaining influence relative to the liberals. For example, despite incredible media attention to conservatives such as Jerry Falwell and Pat Robertson, their political involvement had little impact on the makeup of the Congress. The Democrats' majority increased by 11 percent between 1973 and 1989. And though the liberal mainline denominations did drop from 47 percent of the Congress in 1973 to 38 percent in 1989, the conservative churches did not pick up these losses—they experienced a slight loss to 18 percent. The real gainers were Roman Catholics and Jews, hardly a conservative lot. Looking at the outcome of congressional actions—such as aid to the Contras—and at public opinion polls—on abortion, for example—there is no strong evidence that the conservative religious forces are gaining in influence. In fact from 1975 to 1988 the percentage supporting legal abortion under any circumstances climbed from 21 to 24 percent, and the percentage wanting it illegal in all circumstances dropped from 22 to 17 percent (Princeton Religious Research Institute, 1989a). And while in 1980, 9 percent said they would be less likely to vote for a person who is an evangelical Christian, in 1987, 29 percent said they would be less likely to do so (Princeton Religious Research Center, 1987).

Clearly, the liberal mainline denominations' influence cannot be taken for granted. These denominations will never again have center stage to themselves. Not only are conservative Protestants demanding a larger role but so too are new actors. The religious scene is becoming more diverse as Catholics, Mormons, and those who are either antireligious, not religious, or not traditionally religious increase in number.

Though it is popular to relate the decline of the liberal churches to their liberalism, the downturn in membership probably has more to do with demographics (geographical location and birthrates) than with involvement in social issues (see Hoge and Roozen, 1979). Undoubtedly, there is some relationship between liberalism and decline. Certainly some members and some congregations left the liberal denominations because of liberal social action. Perhaps more important, many young people who have grown up in the liberal tradition and may cherish its values feel little loyalty to organized religion. Though, ironically, this situation may partly result from these churches' success in teaching youth the prophetic message that social action is more important than ritual, it is a serious matter. There is a strong relationship between church participation and both giving and volunteering to nonreligious philanthropic causes. If these young people remain uninvolved in the organizational church, they will likely be less personally involved in pursuing the church's liberal social agenda at the same time that their lack of participation in the church weakens its influence on public policy.

The decline in the liberal mainline denominations may

Table 8.1. United Methodist Church Income Figures.

	1984	1985	1986	1987
Board of Church and Society	$2,915,943	$3,669,615	$3,695,597	$3,710,921
Commission on Religion and Race	$1,436,618	$1,460,231	$1,518,497	$1,829,592
Commission on Status and Role of Women	$282,380	$451,365	$376,045	$493,579

continue. Roof and McKinney believe that these denominations "will continue to lose ground both in numbers and in social power and influence" (1987, p. 233). Still, there are several reasons to expect that the influence of the liberal churches will remain strong. In the first place, the liberal churches remain committed to their agenda. For example, Table 8.1 shows the total income figures, 1984–1987, for the United Methodist Board of Church and Society, Commission on Religion and Race, and Commission on the Status and Role of Women (Peck, 1988, pp. H-2-16–H-2-29).

The church has provided stable resources to these units despite their being involved in matters that are controversial in our society. Moreover, the General Council of Finance and Administration has proposed that the basic funding for each of these units be increased each year through 1992.

A second reason for expecting liberal mainline influence to remain strong is that the United Methodist Church, the largest of the liberal mainline denominations, is well planted in every state (and in almost every *county*) in the United States. Its statements on social issues are informed by Americans with diverse perspectives. Though the Southern Baptist Convention is larger, the United Methodist Church is far more geographically representative. I compared the proportion of delegates from each state to the 1988 Southern Baptist Convention and United Methodist Church General Conference with each state's proportion of representatives in the U.S. House of Representatives (which is determined by population distribution). Clearly, the United Methodist Church is more representative.

The Methodist proportion is closer to the proportion of members in the U.S. House of Representatives in forty of the fifty states, and there are three ties. Moreover, Methodists, compared with Baptists, have far larger proportions of delegates from five of the six most populous states.

In the third place, coalitions with the Roman Catholic Church, the nation's largest religious body, may assure continued influence. Cooperative relationships with Catholics are increasing. Such coalitions are facilitated by the fact that, since the Second Vatican Council, American Catholicism has become more open in authority structure and the American Catholic bishops' letters on such subjects as nuclear war and the economy have been congruent with the Protestant mainline positions.

A fourth reason liberal mainline influence may remain strong is that the conservative challenge may subside. Three separate studies point in this direction. Hunter (1987) sees among the younger generation of evangelicals "a broadening of the meaning of some of Evangelicalism's fundamental religious symbols" (p. 162) and a "code of political civility. . . so deeply ingrained that they are ethically constrained *not* to mobilize publicly (and even politically) against" cultural changes they strongly oppose (p. 164). Johnson and Tamney's study of Moral Majority sympathizers suggests that over the long term support for the Moral Majority will decline because the sources of Moral Majority support are negatively related to education and cosmopolitanism, which appear to be increasing through time in the United States (Johnson and Tamney, 1985). Finally, Ammerman (1986, p. 487) sees the major source of fundamentalism's rise in the Southern Baptist Convention as a reaction to the erosion of cultural support for traditional beliefs:

> First, it is apparent that the forces creating a new South are also eroding fundamentalist theology. As the level of education increases, fundamentalism decreases. Clergy with master's and doctoral degrees are eight times as likely to hold a moderate theology as are those with less than a bachelor's degree. . . . Lay people in households headed by

professionals or managers are five time as likely to
be moderate as those in farm and blue-collar
households. . . . And people with family incomes
of $35,000-plus are more than twice as likely to be
theologically moderate as those with family incomes of less than $10,000. . . . As Southerners
move toward the higher educational levels and income that accompany a white-collar, professional
economy, fewer and fewer will maintain a fundamentalist theology. But at the same time, many at
the edges of this transition are likely to respond by
embracing fundamentalist beliefs more vigorously
than ever.

The number claiming a fundamentalist identity is significantly higher among the newly urban people, and within this
group it is highest among those with less than a college education. "The data suggest that those in the new South with the
education, income, and successful careers have moved rather
easily into a theology that is less grounded in old assumptions"
(Ammerman, 1986, p. 487). It is those who are exposed to the
modern urban South but do not have a secure place there who
form the core of the movement. As newcomers become better
integrated into the dominant urban culture, they should become less susceptible to the fundamentalist movement.

Ammerman's argument is consistent with Joseph Gusfield's reflections on another conservative social movement—the
temperance movement. He stresses the importance of public
affirmation of norms as "a positive statement of the worth or
value of the particular subculture vis-à-vis other subcultures in
the society" (1963, p. 116). Johnson and Tamney's work discussed
above (see also Mueller, 1983) fits this emerging interpretation
that support for at least the narrowest values and views of the
conservatives will eventually decline.

Marty (1987, p. 343) sees the mainline religionists on the
new religious scene playing "a more modest but still important
role as advocates of sorts of tolerance in an increasingly tribal
world." He understates the case. Attitudes of tolerance and

consensus-forming structures are critical in an increasingly diverse society, one in which groups with a broad range of interests and values have a voice. The liberal mainline denominations can be an important resource for such a society. Words from an eighteen-page Disciples of Christ study document on economic systems typify the liberal churches' approach to complex, controversial subjects: "A study document is not a statement of the point of view of some individual or group. It should manifest openness and respect diversity. . . . It must clearly and fairly set forth various points of view held by competent and sincere Christians" (Office of the General Minister and President, 1988, p. 284). "We may believe that our faith leads us to prefer some particular [economic] model. If so, we will want to advocate that approach and debate its merits with those who believe their faith supports other models. However, in doing so we should keep in mind the basic moral values our faith implies — standing with the poor, community, human dignity, and social realism. We can advance these values by being true to the ones our chosen model stresses and being sensitive to the ones it tends to minimize. In this way the strengths of each model are maximized, the people of the world may realize some value from each, and an overall result will be a more just world economy" (p. 301).

The future is never clear, but clearly the liberal mainline denominations possess resources that are vital for a society that would embody diversity, and freedom, and justice.

References

Ahlstrom, S. E. *A Religious History of the American People*. New Haven, Conn.: Yale University Press, 1972.

Ammerman, N. T. "The New South and the New Baptists." *Christian Century*, May 14, 1986, pp. 486–488.

Barrett, D. B. "Adherents of All Religions by Eight Continental Areas, 1988." In D. Daume (ed.), *Britannica Book of the Year*. Chicago: Encyclopaedia Britannica, 1989.

Executive Committee, Southern Baptist Convention. *Annual of the Southern Baptist Convention, 1988.* Nashville, Tenn.: Executive Committee, Southern Baptist Convention, 1988.

Gusfield, J. *Symbolic Crusade.* Berkeley: University of California Press, 1963.

Hodgkinson, V. A., Weitzman, M. S., and Kirsch, A. D. *From Belief to Commitment: The Activities and Finances of Religious Congregations in the United States.* Washington, D.C.: INDEPENDENT SECTOR, 1988.

Hoge, D., and Roozen, D. A. *Understanding Church Growth and Decline: 1950–1978.* New York: Pilgrim Press, 1979.

Hunter, J. D. *Evangelicalism: The Coming Generation.* Chicago: University of Chicago Press, 1987.

Jacquet, C., Jr. (ed.). *Yearbook of American & Canadian Churches.* Nashville, Tenn.: Abingdon Press, 1988.

Johnson, S. D., and Tamney, J. B. "The Christian Right and the 1984 Presidential Election." *Review of Religious Research,* 1985, *27,* 124–133.

Kelley, D. *Why Conservative Churches Are Growing.* San Francisco: Harper & Row, 1972.

Marty, M. E. *Religion and Republic: The American Circumstance.* Boston: Beacon Press, 1987.

Mueller, C. "In Search of a Constituency for the 'New Christian Right.'" *Public Opinion Quarterly,* 1983, *47,* 213–229.

Office of the General Assembly. *Presbyterian Church (USA): Minutes 200th General Assembly.* Louisville, Ky.: Office of the General Assembly, 1988.

Office of the General Minister and President. *1988 Year Book & Directory of the Christian Church (Disciples of Christ).* Indianapolis, Ind.: Office of the General Minister and President, 1988.

Ostling, R. N. "Those Mainline Blues." *Time,* May 22, 1989, pp. 94–96.

Peck, J. R. (ed.). *1988 Journal General Conference The United Methodist Church.* Vol. 1. Nashville, Tenn.: United Methodist Publishing House, 1988.

Princeton Religious Research Center. "Support for an Evangelical Candidate Declines Sharply." *Emerging Trends,* Apr. 1987, *9,* 5.

Princeton Religious Research Center. "Attitudes on Abortion Little Changed Since Supreme Court's 1973 Ruling." *Emerging Trends*, Feb. 1989a, *11*, 5.

Princeton Religious Research Center. "Little Change in Major Faiths." *Emerging Trends*, Feb. 1989b, *11*, 3.

Princeton Religious Research Center. "'Mainline' Church Membership Still Below Level of 1960s, 1970s." *Emerging Trends*, May 1989c. *11*, 1.

Rauschenbusch, W. *The Righteousness of the Kingdom*. New York: Harper & Row, 1968.

Roof, W. C., and McKinney, W. *American Mainline Religion: Its Changing Shape and Future*. New Brunswick, N. J.: Rutgers University Press, 1987.

Wood, J. R. "Unanticipated Consequences of Organizational Coalitions: Ecumenical Cooperation and Civil Rights Policy." *Social Forces*, 1972, *50*, 512–521.

Chapter 9

Timothy T. Clydesdale

Soul-Winning and Social Work: Giving and Caring in the Evangelical Tradition

In a word: *regeneration*. The issue is not poverty or hunger, but faith and ethics. The present-oriented slave [the person in poverty] cannot . . . be helped by handouts — they will only reinforce his moral defects. . . . The poor must learn the relationship of salvation to family life, work, debt, responsibility, thrift, saving, and everything else.

> David Chilton
> *Productive Christians in an*
> *Age of Guilt Manipulators*

The Gospel is clearly biased in favor of the poor and oppressed. There is a biblical mandate to support the cause of the poor against the abuses of wealth and power. . . . We pursue our material comfort at the cost of impoverishing others. . . . A vital relationship to God will evidence itself in an active serving of social and political justice.

> Jim Wallis
> *Agenda for Biblical People*

On the surface, one might assume that these quotations are from two Christian authors with quite different views of poverty. One might further speculate that the first quote is from an evangelical, while the second is from a religious liberal. The first assumption is correct, but the second is not. Both quotes are from evangelicals (that is, theologically conservative Christians). And while this revelation might strike some as surprising, religious historians have long told the story of how evangelicals have practiced diverse forms of giving and caring. Evangelicals, in various times and ways, have involved themselves in everything from individual, personal acts of charity to prophetic crusades against oppression and injustice, varying with how evangelicals understood the conditions and causes of poverty. In this chapter, I will first provide a general introduction to this tradition of giving and caring by evangelicals, presenting several different responses that American evangelicals have made to the issue of poverty. Then, I will discuss current patterns of giving and caring, using recent national surveys and examining the practices of evangelical philanthropic foundations.

A Long (and Variegated) Tradition

To begin, one cannot speak of a single history of giving and caring in the evangelical tradition, for there are really several different histories. Some evangelicals emphasize individual acts of charity to those in need. Others seek to expose oppressors and injustice, fighting the plague of poverty wherever it rears its head. In common to all is a desire to be obedient to the Bible (held in highest esteem by evangelicals) and its commands to "love your neighbor" and "give to the poor." The variety is born in the application of these commands to the world; that is "who" is our neighbor and "how" should we give to the poor. What follows here, then, is a compressed introduction to four different responses evangelicals have made to the above biblical commands.

American Puritanism. The American colonies promised to be a new society to the Puritans who fled the religious persecution of seventeenth-century England. This new society would be founded on the Truth, as contained in the Puritans' Bible and expounded by their preachers. To a degree, the Puritans realized their vision. They maintained a general cultural hegemony throughout New England, up to and including the mid-eighteenth century, where we can find two early forms of evangelical giving and caring.

One of the most prominent preachers during the eighteenth century was "the Grand Itinerant"—George Whitefield (Ahlstrom, 1972, p. 238). Whitefield earned this title because he traveled extensively throughout prerevolutionary America to preach and convert sinners. Born and trained in England, Whitefield was neither an ordinary preacher nor a typical revivalist. Many historians credit Whitefield with triggering the first Great Awakening, a religious revival that swept across the colonies in such a dramatic way that H. Richard Niebuhr (1959, p. 126) later referred to it as the "national conversion" of the United States. Yet, how did a prominent preacher like Whitefield view the needs of the world and the response Christians should make to them? The answer to this question is found in one of his few written sermons.

"Regeneration" summarizes Whitefield's understanding of the needs of the world. Every person needs "regeneration," that is, an intensely transforming personal experience when he or she repents from sin and believes in Jesus Christ as Savior (Whitefield, [c. 1760] 1906). "We [the regenerated] must be so altered as to the qualities and tempers of our minds, that we must entirely forget what manner of persons we once were" (p. 59). Once people were so transformed, preached Whitefield, they could be "infallibly certain of being as happy, both here and hereafter, as an all-wise, all-gracious, all-powerful God can make them" (p. 58). His foundational concern was the regeneration of all people (or "souls" as they are sometimes called by evangelicals)—regeneration was the key factor to personal happiness. Therefore, to persons in this tradition, the ultimate need of all people was regeneration, for following regeneration would come certain happiness; all other needs were either unimportant or, at best, not of high priority. And while Whitefield never completely ignored the physical needs of his listeners, his response to their needs was sporadic and poorly organized (Bremner, 1961). The "poor" (in this tradition) are "spiritualized"; that is, those who are unregenerated are considered "poor" rather than those who lack basic economic resources.

Whitefield was so preoccupied with the spiritual realm that he effectively had blinders on—gazing solely on his spiritual mission and indifferent to all else.

Dwight L. Moody, a late nineteenth century evangelist, did not start out in the footsteps of Whitefield. Indeed, his early ministry through the YMCA involved him greatly in relief and assistance to the urban poor. But this did not last. Moody gave the following reason for abandoning his combined relief and revivalism ministry for an exclusively evangelistic one: "If I had the Bible in one hand and a loaf in the other, the people always looked first at the loaf; and that was just contrary of the order laid down in the Gospel" (Marsden, 1980, p. 37). Evangelism (getting people to believe in Jesus as personal Savior) was the key to social change, Moody believed, and once the poor converted and "acquired the sense of responsibility found in strong Christian families, poverty would cease" (Marsden, 1980, p. 37). He viewed the causes of poverty as individual and moral and ended up joining the tradition of Whitefield, maintaining that the solution to all needs was the conversion of souls.

A contemporary spokesperson, David Chilton, quoted at the beginning of this chapter, also illustrates this tradition. This strand of giving and caring merges a "blame the victim" view of poverty with a singular emphasis upon evangelism as the appropriate response to poverty. As a proponent of the free market system, Chilton holds a private, individuated understanding of poverty. It is the poor's moral inferiority that has kept them from participating fully in capitalism, Chilton (1981) argues, and he chastises Christians for doing charitable work when evangelism is the only solution to poverty. Chilton, along with Whitefield and Moody, stands in a tradition that can be labeled "indifferent evangelists"—"indifferent" because of their lack of interest in or discouragement of poor relief, and "evangelists" because they focus on spiritual issues only.

Jonathan Edwards, a contemporary and friend of Whitefield, provides a contrast to "indifferent evangelists." Edwards did not travel widely but rather maintained a stable occupational life as a pastor and later as a professor. As a writer, Edwards is well regarded even today. His response to poverty is

found in a five-week sermon series preached to his Northampton, Massachusetts, congregation, titled "The Duty of Charity to
the Poor, Explained and Enforced" (Edwards, 1971, pp. 172ff.).

Duty was a word that rang clearly in the ears of a good
Northampton parishioner. Duties of diligence and simplicity
were proclaimed to Puritans as symbols of their salvation (and
membership in the "elect"), and so was giving to the poor an
outward sign of salvation. "This duty is absolutely commanded,
and much insisted on, in the word of God. Where have we any
command in the Bible laid down in stronger terms, and in a
more peremptory urgent manner, than the command of giving
to the poor?" (Edwards, 1971, p. 172). Edwards reasoned with his
parishioners that charity was essential, invoking Jesus's "Golden
Rule," the promise of God's blessings, the example of Christ, and
the biblical view of Christians as stewards (caretakers, not
owners) of personal belongings. The obedient Christian, Edwards stressed, was one who recognized that he was only the
keeper of personal belongings (their true owner was God), who
realized that he would give an account to God for the use of his
possessions, and who therefore gave generously to those in need.

Edwards, in contrast to Whitefield, understood the poor
to have both spiritual and economic needs. He saw them as a
group for whom Christians needed to have a special concern.
Yet he remained ambivalent toward the role of the law, state, or
other structures in perpetuating or constraining poverty (Edwards, 1971). Instead, his emphasis was on the importance of
acts of charity in the life of the believer, not on "how" or "why" the
poor were in poverty. Certainly, Edwards shared Whitefield's
concern for the conversion of souls and was pivotal in triggering
a revival himself in Northampton prior to the first Great Awakening (Tracy, 1980). But unlike "indifferent evangelists," Edwards
saw the poor in need of special assistance beyond the spiritual,
and in this regard, Edwards demonstrated a more specific understanding of poverty and the necessity of charitable acts in
response.

This idea of the Christian as steward can also be seen in
the writings of Larry Burkett. Burkett is the founder and director
of Christian Financial Concepts, Inc., and an author of financial

advice books for evangelicals. Counseling his readers on "God's View of Success," he states, "Those who are truly being blessed by God have demonstrated a willingness to use their material resources for God" (1986, p. 28). Burkett encourages giving to the poor; however, his understanding of poverty is not very different from Chilton's "blame the victim" response. He warns his readers to give to the "poor, not lazy" (p. 52) and implies that many poor are just lazy. With a focus on the Christian as steward and an economic view of the poor (though one that separates them into "lazy" and "nonlazy"), Burkett and Edwards represent a tradition we can label "dutiful stewards."

The next two types of giving and caring developed much later and are quite different. These later types hold a broader understanding of the "how" and "why" of poverty than indifferent evangelists or dutiful stewards. To understand how these two emerged, we need to look at their historical antecedents, asking what factors influenced a broader understanding of poverty. The first of the two types did not crystallize until the 1840s, almost a century after Whitefield and Edwards' era. What happened in that century? Obviously, many things, but for our purposes, the influences of the second Great Awakening will be most helpful.

Impact of the Second Great Awakening. The second Great Awakening was qualitatively different from the first. While much of the groundwork for the second Great Awakening was laid by Whitefield and Edwards, the second revival itself was largely the work of local pastors and laity in their own parishes (Ahlstrom, 1972). Missing was the intense sensationalism of the first Great Awakening, as "over and over again the effects on individual behavior were attested as permanent, while undue excess and the reaction it would have caused were rare" (Ahlstrom, 1972, p. 417). As this revival took root, the revived were eager to show the "fruits of conversion" and quickly set about doing good works.

Soon, these doers of good works formed various societies and associations that focused on social and spiritual concerns. Four kinds of religious association developed out of the awakening: missionary societies, religious education and publication

societies, moral reform societies, and societies for the promotion of humanitarian interests. These associations must be understood if, in Ahlstrom's words, "the significance of the Second
Awakening is to be grasped" (p. 423). The first two categories
were by far the most popular, and they continued the giving and
caring patterns of Whitefield and Edwards. The latter two categories, however, are of special interest, for in them we find the
seeds of a different type of giving and caring that would attain
prominence around the 1840s.

The societies for humanitarian interests focused on the
needy and made many contributions to the understanding and
care of people with physical or mental disabilities. In the years
following the second Great Awakening, these societies became
involved in pressuring for reform legislation at the local, state,
and national levels—signifying a more structural understanding of the causes of poverty. Many of the moral reform societies
targeted intemperance, a "sin" theme that would continue to
rally evangelicals for the entire century. But by 1817, it became
clear to many reformers in both categories that the practice of
slavery could no longer be condoned; "indeed, the entire impulse for humanitarian and moral reform was inexorably con-
verging on this nation-shaking question" (Ahlstrom, 1972, p.
428). While conservative Protestants were certainly on both
sides of the slavery debate, within the abolitionists' camp we find
examples of conservative Protestants with a broader, more public understanding of poverty.

Jonathan Blanchard (1811–1892), one of these abolitionists, had a distinguished career as a Presbyterian minister, and
later as the president of Knox and Wheaton colleges. He deeply
involved himself in the abolitionist movement, even assisting in
founding the abolitionist Liberty party, and also advocated
world peace (Marsden, 1980). Both his political involvements
(startling for a minister at that time) and the following excerpts
from a debate over the justice of slavery outline a broader and
newer type of Christian caring.

"Now, the question is, whether Humanity can look to
Christianity and find protection? Whether the oppressed can
flee to the sanctuary of the Gospel of Christ and find a refuge

there—or whether religion affords no protection to human rights? In other words, whether the religion we profess is a humane or an inhumane religion?" (Blanchard, 1846, p. 80). Here we see a much different view of the poor. Blanchard is concerned about the "oppressed." The oppressed need "protection" and "sanctuary." This is a very different understanding than Whitefield's focus on spiritual change or Edwards' concern for charitable deeds. Blanchard's God was especially concerned with the oppressed and unprotected. Here Christian caring included issues of injustice and oppression. Blanchard understood slavery to be a structural, societal evil necessitating a societal response. Yet Blanchard did not sacrifice his conservative theology. Note the combined language of theology and oppression: "It is precisely that class [slaves] in whom Jesus Christ, the Son of God, did, while on earth, and does now, (for his disposition is unchanged), take the deepest interest. For surely the lowest and most oppressed conditions of mankind received his most tender regards. For Christians, therefore, no question can be raised more fit to occupy their attention than this" (p. 13).

Blanchard knew no disjuncture between his Christian faith and his social action; indeed, his theology undergirded and motivated his abolitionist activism. He played a prophetic role in the slavery debate, demanding justice be given to slaves.

Jim Wallis, founder of *Sojourners* magazine, a publication of the evangelical political left, is a contemporary example of Blanchard's approach. Further along in an *Agenda for Biblical People* (cited earlier), Wallis (1976, p. 126) states, "The church must remember...to be obedient to its prophetic role and calling." Wallis concerns himself with, among other things, world hunger, Central America, and peace issues. Blanchard and Wallis represent a tradition of evangelicalism we can label "prophets of justice." Prophets of justice view poverty structurally, calling Christians not to miscellaneous acts of charity, but rather calling them to live a life of "radical obedience" to Christ, speaking out and fighting injustice and oppression worldwide.

The last type of caring and giving emerged relatively

recently. Closely related to the prophet of justice type, it never-theless has its own unique features and development. Its story begins in the late nineteenth century, when many conservative Protestants heard the call of the prophets of justice following the Civil War and involved themselves in issues such as monopoly reform, tax inequities, or working conditions in factories. The *Christian Herald* (a well-received evangelical weekly) in 1910 sup-ported "labor unions, worked for legislation concerning women's and children's labor, advocated better treatment of immigrants and blacks, and waged an unceasing campaign for world peace" (Marsden, 1980, pp. 84–85). However, conservative Protestantism abandoned these and other such activities be-tween 1910 and 1930, during the "Modernist–Fundamentalist" debate, in a striking reversal.

The "Great Reversal." What was the cause of conservative Protes-tantism's abandonment of social and political justice issues dur-ing the period 1910–1930? The key to understanding this aban-donment, labeled by some the "great reversal" (Moberg, 1977), is in the conservatives' reaction to liberal church support of a "Social Gospel." The Social Gospel was championed by the-ologian Walter Rauschenbusch. "Following the lead of philo-sophical pragmatism, proponents of the Social Gospel held that the only test of truth was action. 'Religious morality,' said Walter Rauschenbusch, is 'the only thing God cares about'" (Marsden, 1980, pp. 92–92). Doctrine was important only insofar as it inspired believers to social action. This idea is in radical contrast to conservative Protestants like Blanchard, who saw his activities as complementary to those of evangelism. Concerning such Christians' view of social action, Marsden writes: "The necessary first step in the Christian's life was repentance for sin and total dependence on God's grace. Good works should follow. The only question was what form these should take—individual or pub-lic, private or political" (p. 91).

Prior to Rauschenbusch, conservative Protestants en-gaged in both public and private good deeds. When liberal churches became enamored of the Social Gospel, however, con-servative Protestants were forced to distinguish themselves from their foes. They chose to renounce social action and emphasized purely evangelistic concerns. This abandonment of social action virtually dominated conservative Protestantism until a new generation picked up the earlier legacy of evangelism and social involvement.

The Role of Educational Expansion. The enormous expense of education following World War II and especially during the 1960s has been well-documented (Craig, 1981; Wuthnow, 1988). The last type of giving and caring, which can be labeled the "professional care givers," developed concurrently with this expansion of education. Hunter (1987, p. 168) highlights an "irony in...Christian higher education," where evangelical colleges (the producers of many evangelical leaders) turn out graduates who reject various dimensions of the popular evangelical world view, such as the private view of poverty of an indifferent evangelist or a dutiful steward. Not atypical is the case of a promising young believer who attended an evangelical college because she wanted to be a missionary. By graduation, however, her occupational goal shifted to social work or Third World development, though still including an evangelistic dimension. For the most part, the former potential missionary's faith commitments remained the same; her educational experience did not secularize her religious foundation. Rather, she chose the greater legitimacy of a professional occupation over that of a missionary in applying her commitment. Evangelicals like this woman choose a variety of human service occupations such as counseling, relief work, or development. "Professional care givers" have a broader understanding of poverty and commit themselves to alleviating the harmful effects of poverty through the standardized techniques of their profession.

Often, professional care givers are employed by religious organizations with a commitment to serving the poor and needy. Some of these organizations, previously traditional missionary societies with a minor relief focus, have transformed into comprehensive relief and development associations (Youngren, 1982). Compassion International is an example of a professional care giver approach at an organizational level. This organization grew out of relief work initiated in the wake of the Korean War, and is now broadly concerned with Third World relief and development. In a self-conscious reference to the "great reversal," Compassion International (1989, p. 7) stated, "Earlier in this century a debate over a 'social gospel' and a 'spiritual gospel' split the church. But we see no such dichotomy. And Christ didn't either." Compassion International expresses its concern for the poor by focusing on the spiritual, physical, economic, and social development of Third World countries.

This model has not abandoned evangelism, as an indifferent evangelist might charge. Professional care givers remain committed. Jubilee Fund, for example, emphasizes "the whole Gospel" and "wholistic practice of faith." States John Alexander (1980, p. 24), its director: "We do not believe that the needs of the poor and oppressed will be met simply by development projects; their needs, like everyone else's, have spiritual roots. Those needs must be addressed by evangelism, church planting, and community building. Further, we do not believe that the needs of the poor can be met by a gospel that doesn't touch the earth; there must be structural change, nutrition training, jobs, prophetic confrontation with the oppressors."

Alexander understands the needs of the poor to be public and social as well as personal and spiritual. The more inclusive response of these care givers results from their professional training combined with their religious commitments. The products of and participants in institutionalized evangelicalism, they provide an institutional, bureaucratic response to poverty.

Placing the Four Types. The major difference among the four responses of giving and caring varies with how each has understood the conditions and causes of poverty. The responses range from private and individuated, on the one hand, to public and societal on the other. However, view of poverty alone cannot fully account for the four differing responses to it. For example, the prophet of justice and the professional care giver have the same understanding, yet they have different agendas in response to it—prophetic confrontation versus professional intervention. I argue that another factor, religious form, is involved here. Re-

ligious form is a measure of structure, spanning from institutional (that is, ordered, bureaucratic) to nascent (that is, unstruc-
tured, "effervescent"—Warner, 1988, p. 34). The dutiful steward
and the professional care giver are institutional; that is, they are
concrete and ordered. These types have a rational, teachable
nature to them, reflecting their development out of bureaucratic
forms of religion. By contrast, the indifferent evangelist and
prophet of justice have a charisma-like nature. These nascent
types resist bureaucratization (that is, rational ordering), just as
the people who formed them resist the constraints of
institutions. Thus, two factors appear to be at work here, and
locating where an evangelical would fit in this typology can be
done by identifying his or her view of poverty and combining it
with the degree of institutionalization of his or her religious
involvements.

Where, then, do today's evangelicals fit? Which type or
types describe them best? For that matter, just how involved are
evangelicals in giving and caring activities? Are they more or
less involved in these activities than nonevangelicals? Than
other religious groups? These questions have been explored in
surveys conducted by the Gallup Organization.

Recent Survey Findings

What defines a person as an evangelical? Both evangelicals and
their observers have discussed this issue for years. While there is
no one single definition, most agree that evangelicals believe
firmly that Jesus Christ is the Son of God, that his death and
resurrection pay the penalty of a person's sin and restore his or
her relationship with God, that the Bible is God's inspired word,
and that one should live in such a way that demonstrates and
convinces others of the above. Members of each of the four types
would affirm these beliefs.

How many evangelicals exist in America today? The Gallup Organization has estimated the number of evangelicals at
between 17 and 35 percent of the U.S. population, and James
Davison Hunter, a leading observer of evangelicals, has estimated 21 percent (Gallup, 1982, 1984; Hunter, 1983). Their

estimates vary depending on how each has defined evangelicalism, and the Gallup Organization has continually refined its criteria. For the following analyses, I defined evangelicalism by using responses to six cognitive and behavioral items. An evangelical is a person who (1) believes in the divinity of Jesus Christ, (2) has "made a commitment to Jesus Christ," (3) believes in life after death, (4) believes the Bible to be the inspired and inerrant word of God, (5) prays to God, and (6) would invite others to join his or her denomination or church. According to a December 1988 Gallup survey of 2,556 adults, 765 respondents (29.9 percent) met all six of these evangelical requirements.[1]

Evangelicals in this 1988 Gallup survey had the following characteristics. They were highly concentrated in the South (41 percent) and Midwest (29 percent), while their lowest concentrations were in New England (17 percent). Evangelicals were also more likely to be over fifty years old (47 percent) than nonevangelicals (35 percent), and less likely to be under thirty (16 percent) than nonevangelicals (24 percent). Perhaps as a function of their age, evangelicals were also more likely to be either married (68 percent) or widowed (12 percent) than nonevangelicals (61 percent and 7 percent, respectively). More evangelicals (56 percent) than nonevangelicals (48 percent) were women, and more nonevangelicals (52 percent) than evangelicals (44 percent) were men. Comparing educational attainments and income, there was no statistically significant difference between the two groups (that is, evangelicals were just as likely as nonevangelicals to be college educated or highly paid).

Perhaps the most striking difference between groups, however, is not in their background characteristics (for example, sex ratio) but rather in the importance they ascribe to religion. Attitudinally, evangelicals responded that religion is "very important" twice as frequently as did nonevangelicals (84 percent to 43 percent). And behaviorally, they were three times as likely to attend church weekly as were nonevangelicals (60 percent to 20 percent). Does this high respect for and involvement in religion make a difference in evangelicals' levels of giving and caring? Based on the 1988 survey and other recent polls, the answer is yes.

Caring and Giving Activities. According to a Gallup poll conducted in 1981, evangelicals were "more likely to be involved in
charitable activities" and "more likely to place importance on
'working for the betterment of society'" (Gallup, 1982, p. 33).
When asked, "Do you, yourself, happen to be involved in any
charity or social service activities, such as helping the poor, the
sick, or the elderly," 42 percent of evangelicals responded yes
compared to 30 percent of nonevangelicals (Gallup, 1982). In
1983, this pattern was seen again, with 88 percent of evangelicals
stating that they "donated time to help someone, other than a
family member, who was sick or in need" compared to 73 percent of nonevangelicals. Evangelicals were also more involved in
formal helping activities, with 53 percent of evangelicals stating
that they did "volunteer work for a community organization
other than a church, such as a civic group or charity," while only
42 percent of nonevangelicals reported doing the same. Further,
evangelicals were more likely than nonevangelicals to do both
activities (52 percent compared to 37 percent). This pattern
persisted (that is, remained statistically significant at $p < 0.01$)
even after a comparison of only those individuals who attended
church weekly or responded that religion was "very important"
in their life.[2]

From this finding, it might appear that evangelical faith is
an important predictor of a person's involvement in giving and
caring activities. Did this pattern continue to the end of the
1980s? Again, the answer is yes. Asked about their involvement
in charitable activities during the past year, 37 percent of evangelicals compared to 22 percent of nonevangelicals said they
were either fairly involved or very involved in "civic, social, and
other charitable activities in [their] community or neighborhood" (see Table 9.1). This difference continued as the questions
became more specific. When asked about personal goals, 50
percent of evangelicals compared to 31 percent of nonevangelicals responded that "giving time through volunteer
work to charitable and religious organizations" was "absolutely
essential" or "very important." Sixty-two percent of evangelicals
compared to 41 percent of nonevangelicals responded in the
same manner to "making contributions to charities, institutions,

Table 9.1. Evangelicals and Nonevangelicals:
Comparing Giving and Caring Attitudes and Activities.

	Evangelical (N = 765)	Nonevangelical (N = 1791)
Charitable Activities		
(% responding "very" or "fairly" active)	36.6	22.1
Volunteering as a Value		
(% responding volunteer work is "absolutely essential" or "very important")	49.6	30.8
Volunteers		
(% volunteering in organizations during the past year)	49.4	38.1
Giving as a Value		
(% responding making contributions is "absolutely essential" or "very important")	62.1	40.6
Givers		
(% making a contribution to charitable organizations during the past year)	79.1	63.0

Source: Author's analyses of the Gallup Organization Survey GO 100-AP, Dec. 1988.

religious organizations, or causes you agree with." And when it came to applying these values, more evangelicals than nonevangelicals volunteered (49 percent versus 38 percent) and gave (79 percent versus 63 percent).

Of course, one can raise the objection that recipients of giving and caring included religious organizations: Certainly evangelicals do not volunteer more or give more to nonreligious organizations than nonevangelicals. True, they do not give or volunteer *more* when religious organizations are not included; but neither do they give or volunteer *less*—they give and volunteer at the same rates as nonevangelicals. Counting out religious volunteering, 41 percent of evangelicals volunteered and 38 percent of nonevangelicals volunteered. (Given sampling margins of error, these numbers are statistically the same.) Counting out religious contributions, 53 percent of evangelicals gave and 51 percent of nonevangelicals gave to charitable organizations. (Again, these numbers are statistically equal.) Hence, evangelicals give and volunteer to nonreligious organizations as readily as nonevangelicals do, and at the same time maintain high levels of giving and volunteering in religious organizations.

Using a multivariate statistical procedure called analysis of covariance, I was able to determine whether a person's evangelicalism remained a significant predictor of charitable activities, volunteer work, and giving even with age, income, marital status, gender, and education held constant simultaneously. It was. Evangelicals are more likely to be volunteers and givers even when compared to people of the same age, income, marital status, gender, and education. (For the statistically trained reader, F-ratios were 176.6 for charitable activities, 84.5 for volunteers, and 202.9 for givers. All F-ratios were significant at $p < 0.0001$.)

Thus, a higher percentage of evangelicals give and volunteer, even holding many variables constant. But what about their view of poverty? Do they largely "blame the victim"? Or do they hold broader views of what causes poverty? While a survey is not the best instrument to discover these things, we can gain a general sense of how public or private their view is.

Current Views on Poverty. In 1983, the Gallup Organization asked what should be the three top priorities for the church. Eighty-five percent of evangelicals responded, "helping individuals grow spiritually," 50 percent responded "evangelism and missionary work," and 21 percent responded "working for social justice" as one of the top three priorities. In 1988, 32 percent of evangelicals agreed with the statement "Most churches are not concerned enough with social justice." Thirty-one percent of evangelicals strongly disagreed with the statement "The government is spending too much money on programs to help the poor." Thirty-one percent of evangelicals strongly agreed that "the government should guarantee that every citizen has enough to eat and a place to live." Thirty-nine percent of evangelicals agreed and 8 percent strongly agreed that "the government and individual Americans have special responsibilities to spend money helping the poor in other countries." On the basis of these responses, we can speculate that about 20 to 30 percent of evangelicals hold a more public response to poverty. These evangelicals would fit in either the prophet of justice or the professional care giver category.

The majority of evangelicals, however, would fit into the indifferent evangelist or the dutiful steward category. Looking at this group, we find that 6 percent of evangelicals strongly agreed with the statement "The government is spending too much money on programs to help the poor," and 3 percent strongly disagreed with the statement "The government has a basic responsibility to take care of people who can't take care of themselves." This 3 to 6 percent group can probably be considered indifferent evangelists. The remaining 65 percent or so, who hold more private, though not extremely private, understandings of poverty, can be considered dutiful stewards. Thus, the bulk of evangelicals would view poverty as the result of individual circumstances and not as a broader issue of injustice, oppression, or economic factors.

This "bulk" of evangelicals, who in general are more likely to be volunteers and givers than nonevangelicals, would most likely work for and support organizations that align with their stated priorities of "helping individuals grow spiritually" and emphasize "evangelism and missionary work." However, a smaller (though not negligible) minority of evangelicals would be concerned with broader, more structural social justice issues. To confirm this, we could examine the types and goals of organizations to which evangelicals volunteer and give, and ask evangelicals why they choose to volunteer and give to the organizations that they do. Unfortunately, these questions cannot be answered with the information currently available; they would also take us beyond the scope of an introductory chapter. We can check some of these patterns, however, by moving our examination to an institutional level. By looking at the giving priorities of evangelical institutions, we should see a reflection of a strong concern for evangelism and missionary work and a varying degree of concern for broader issues like relief and development.

Giving To and Through Institutions. Several institutions to which evangelicals give money have had sensational media coverage. From television evangelists such as Jimmy Swaggart and Jerry

Falwell to political action groups such as the Moral Majority and Christian Voice, these organizations have occupied a prominent public position in headlines and conversations throughout the United States. Some TV evangelists bring in lucrative support, ranging up to the tens of millions of dollars annually (Horsfield, 1984). The majority of this money is earmarked for operational costs and the purchase of additional air time, ostensibly for further evangelism. The Moral Majority and the Christian Voice also maintain fairly large budgets. Concerned with a specific agenda of "moral" issues (such as abortion and school prayer), these two organizations have sought to influence both elections and legislation. The Moral Majority operated on $2 million and $6 million its first and second years, respectively, and used high-profile evangelists, media-attracting techniques, and a mass mailing list to gain the voting population's attention (Liebman, 1983).

However, there is another, less publicized type of institution through which and to which evangelicals give. Taking a cue from Henry Ford and others, a number of wealthy evangelicals have established philanthropic foundations. Through the use of the *Foundation Directory* and referrals, twenty-five self-described evangelical foundations were identified. Letters requesting annual reports, historical information, and giving priorities were sent to all twenty-five organizations. Follow-up telephone calls were made. Of the twenty-five foundations, four were no longer in existence, and twelve responded to the request. The four largest and most frequently referred to foundations (DeMoss, Stewardship, Chatlos, and Maclellan) were among the respondents.

As expected, these foundations gave priority to (1) missionary work and evangelistic activities, (2) evangelical educational institutions, such as Bible colleges and seminaries, and then (3) general human welfare organizations engaged in poor relief, development, or other social services. Some foundations also gave to local community organizations (for example, a hospital) and two gave to political lobby groups (see Table 9.2). Eighty-three percent of these foundations support evangelistic activities within the United States, and two-thirds support the same overseas. Seventy-five percent of foundations support evangelical educational institutions (often the alma mater of the founder), where future evangelists and missionaries are trained. Two-thirds of the foundations do recognize some responsibility to the poor, donating money to organizations for relief, development, and social services; however, only one foundation (Jubilee) places a high priority on supporting these groups.

Missionary activities received the highest priority for support, with foundations either directly funding evangelistic work or funding the schools training evangelicals who will do it. Approximately 88 percent of high-priority giving marks are in the first three categories (that is, the evangelism, missionary, and educational organizations). By highlighting two typical foundations, Maclellan and Stewardship, we get a closer look at foundations that fit the dutiful steward pattern.

The Maclellan Foundation was founded by Robert J. Maclellan in 1945 and currently has sizable assets of $26.6 million. (Though one often thinks of foundations like the Ford Foundation with its $4.8 billion endowment, 87 percent of foundations have less than a $1 million endowment [Butler and Farrell, 1987].) "The purpose of the [Maclellan] Foundation is to give primarily to Christian causes. . . . This giving is divided in three categories: education, home missions, and world missions" (Maclellan, 1989). Elaborating, Maclellan stated: "The Foundation supports approximately 100 organizations. With few exceptions, these organizations are characterized as Christian. . . . [W]e would hope that all recipient organizations are evangelistically oriented. . . the purpose behind each grant is to enable the organization to evangelize and disciple the world both at home and abroad." Further on, Maclellan notes that Christians do have a responsibility to relieve the suffering of others, but that the foundation usually tries to give relief money through an evangelistic or church planting organization. Maclellan senses his responsibility to be a "good steward" of his money and does recognize the need for charity; however, with a foremost concern for evangelism, he demonstrates the private, nonstructural understanding of poverty of most evangelicals.

The Stewardship Foundation was begun in 1947 by C. Davis Weyerhauser and has assets of $63 million. According to

Table 9.2. Giving Patterns and Priorities for Selected Evangelical Foundations.

Foundation (Assets)	Foreign Missions/ Evangelism	U.S. Missionary/ Evangelism/ Church Planting	Evangelical Educational Institution	Political Lobby Group	Poor Relief/ Development/ Social Svcs.	Local Community Giving
Anderson Family ($1.5M)	Y	Y	Y	N	Y	N
Beuford (N/A)	N	Y*	N	N	Y	N
D. M. Brown ($9.5M)	Y	Y*	Y*	N	Y	Y
Chatlos ($67M)	N	N	Y*	N	Y	Y
DeMoss ($185M)	Y*	Y*	N	N	N	N
Eckerd ($0.4M)	Y	Y	Y	N	Y	N
Heath ($2.0M)	N	Y	N	N	Y	Y*
Jubilee ($1.5M)	Y*	Y*	Y	N	Y*	N
Maclellan ($26.6M)	Y*	Y*	Y*	Y	Y	Y
Rainbow Fund ($0.00)	Y	Y	Y	N	N	N
Staley ($4.0M)	N	N	Y*	N	N	N
Stewardship ($63M)	Y	Y*	Y*	Y	Y	Y
Totals (out of 12)	8	10	9	2	8	4

Sources: Foundation Directory, 1986; author's survey.

Y = Yes, give
N = No, do not give
Y* = High-priority giving

its charter, the Stewardship Foundation must give 86 percent of its annual grants to evangelical purposes (Kovatz, 1989). The majority of its giving, similar to Maclellan's, is allocated to missions and educational institutions. The recipients of Stewardship's largest annual support are Young Life (a youth evangelistic organization), Fuller Theological Seminary (of which Weyerhauser was a founder), and Whitworth College (an evangelical liberal arts college). Stewardship Foundation also supports a few political action groups, most notably the National Coalition Against Pornography, and gives a sizable amount of money to various poor relief and development projects at home and abroad. The very name of this foundation illustrates its type.

The Maclellan and Stewardship foundations demonstrate predominant evangelical patterns of giving. The Jubilee Foundation, however, provides a dynamic contrast to Maclellan and Stewardship. The Jubilee Foundation, with only $1.5 million in assets, is unique among evangelical foundations not only in its giving priorities but also in its goal of advising and streamlining the work of other evangelical foundations. Robin Wainwright (1989), Jubilee's executive director, stresses "holistic world mission," and encourages foundations to try new methods of giving, such as economic development as a tool for church planting. An evangelical seminary graduate, Wainwright combines his religious worldview with the latest business jargon when trying to persuade other foundation professionals. Employing terms such as *strategic planning* and *cost effectiveness*, he has been generally welcomed by evangelical philanthropists, themselves businessmen. Yet Wainwright is no mainstream executive, for he describes his own view of poverty and its causes as "quite broad" and "politically liberal." Very much the professional, Wainwright and Jubilee Foundation fit our professional care giver type. Certainly, they are something of an anomaly, especially among foundations, which are notorious for their conservatism. Jubilee represents at the foundation level the 20 to 30 percent of evangelicals who hold broader understandings of poverty than their fellow evangelicals. Thus, we find confirmation here of the dominant stewardship motif yet see evidence of some diversity among foundations in their patterns of giving.

Summary

American evangelicals possess a diverse tradition of giving and caring and are by no means monolithic in their view of poverty and/or the proper response to it. George Whitefield believed he was helping the poor when he preached repentance for sin and saving faith in Jesus to them. Jonathan Edwards concurred with Whitefield that the poor needed regeneration but emphasized responsible stewardship to fellow Christians and encouraged them to practice charity. Jonathan Blanchard rose to the defense of slaves, proclaiming the rights of the poor and oppressed against the oppressors. Compassion International enters various Third World communities, assisting the villagers in agricultural techniques, setting up schools and medical clinics, and supporting local churches in their endeavors to proclaim the Lordship of Jesus Christ.

Evangelicals are deeply concerned with telling others the Gospel of Jesus Christ. Some do so through holistic ministries to communities and individuals, employing professional techniques to combat individual and structural forces of poverty. Others may cry out and condemn classes or societies that oppress the poor, calling their hearers to radical obedience to Christ. Most evangelicals, however, are concerned simply with the spiritual condition of individuals within and without their communities, not with various forces of poverty or oppression. This majority of evangelicals want people to hear about Jesus and place a high priority on evangelism and missionary work. For them, the highest act of caring is the regeneration of a person.

The difference between these approaches lies in how each understands the object of their giving and caring. Evangelicals with a private view of poverty believe evangelicalism is the key to its eradication. Evangelicals with a broader understanding of poverty recognize the need for both spiritual *and* structural change. In which direction evangelicalism is moving or will move is difficult to tell. One point can definitely be stated, however. Regardless of which view evangelicals take, they certainly put it into action. And that is a lesson everyone can learn.

Notes

1. The author is grateful to the Gallup Organization, INDEPENDENT SECTOR, and Professor Robert Wuthnow for making available the 1988 survey used in this chapter. Errors in analysis and interpretation of this survey are the sole responsibility of the author.
2. The author wishes to thank Professor Robert Wuthnow and the Gallup Organization for making the 1983 survey available. Errors in analysis and interpretation are the sole responsibility of the author.

References

Ahlstrom, S. *A Religious History of the American People*. New Haven, Conn.: Yale University Press, 1972.

Alexander, J. "Challenging Charity." *Sojourners*, 1980, *4*, 24.

Blanchard, J. "Opening Remarks." *A Debate on Slavery*. Cincinnati, Ohio: Wm. H. Moore, 1846.

Bremner, R. H. *American Philanthropy*. Chicago: University of Chicago Press, 1961.

Burkett, L. *Using Your Money Wisely*. Chicago: Moody Press, 1986.

Butler, F. J., and Farrell, C. E. (eds.). *Foundation Guide for Religious Grant Seekers*. Atlanta: Scholars Press, 1987.

"Child Development: Helping Children in All Ways." *Compassion Update*, Jan./Feb. 1989, p. 7.

Chilton, D. *Productive Christians in an Age of Guilt Manipulators*. Tyler, Tex.: Institute for Christian Economics, 1981.

Compassion International. Program statement. Washington, D.C., 1989.

Craig, J. E. "The Expansion of Education." *Review of Research in Education*, 1981, *9*, 151–213.

Edwards, J. "Duty of Charity to the Poor, Explained and Enforced." *The Works of Jonathan Edwards.* Vol. 2. Philadelphia: Banner of Truth Press, 1971.

Gallup, G., Jr. *Religion in America.* Princeton, N.J.: Princeton Religious Research Center, 1982, 1984.

Horsfield, P. G. *Religious Television: The American Experience.* New York: Longman, 1984.

Hunter, J. D. *American Evangelicalism: Conservative Religion in the Quandary of Modernity.* New Brunswick, N.J.: Rutgers University Press, 1983.

Hunter, J. D. *Evangelicalism: The Coming Generation.* Chicago: University of Chicago Press, 1987.

Kovatz, S. Correspondence with the author. Feb. 2, 1989.

Liebman, R. C. "Mobilizing the Moral Majority." In R. C. Liebman and R. Wuthnow (eds.), *The New Christian Right.* Hawthorne, N.Y.: Aldine, 1983.

Maclellan, R. J. Correspondence with the author. Feb. 8, 1989.

Marsden, G. M. *Fundamentalism and American Culture.* New York: Oxford University Press, 1980.

Moberg, D. O. *The Great Reversal.* (Rev. ed.) Philadelphia: A. J. Holman, 1977.

Niebuhr, H. R. *The Kingdom of God in America.* New York: Harper Torchbooks, 1959.

Tracy, P. J. *Jonathan Edwards, Pastor.* New York: Hill and Wang, 1980.

Wainwright, R. Correspondence with the author. Feb. 16, 1989.

Wallis, J. *Agenda for Biblical People.* New York: Harper & Row, 1976.

Warner, R. S. *New Wine in Old Wineskins.* Berkeley: University of California Press, 1988.

Whitefield, G. "Regeneration." In A. R. Buckland (ed.), *Selected Sermons of George Whitefield.* Philadelphia: Union Press, 1904. (Originally published c. 1760.)

Wuthnow, R. *The Restructuring of American Religion.* Princeton, N.J.: Princeton University Press, 1988.

Youngren, J. A. "The Shell Game Donors Love to Lose." *Christianity Today,* 1982, *26*, 39–41.

Chapter 10

Dean L. May

The Philanthropy Dilemma:
The Mormon Church Experience

The choosing of the first deacons of the Christian faith, as described in Acts 6, was precipitated by complaints that certain widows were being neglected in the ministration of common goods. The apostles countered that "it is not reason that we should leave the word of God, and serve tables" and appointed the first deacons to take over the task. Christians since that time have been similarly divided within and among themselves by their efforts to fulfill the two fundamental callings: to preach the gospel to the unconverted and to care for the material needs of the faithful. This tension is particularly evident in groups that place great stress upon evangelical outreach, such as the Latter-day Saints. The Mormon experience is in some respects unique, but it offers insights into the problems of all religious bodies that try to strike a balance between spreading the gospel and providing for the poor.*

* An early version of this chapter was delivered at the annual meeting of the American Society of Church History, San Francisco, December 1983. Portions were printed in *Church History* (September 1988, pp. 322–336) as "Body and Soul: The Record of Mormon Religious Philanthropy." The editors of *Church History* have graciously given permission to use parts of that text in the present manuscript, which was presented at the 1989 Spring Research Forum of INDEPENDENT SECTOR on "Philanthropy and the Religious Tradition" held in Chicago, March 10–11, 1989.

The author wishes to thank Davis Bitton, Robert A. Goldberg, and Marion D. Hanks for thoughtful and helpful comments on earlier drafts of this chapter. None is, of course, responsible for the final product. Betty Sedgley Kenyon typed the manuscript with her unfailing skill and good cheer, and Crista Thompson assisted with preparing final copy.

As he was founding Mormonism in the 1830s, Joseph
Smith announced doctrines that prepared the way for his faith
to go well beyond the traditional call to charitable giving common among most religions. The direction was set in September
1830, when Smith received a revelation (Doctrine and Covenants 29:34) in which God announced that "all things unto me
are spiritual, and not at any time have I given unto you a law
which was temporal." Mormons took this somewhat ambiguous
statement to mean that spirit is only a different type of matter. As
Smith phrased it in a revelation some years later (Doctrine and
Covenants 131:7), "all spirit is matter, but it is more fine or pure,
and can only be discerned by purer eyes." In thus denying that
body and spirit belong to separate spheres, Joseph Smith was
laying open the way for a preoccupation with the physical and
material conditions of human life unusual among Christian
religions (McMurrin, 1959, pp. 6–10). Smith's successor, Brigham Young, broadened and extended that preoccupation in the
Great Basin (*Journal of Discourses* 18:243), insisting that "in every
case the man that dictates the spiritual kingdom of God [that is,
the prophet] must dictate the temporal affairs; it cannot be
otherwise."

A denial of differences between matter and spirit need
not, however, lead to philanthropic teachings or activities. It
could as easily lead to a self-indulgent materialism. Indeed,
some maintain that that is precisely what has happened in the
Mormon case: The Saints as individuals and their church as an
institution have become unduly concerned with the pursuits of
worldly gain and have neglected more humanitarian religious
values. Whether this assessment is true or not, there is ample
evidence that the naturalistic element in Mormon theology has
led the Saints historically to see the saving of the human body to
be as much a religious obligation as the saving of the soul. Latter-
day Saint teachings from the outset focused a part of the naturalistic monism described above upon concern for the poor. The
Book of Mormon (1956), originally published early in 1830,
frequently comments upon care of the poor as an obligation,
indeed an identifying feature, of a covenant people. Passages in
the book of Fourth Nephi (verse 3) refer to a perfect society

created through the direct ministry of Jesus Christ in which "They had all things common among them; therefore there were not rich and poor, bond and free, but they were all made free, and partakers of the heavenly gift." Book of Mormon leader King Benjamin offered his people a compelling sermon on charity (Mosiah 4:16-19), often cited by Mormons as the foundation of their philanthropic enterprises. In it, King Benjamin condemned all who justify limiting charitable giving with the argument "the man has brought upon himself his misery." A person withholding charity on these grounds "hath great cause to repent for behold, are we not all beggars? Do we not all depend upon the same Being, even God, for all the substance we have?" In December 1830, Joseph Smith received another revelation, eventually published in a book of Mormon scripture, the Pearl of Great Price ([1851] 1956) as part of the Book of Moses. Smith was profoundly struck by sections of the text (Moses 7:18) describing the career of the Old Testament prophet Enoch. Much of Smith's subsequent life and teaching was shaped by his vision of the perfect society that Enoch realized in the ancient city of Zion. Enoch's accomplishment was summarized in one verse: "And the Lord called his people Zion, because they were of one heart and one mind, and dwelt in righteousness; and there was no poor among them."

Offering the aim of unity as a social value ("one heart and one mind"), a high ethical character as a religious value ("dwelt in righteousness"), and the elimination of poverty as an economic value ("there was no poor among them"), this brief passage set the agenda for Joseph Smith's lifework and greatly influenced his successors in the leadership of the Mormon church. Moreover, it seemed clearly to shift responsibility for care of the poor from individual charity, which could be interpreted as the intent of King Benjamin's sermon, to the community. The emphasis upon the material was thus joined to the traditional religious call to charitable giving and then made a community responsibility, the combined three elements thereby laying the foundation for Mormon religious philanthropy. In effect, the Saints were enjoined to express their deepest love for humankind by converting all to the gospel; the converts would then enter a community where social, spiritual, and material needs could be effectively nourished. This understanding was not philanthropy in the more common present use of the term, which suggests that ideally, the giver should have no other motivation than doing good. Yet as we shall see, from the Latter-day Saint perspective, philanthropic ministrations were not hostage to conversion, but ineffectual in the absence of it.

Smith created the instrument for accomplishing Enoch's work among the Latter-day Saints only two months after the Enoch revelation. In early February 1831, he published a revelation called "The Law of the Church." In it, he adumbrated the economic communalism later known as Consecration and a Stewardship. The section of the revelation dealing with economics (Doctrine and Covenants 42:30) began: "And behold, thou wilt remember the poor, and consecrate of thy properties for their support that which thou hast to impart unto them, with a covenant and a deed which cannot be broken." The economic system, as later elaborated by subsequent revelations and Smith's instructions, required members to donate all their possessions to the church, an act that formally acknowledged that all earthly things belong to God. The bishop was then to return to them personal belongings and the means to house their families and make a living in their chosen profession. This grant from the bishop was called a Stewardship. It was then the responsibility of the communicant to exercise whatever talent and entrepreneurial skills he or she might possess during the ensuing year to improve that stewardship and at the end of the year account to the bishop for his or her labor. If a surplus had been gained beyond the reasonable "circumstances, . . . wants and needs" of the family, the steward was to consecrate the surplus voluntarily to the "Lord's Storehouse," where it would be used to care for the poor, promote missionary work, build churches, and support other church needs.

Thus, surplus capital was to flow annually into the Lord's Storehouse, where it would be administered by church leaders according to their perceptions of community needs, including especially care of the poor. Individual responsibility for economic progress was maintained and the market was to control wages and prices, but investment capital (the surplus) was to be allocated by church leaders on behalf of the community. In Jackson County, Missouri, which Joseph Smith designated in 1831 as the site for his City of Zion, printed forms were used to accomplish the transactions of Consecration and Stewardship. According to the documents (Arrington, Fox, and May, 1976, pp. 15–40, 365–372), the offerings thus given were to be used "for the purpose of purchasing lands in Jackson County, Missouri, and building up the New Jerusalem, even Zion, and for relieving the wants of the poor and needy." The overall effect was to foster among Mormons the idea that economic activity is a religious responsibility and communicants are accountable in the conduct of their secular lives to church authority. And, of course, an essential and paramount aim of Consecration and Stewardship was to provide an effective reserve of capital to be used in caring for the poor—unquestionably a church responsibility.

Consecration failed as an economic system when the Mormons were driven from Jackson County, Missouri, in 1833. Parts of the system were revived at various times, and a strenuous effort was made in the 1870s to reshape the Great Basin economy according to its principles, but none of these were of lasting economic consequence (Arrington, Fox, and May, 1976). The tradition of instituting church programs to care for the poor was well established, however, and continued. Mormons fleeing from Missouri into Illinois in September 1838 made a pledge (Smith, 3:249–250) "that we will never desert the poor who are worthy, till they shall be out of the reach of the general exterminating order." After founding the town of Nauvoo, Illinois, Joseph Smith began the practice of designating one day a month as a "fast day" during which the faithful would refrain from eating. As described by Arrington and Bitton (1979), the practice soon developed of contributing the food thus saved for poor relief, to be administered by church leaders, including especially the bishops of the various congregations or wards.

The most important innovation of the Nauvoo period, however, was the founding in 1842 of the Relief Society, a women's organization charged by Joseph Smith (May, 1976) to "provoke the brethren to good works in looking to the wants of the poor, searching after objects of charity, and in administering to their wants." Smith's wife, Emma, presided over the organization. Under its auspices a program was organized to provide regular visits to the homes of the poor and ill, and funds were raised to help care for their needs. The organization was given new life in Utah in the 1870s, its membership broadened, and its range of interests expanded. Its work since that time has been an essential element of the Mormon church welfare program (Beecher, 1982; Blumell, 1979).

As the Mormons fled westward from Illinois in 1846, they again made special provisions under Brigham Young's direction for transporting the poor to the new gathering place. Once established in Utah, the church instituted over the next century a variety of programs to care for the material needs of those who gathered to the new Zion. These programs began to coalesce in 1936, when church leaders launched the Church Welfare Program. Under its provisions each "stake" (several congregations or wards) was to purchase and manage a producing enterprise such as a farm, dairy, or small factory. They were then to ship the products of these cooperatives to a general distribution center in Salt Lake City, where workers redistributed them to local areas. Thus all bishops could draw upon a well-stocked storehouse to care for the poor in their wards. Combined with fast offerings and the Deseret Industries (a handicapped rehabilitation system similar to Goodwill Industries), the Church Welfare Program has been of considerable economic importance in areas heavily populated by Latter-day Saints. It is largely responsible for the (only partly accurate) popular notion that the Mormons "take care of their own." Though the ability of the program to handle all welfare needs of Mormons has been overstated, it is nonetheless an effort of considerable dimensions and solid accomplishment, of which Mormon leaders are justly proud (Arrington, Fox, and May, 1976, pp. 337–358).

All of this indicates that Mormon religious philanthropy has consisted of much more than pious sermons and unapproached ideals. Persistent efforts have been made since the very inception of Mormonism for the church to take responsibility for the material as well as the spiritual welfare of its people — to care for both body and soul. Yet there has been a well-defined limit to this considerable record of philanthropy. With a few exceptions, official church programs have been designed to assist members of the Mormon faith, leaving non-Mormons almost entirely untouched. Though leaders urge individual Mormons to support public charities, such as United Way, and they have a commendable record of doing so, official church philanthropy of the Good Samaritan variety has clearly taken a back seat to the "we take care of our own" philosophy. The Mormon church has rarely sponsored on an ongoing basis projects similar to those of the United Jewish Appeal, the Catholic Relief Fund, or the American Friends Service Committee — relief organizations that work in an essentially nondenominational way to alleviate human suffering around the world. Until very recent years, such efforts by the Mormons have been either carried out among present members or tied clearly to proselytizing or conversion efforts: the hope of future members. Just as one set of doctrinal teachings and historical experiences combined to promote a vigorous program of caring for the material needs of Mormons, another set made them rather singly devoted to being their "brothers' keepers" in a fairly limited sense of the term.

How, then, did Mormon philanthropy come to be focused so unremittingly inward? Very little of Mormonism can be understood without fully taking into account the fact that it began as a millenarian movement and remains to this day firmly attached to its millenarian roots (Underwood, 1982; Shipps, 1985). Perhaps the clearest of many early expressions of this aspect of Latter-day Saint teachings is in a revelation Joseph Smith received in September 1830 (Doctrine and Covenants 2:7-11):

> And ye are called to bring to pass the gathering of mine elect; for mine elect hear my voice and harden not their hearts; Wherefore the decree hath gone forth from the Father that they shall be gathered in unto one place upon the face of this land, to prepare their hearts and be prepared in all things against the day when tribulation and desola-

tion are sent forth upon the wicked. . . . For the
hour is nigh and the day soon at hand when the
earth is ripe; and. . .I will reveal myself from
heaven with power and great glory, with all the hosts
thereof, and dwell in righteousness with men on
earth a thousand years, and the wicked shall not
stand.

Mormon converts of the nineteenth century were accordingly warned to prepare for the coming millennium and, more
importantly to the present discussion, warned to flee the world
and "gather" with the Saints where they would be prepared for
Christ's Coming. The vigorous missionary effort launched at
that time saw conversion not as a metaphorical gathering but
the preparation for a literal gathering. The new convert became,
in a sense, a sojourner in his or her native land, and was urged to
bend all efforts from the time of conversion to finding the
means to gather with the Saints, wherever they may be found.
William Mulder expressed the idea perfectly when he chose to
title his 1957 study of Mormon Scandinavian migration to Utah
Homeward to Zion. With the skill of a poet, he reminds us of the
profoundly important fact that Mormon Danes, Norwegians,
Swedes, and Icelanders took leave of their kin and native lands
for a difficult journey that they seldom doubted was leading
them "homeward."
    This teaching of the gathering imparted a powerfully
centripetal thrust to the Saints' worldview. The outside world, for
committed Mormons, had but one relevant dimension — it was a
field of possible converts, souls to be set on their homeward
path. The benefits of conversion, as the missionaries saw it,
extended well beyond freedom from false doctrine and bestowal
of true priesthood. Mormonism would effect no less than a
regeneration of the convert's whole life, temporal as well as
spiritual. "Now go and take this, ye swift messengers," said Mormon Apostle Orson Hyde in 1854 (*Journal of Discourses* 2:66):
"you faithful agents. . . be messengers of glad tidings to the poor,
and wretched, and oppressed, and meek of the earth. It is an

honor to be a messenger, bearing to them the means of taking them out of their poverty, wretchedness, and oppression."

Appalled by the privation of the working classes of Europe, Mormon missionaries, including Brigham Young, felt that they were bringing the Old World a social as well as a spiritual gospel. The condition for the full implementation of both, however, was that the converts must gather, where they could "be prepared in all things"—that is, participate in the elaborate, all-encompassing environment in towns and villages of the Mormon Zion.

With this perspective, it is easy to understand why virtually the sole European-based social program of Mormonism was the establishment of savings banks, in which the poor deposited a few pence each month toward their eventual emigration. The European churches of the nineteenth century were distant outposts—conduits really—designed, once their purpose was fulfilled, to pass away. Few meeting houses were built, no temples erected, no charities founded, for all resources were applied to the costly task of bringing the convert to Utah.

Once committed to that venture, the faithful immediately became subjects of Mormonism's paternalistic social welfare program. Church periodicals kept the European converts informed of forthcoming travel opportunities. As savings mounted or when chosen as recipients of assistance from the Utah-based Perpetual Emigrating Fund, converts left their homes for Liverpool. There agents of the Perpetual Emigrating Fund company arranged accommodations while families awaited the sailing of vessels chartered specifically for Mormon emigration. As they embarked, the several hundred passengers were organized into temporary congregations and grouped, each under a priesthood leader who helped plan meal preparation, arranged sleeping facilities, conducted religious services, mediated disputes, performed marriages, blessed infants, and presided at funerals.

When the emigrants disembarked in New Orleans, Boston, New York, or Philadelphia, agents again were on hand to help find accommodations and procure steamboat or rail passage to Council Bluffs or the rail head. There, still others assisted in outfitting them for overland travel, dividing the families into immigrant "companies," each comprised of a strictly limited number of wagons under the supervision of a returning missionary or company agent. (Many old-line Mormons can name the company with which their ancestor traveled.) When they finally arrived in Salt Lake City, they commonly were met by high church officials and bishops from several regions, who informed them of possible settlement opportunities and helped them find employment, sometimes at first on a church public works project. If they arrived in difficult times, their local bishop might be called upon to provide for their welfare through resources contributed as tithes to each "bishop's storehouse." During the nineteenth century, some 85,000 people were brought to "Zion" in this way, a good many of them with advances provided by the Perpetual Emigrating Fund (Mulder, 1957; Taylor, 1965; Larsen, 1947; Jensen, 1982).

The workings of that system communicate clearly the inwardly directed nature of Mormonism's early philanthropic endeavor. In the Mormon view the world was Babylon. It could be regenerated only as individuals were converted and submitted themselves to the Mormon system. Once within that system, they were cared for under a social welfare program administered by the church, which attended carefully to economic and social as well as religious needs.

The church thus set a pattern early on of using its finite resources primarily for missionary work and for bringing converts under the influence of the Mormon system. Though established in the nineteenth century, the pattern persists with some modification in the twentieth century — modern-day Mormon church leaders, after all, being only one generation removed from the workings of this system in its full nineteenth-century flower. The major modification is that the massive emigration program — bringing the convert to Zion — has been replaced by a massive program of building meeting houses, welfare storehouses, social service offices, and temples wherever groups of Mormons are located — bringing Zion to the convert. The fundamental aim of distancing the faithful from the world was attenuated, but by no means lost, through the cessation of the gathering to Utah at the turn of the century. Converts of the twentieth century are surrounded by a whole set of Mormon institutions that have the effect of drawing them into a Mormon system and distancing them from others.

This shift in strategies points to another important influence upon Mormon philanthropic endeavor. Contrary to popular opinion, the Mormon church does not wallow in riches; in fact, historically quite the opposite has been the case. Before 1847, the Mormon role in American philanthropy had been to solicit it from others. As Davis Bitton (1980) has pointed out, concerted efforts were made to secure public support for those of their faith who were refugees; first those from Missouri in 1838–39 and then those from Illinois in 1846. From 1847 to the turn of the century, a very heavy drain was made on church revenues by the gathering process itself, since a high proportion of those brought to Utah under the Perpetual Emigrating Fund were never able or willing to repay their debt.

The relative poverty of the church is not surprising if data from the author's ongoing comparative study of an Idaho non-Mormon farm town and a Utah Mormon farm town are at all representative. In 1870, the average farm in the non-Mormon town was 182 acres, while that of the Mormon town was 31. The Utah farmers reported a total annual income ten times less than the Idaho farmers paid for hired help (which did not exist in the Utah town). Utah continued into the twentieth century to rank among the lowest states of the United States in per capita income, reaching fiftieth among the fifty states by 1987 (Utah Industrial Promotion Division, 1978). The fact is, that despite considerable generosity on the part of members, the Mormon church had a relatively poor population from which to draw its tithes.

It is thus not surprising to learn that the church barely avoided bankruptcy in the 1890s, when federal control of church assets under the Edmunds-Tucker (antipolygamy) Act of 1887 deprived the institution of traditional rental and investment income. Financial stability did not return until the late teens and early twenties, but general economic malaise in Utah continued through much of the twentieth century, limiting the base from which church tithes were drawn (May, 1974). The costs of the gathering were replaced by greatly expanded building, missionary, and welfare programs in the twentieth century, but the financial base to support these was still relatively low. Thus there were in this small population—not to exceed a million members worldwide before 1950—barely enough resources to maintain internal philanthropies.

There was another factor limiting Mormon philanthropic endeavor. The Mormon population was small in numbers, but perhaps equally important, most Mormons lived in the Great Basin area of the United States, remote and isolated geographically, and also, because of local conditions, remote from many of the social problems of early twentieth-century America. Though they were informed through the press and other media of urban poverty, the scale of the problem was sufficiently limited locally as to be unnoticed and beyond the experience of most Utahns. Most of the state's citizens were poor compared to those of many other states, and wealth was very evenly distributed, thus diminishing visible poverty, even in the two cities of Salt Lake and Ogden (Sale, 1974). The Mormon population simply did not have anything to compare with New York's West Side, Chicago's South Side, Boston's South End, or similarly poor areas of Detroit, Cleveland, or Cincinnati. Only missionaries working outside Utah had a sense of what urban poverty was.

We therefore can see that Mormon attitudes toward philanthropy were shaped historically by several factors. The naturalistic monism of Mormon doctrine combined with scriptural examples of organized community responsibility for the poor led to the establishment of social and economic welfare programs for church members. At the same time, millennial exclusiveness and the doctrine of gathering focused those philanthropic energies inward. This tendency was reinforced by a growing feeling that the Mormon system was entirely separate and different from that of the world. Regeneration that comes from conversion and entry into the Mormon system offered the only hope of ameliorating world poverty. All other systems were merely "utopian," to use the term in Marx's pejorative sense. Finally, poverty and physical isolation both worked to limit awareness of external needs and the possibility of serving them, even had they been recognized.

The Mormon response, or lack thereof, to the new social awareness of American churches in the late nineteenth and early twentieth centuries is thus no surprise. Though at least a platoon of Mormon missionaries worked in close proximity to William Booth's Salvation Army in London in the 1860s, they saw themselves as agents of a gospel at once spiritual and social, far superior to what Booth's army could offer. Rather than found settlement houses, the Mormons offered a means of *re*settlement, bringing the converted out of the environment of poverty and error to Zion. When Walter Rauschenbusch proclaimed the Social Gospel in 1907, he had concluded from a review of the early Christian church that "the essential purpose of Christianity was to transform human society into the Kingdom of God by regenerating all human relations and reconstituting them in accordance with the will of God" (p. xiii). His call that Christianity take up this task had no meaning for the Mormons, for they felt that they had already brought it well along. When he further lamented that the "older conception of religion views as religious only what ministered to the souls of men or what served the church" (p. 335), the Mormons could, with some justice, look at their own array of social welfare programs and find themselves innocent of his indictment. The plea of Boris Bogen in 1917 that Jewish philanthropy be brought once again under the animating spirit of the synagogue and dispensed through the rabbi could have no meaning to Mormons, where the ward had long been the primary unit of society and the local bishop had never ceased dispensing temporal as well as spiritual salvation to his parishioners.

It seems evident to me that external philanthropy—the caring for the needs of the poor not of the faith, and without an explicit proselytizing component—received great impetus from the Progressive movement, when social justice was a watchword of a national enthusiasm for reform. And both Rauschenbusch and Bogen were motivated by a feeling that the churches were

being placed on the defensive and that if they did not make
social concerns an integral part of the church program, they
would see secular organizations become the administrators of
compassion and humanitarian needs in society. The churches
might thus become increasingly irrelevant. Part of the response
of many established churches, within that context, was to seek
consciously to avoid the charge that their philanthropies were
fired by sectarian partisanship. They wanted the churches to
avoid co-optation by secular philanthropy but in the process
were willing to tolerate a certain amount of secularization of
their own charitable impulses.

As we have seen, the Mormons had long assumed responsibility for the social welfare of their members and in so doing
were remarkably advanced. Yet their efforts toward external
philanthropy had been minimal. Though they took great pride
in shipping grain and other supplies to victims of both wars,
these shipments were sporadic responses to calamitous events
and in no way indicated a trend in the direction of sustained
external philanthropy. Since World War II the church welfare
system has often aided victims of floods, earthquakes, and other
disasters in many parts of the world. Yet these ministrations were
distributed through Mormon networks, which naturally made
Mormons the main recipients of the aid.

As the twentieth century has progressed, however, some
probings in the direction of external philanthropy have become
evident. Though missing the tides that launched established
churches into philanthropic service in the early decades of the
century, the Mormons somewhat belatedly have embarked on a
few such projects of their own. This may be in part a result of a
growing concern for respectability that became evident in the
1930s and has continued—the church endeavoring in many
ways to combat whatever negative stereotypes may exist about
the Mormons and to put itself in the best possible light. Though
the Latter-day Saints have remained aloof from ecumenical
movements, they have indicated some sensitivity to the charge
that their missionary work has been primarily a "sheep-stealing"
enterprise and has neglected humanitarian concerns. The move
toward external philanthropy may also be, as some have sug-

gested, a predictable result of the gradual transition of Mormonism from a provincial sect to an established American church.

Yet the major force causing the church to reconsider its philanthropic mission has been an explosive dynamism brought about by the unprecedented success of its missions in Central America, South America, the Philippines, Africa, and other Third World regions. This growth has caused the church to see itself increasingly as a worldwide religion—a catholic church with responsibilities to all people of the earth. Mormons are less isolated than they once were and more aware of worldwide poverty. Though American Mormons are wealthier than they were previously, per capita church wealth has declined as contributions of North American Mormons are used to finance the extension of church programs of the burgeoning Third World membership.

One consequence of these changes has been the injection of a philanthropic element into the traditional missionary system. Starting in the early 1970s, certain missionaries were chosen because of specialized skills in nursing, public health, education, agriculture, construction, and other areas. They were instructed to teach their skills to the residents of villages and hamlets where they were working. This program grew to about 500 by 1980 and has remained fairly stable since then. In 1980, their assignment was changed somewhat, as reflected in their new designation as "additional assignment missionaries." The new term was clearly to emphasize that their proselyting mission comes first and other aid is "additional" to that primary responsibility. Nevertheless, the program has placed missionaries in Thailand, the Philippines, Taiwan, Hong Kong, West Africa, and other areas, where they promote gardening, beekeeping, nursing, public health, literacy, and other means of improving health and raising standards of living.

Another program began in 1978, under the guidance of a high church official, Marion D. Hanks, who was serving at the time as executive administrator for Southeast Asian activities of the Latter-day Saints. As church leaders visited refugee camps in the area, they became increasingly aware of the pressing need for education of refugees planning to resettle in English-speaking countries. Accordingly, a number of young women already serving as volunteer missionaries were assigned to become teachers in refugee camps, working at various times in Thailand, Hong Kong, and the Philippines. Reaching in some years about thirty in number, they taught English language classes and other skills needed to cope with the new cultural environment for which the refugees were bound. Though the program is being gradually phased out as the flow of refugees bound for the West diminishes, it nonetheless represents a departure from the traditional tie of humanitarian service to conversion efforts (Bishop, 1983; Hanks, 1984).

Rapid church growth in Africa has brought other developments, directed especially toward the poverty of Ghana and Nigeria. In 1977, E. W. "Al" Thrasher, a non-Mormon businessman, endowed the Thrasher Research Fund, which he asked the Mormons to administer. The fund supports research projects that promise to counter persistent problems of malnutrition and infectious disease and to improve health among children throughout the world. The organization has especially supported research that might lead to implementation of low-technology, immediately applicable health care skills among citizens of developing regions (MacMurray, 1983; Thrasher Research Fund, 1987).

Most recently the church employed its traditional fast day method of raising funds for the needy in response to the world famines of 1985. Designating fast days in January and November 1985 and urging its members to contribute what they would otherwise have used for food to a famine relief fund, the church raised more than $10 million. The funds were distributed among Red Cross agencies, Catholic Relief Services, CARE, and Africare and directly to specific Third World countries for development projects. This has led to formal agreements with the American Red Cross and the establishment in the church of the Humanitarian Service Subcommittee to oversee humanitarian relief efforts, including funding for irrigation and other relief efforts in the Third World (*Church News*, 1985; *Ensign*, 1988).

It is too early to tell, however, whether these activities

indicate a direction of the future or are merely episodic. The church is clearly in a period of rapid flux as it copes with the unprecedented strains caused by growth in less-developed regions. It is readjusting the whole range of its welfare programs, those functioning within its own system and those directed outward, seeking to minister equitably to both spiritual and material needs of its members in all parts of the world. One such readjustment has been to limit the extent of its internal welfare operations, cutting back on the number of cooperatives owned and operated by North American congregations and on social welfare services available to them—programs that it had never extended successfully to converts in rapidly growing Third World areas.

These changes may presage not a new period of humanitarian outreach but a more exclusive concentration upon salvation of the soul than Mormonism has ever known. The welfare missionaries have been reminded that their humanitarian work is in addition to their proselyting. And church leaders must certainly be aware that recently initiated external humanitarian programs will spread goodwill in the Third World, where missionary work has been rapidly expanding. Finally, central church leaders have formulated an oft-quoted tripartite statement of their worldwide mission that has been used at times to undercut the humanitarian concerns of some members, paring back all programs that do not contribute directly to "spreading the gospel, perfecting the Saints, and redeeming the dead." It is perhaps indicative of a possible reaction within church councils to purely philanthropic work that Marion D. Hanks was reassigned from Southeast Asia to become president of the Salt Lake Temple—his energies thus somewhat abruptly redirected from the most outward-oriented Mormon activity to the most inward.

It is risky to predict what the future trend of Mormon philanthropy might be. It may be that a growing stress on charitable giving and outward philanthropies and reliance on government and secular welfare programs will eventually supersede the traditional internal system of welfare. Yet because the forces that created the traditional system are deep and persistent in the Mormon consciousness and are intimately interwoven with Mormons' very identity as a "peculiar people," it would seem more likely that the great bulk of church philanthropic endeavor will continue to be carried out primarily within the Mormon system. The vision of Enoch's City of Zion, where unity, righteousness, and elimination of poverty for its citizens were the supreme accomplishments, will probably continue to set the agenda for church philanthropies. In October 1983, Gordon B. Hinckley, counselor in the Mormon First Presidency (and at the time virtually acting president), chose to remind church members of the traditional focus of Mormon outreach by quoting a message issued by his predecessors in 1907:

> In a dark period of our history, when enemies were throwing accusations against the Church, the First Presidency issued a proclamation to the world in which they set forth the dimensions of this work. Said they: "Our motives are not selfish; our purposes not petty and earth-bound; we contemplate the human race — past, present, and yet to come — as immortal beings, for whose salvation it is our mission to labor and to this work, broad as eternity and deep as the love of God, we devote ourselves now and forever" [p. 53].

That statement could have been read in 1907 as Mormonism's answer to the Social Gospel. It could be read today as a comment on its own recent experiments with external philanthropy. And it suggests that Mormon church leaders cling with remarkable tenacity to their deep-seated belief that "poverty, wretchedness, and oppression" will give way only to the personal regeneration that results from conversion and subsequent entry into the community of the Saints. They will likely continue to emphasize philanthropic programs within their system, inviting all to enter it, with complete confidence that true religion saves the body only as it saves the soul.

The Mormon experience dramatically illustrates the fundamental dilemma of religious philanthropy in the late twentieth century. In an age of increasing secularization, the churches that thrive are those that have a strong evangelical bent and claims to exclusiveness of doctrine, authority, or both. Such churches exact strong commitment from their members, enough to provide the resources for philanthropic endeavor of significant dimension. Yet their claim to exclusiveness makes them prone to invest their resources internally, promoting further evangelism or helping those within their own communities. Those churches that are less doctrinaire have a better record of outreach but seem to be declining in numbers and in the commitment of their members—their ability to continue their outreach diminishing. The result may well be that if the process of secularization continues into the twenty-first century as it has during the twentieth, a volume on philanthropy and the religious tradition will be solely of historical interest. External philanthropy, as Boris Bogen feared, will have become principally the domain of social workers and civil servants.

References

Arrington, L. J., and Bitton, D. *The Mormon Experience: A History of the Latter-day Saints.* New York: Knopf, 1979.

Arrington, L. J., Fox, F. Y., and May, D. L. *Building the City of God: Community and Cooperation Among the Mormons.* Salt Lake City, Utah: Deseret, 1976.

Beecher, M. U. "The 'Leading Sisters': A Female Hierarchy in Nineteenth-Century Mormon Society." *Journal of Mormon History,* 1982, *9,* 25–39.

Bishop, C. Interview with author, Dec. 14, 1983.

Bitton, D. "American Philanthropy and Mormon Refugees, 1846–1849." *Journal of Mormon History,* 1980, *7,* 63–81.

Blumell, B. D. "Welfare Before Welfare: Twentieth-Century LDS Church Charity Before the Great Depression." *Journal of Mormon History,* 1979, *6,* 89–106.

Bogen, B. D. *Jewish Philanthropy: An Exposition of Principles and Methods of Jewish Social Service in the United States.* New York: Macmillan, 1917.

Book of Mormon. Salt Lake City, Utah: The Church of Jesus
  Christ of Latter-day Saints, 1956. (Originally published 1830.)
Church News, Dec. 29, 1985, pp. 3, 10.
Doctrine and Covenants. Salt Lake City, Utah: Church of Jesus
  Christ of Latter-day Saints, 1956. (Originally published 1833.)
Ensign, May 1988, p. 94.
Hanks, M. D. Letter to author, Jan. 26, 1984.
Hinckley, G. B. "God Grant Us Faith." *Ensign*, Nov. 1983, p. 53.
Jensen, R. L. "Steaming Through: Arrangements for Mormon
  Emigration from Europe, 1869–1887." *Journal of Mormon His-
  tory*, 1982, *9*, 3–23.
Journal of Discourses. 26 vols. London: Latter-day Saint Book
  Depot, 1854–1886; rpt. ed., Salt Lake City, Utah: Church of
  Jesus Christ of Latter-day Saints, 1967.
Larsen, G. O. *Prelude to the Kingdom: Mormon Desert Conquest. A
  Chapter in American Cooperative Experience*. Francestown, N.H.:
  Smith, 1947.
MacMurray, V. D. "Christian Service in Developing Nations:
  Problems and Prospects in West Africa." Paper delivered at
  Brigham Young University, Provo, Utah, July 6, 1983.
McMurrin, S. M. *The Philosophical Foundations of Mormon Theology*.
  Salt Lake City: University of Utah Press, 1959.
May, C. L. "Charitable Sisters." In C. L. Bushman (ed.), *Mormon
  Sisters*. Cambridge, Mass.: Emmeline Press, 1976.
May, D. L. (ed.). *A Dependent Commonwealth: Utah's Economy from
  Statehood to the Great Depression*. Provo, Utah: Brigham Young
  University Press, 1974.
Mulder, W. *Homeward to Zion: The Mormon Migration from Scan-
  dinavia*. Minneapolis: University of Minnesota Press, 1957.
The Pearl of Great Price. Salt Lake City, Utah: The Church of
  Jesus Christ of Latter-day Saints, 1956. (Originally published
  1851.)
Rauschenbusch, W. *Christianity and the Social Crisis*. New York:
  Hodder & Stoughton, 1907.
Sale, T. S., III. "Interstate Analysis of the Size Distribution of
  Family Income, 1950–1970." *Southern Economic Journal*, 1974,
  40, 437.

Shipps, J. *Mormonism: The Story of a New Religious Tradition.* Champaign: University of Illinois Press, 1985.

Smith, J., Jr. *History of the Church of Jesus Christ of Latter-day Saints.* (2nd ed. rev.) 7 vols. Salt Lake City, Utah: Deseret, 1964.

Taylor, P.A.M. *Expectations Westward: The Mormons and the Emigration of Their British Converts in the Nineteenth Century.* Edinburgh and London: Oliver and Boyd, 1965.

Thrasher Research Fund. *Annual Report.* Salt Lake City, Utah: Thrasher Research Fund, 1987.

Underwood, G. "Millenarianism and the Early Mormon Mind." *Journal of Mormon History,* 1982, *9,* 41–51.

Utah Industrial Promotion Division. *Utah! Facts.* Salt Lake City: Utah Industrial Promotion Division, 1978.

Chapter 11

Emmett D. Carson

Patterns of Giving
in Black Churches

In the most comprehensive study of religious institutions to date, INDEPENDENT SECTOR found that of $41.4 billion donated to churches in 1986, 46 percent, or $19.1 billion, was used to support charitable activities and community service (Stehle, 1988, p. 1). When it comes to describing the history of black churches, the important role played by religious institutions in supporting individuals and organizations outside the church is not a novel idea. Much has been written about how black churches provide an essential conduit through which blacks have traditionally channeled their philanthropic efforts to benefit the less fortunate members of both their own community and the larger society. As Lawrence N. Jones, dean of the Divinity School at Howard University, observes in his widely read article "Serving the Least of These": "As the only institution which has proven itself viable and continues to be under the control of its members, black churches have had to assume welfare roles to a degree much greater than that typically required of white congregations" (1984, p. 61). This chapter will examine the degree to which blacks continue to use their churches as a mechanism for supporting individuals and organizations outside the church and whether the level of black activity in this regard exceeds that of whites.

Understanding the contemporary role of the black church in providing charitable services to other organizations is important in two respects. First, because the black church has played a central role in directing the charitable resources of the black community to other organizations, it is important to know whether such activity continues. Second, even as a greater number of black churches, particularly those in poverty-stricken inner-city areas are being called upon to address issues of homelessness, drug abuse, and teenage pregnancy, evidence is emerging that blacks, particularly younger blacks, are attending church in fewer numbers.

Equally noteworthy is the fact that the financial base of many black churches has eroded as middle-class blacks have moved to the suburbs and formed their own churches (Stepp, 1988, p. A1). This declining economic base of inner-city black churches, in addition to putting the future existence of some of these institutions in jeopardy (Hyer, 1989, p. A3), raises serious strategical questions about the extent to which blacks should continue to rely on black churches as a focal point for funneling their charitable resources to black organizations.

It should be stated at the outset that defining exactly what constitutes a "black church" is an admittedly thorny issue. Rather than attempt to resolve the debate here, this chapter assumes that blacks and whites are less likely to attend interracial churches than they are to attend churches where the congregants are predominantly black or white, respectively. The result of this oversimplified definition is that for the purposes of this chapter, any church with a predominantly black congregation, regardless of denomination, is considered a black church.

This chapter draws on two sources of data to begin a preliminary analysis of the thesis that blacks attend churches that have a different outlook about the role of the church in their community than do whites. The primary source of data is the 1988 Joint Center for Political Studies' (JCPS) survey that includes questions on the charitable behavior of a nationally representative sample of 643 black and 695 white Americans in face-to-face personal interviews.[1] The survey has a sampling error of plus or minus 5 percent. The second source of information is drawn from anecdotal examples from case studies conducted by field analysts with selected black churches in Atlanta, Chicago, Detroit, Durham, Houston, New Orleans, Oakland, and Washington, D.C., during the summer months of

1987. These interviews were part of a larger study of black charitable institutions undertaken by the JCPS.

The Role of the Black Church

Without doubt, the most important philanthropic institution within the black community has been, and continues to be, the black church. From slavery to the present, the black church has been an extremely versatile institution through which blacks could channel their philanthropic resources to respond to the changing social and economic conditions that threatened the survival of the black community. There are at least two interrelated reasons why, historically, the black church has been at the center of philanthropic activity within the black community: the indigenous control that blacks have had over the black church and the black church's appeal to different socioeconomic strata within the black community.

The black church is one of the earliest and, collectively, perhaps the largest organization that blacks have controlled. Black ministers have a long tradition of using their pulpits to speak out against social injustice. The church provided ministers with a small measure of safety to speak freely within the church because (1) the minister had some degree of economic independence because his basic necessities were provided by the members of the church, and (2) the symbolism of the church itself provided some insulation from those hostile segments of the larger society that often bore the brunt of criticism in the minister's Sunday sermons.

The other explanation for the success of the black church in providing charitable programs for the community is that because of the traditional attachment of blacks to the church and the overt housing segregation that existed prior to the early 1970s, blacks of all socioeconomic levels found themselves attending a relatively small set of black churches. These two factors, indigenous control and socioeconomic diversity, made the black church a unique forum wherein blacks could privately discuss both secular and nonsecular issues.

American history is filled with examples of how blacks

developed the capabilities of their churches to respond to racism and segregation. Black ministers not only gave their parishioners spiritual and material solace for their present conditions; they also instilled them with hope and engaged them in charitable and other activities so that the black church became a catalyst for the very societal changes that the ministers prayed for in their sermons. For example, many of the early black churches were active stations for runaway slaves on the Underground Railroad.

Racism and segregation are important factors in explaining the development of the early black church and the many black institutions that are patterned after the black church. As E. Franklin Frazier (1974, p. 85) has observed:

> The important role of religion and the Negro church in the social organization of the American Negroes has been due to the restricted participation of Negroes in American society. And as a consequence the Negro church has left its imprint upon practically every aspect of Negro life. The Negro church has provided the pattern for the organization of mutual aid societies and insurance companies. It has provided the pattern of Negro fraternal organizations and Greek letter societies. It has provided the pattern of administration and control of the Negro schools so far as they have been under the control of Negroes.

Often, it is difficult to disentangle the role of the early black churches from the mutual aid organizations that once flourished in the black community. The Free African Society, founded in Philadelphia in 1787, is a good example of the close connection between black churches and mutual aid societies, both of which were often established by ministers and based on religious principles. As Jones (1984, p. 59) notes: "Free African Societies were churches in every sense of the term, save for denominational labels. Qualifications for membership were a list of Christian virtues including sobriety, fidelity within marriage, and abstinence from a variety of 'worldly pleasures.'"

The Free African Society was established after its founders, Richard Allen and Absalom Jones, were refused the right to pray at a local white church. The society was established to provide for the social and economic needs of its members and later spread to many other cities (Frazier, 1974, p. 41). It should be noted, however, that the society was active in providing charitable services to individuals both within and outside the black community.

Soon after the founding of the Free African Society, Jones and Allen each founded in 1787 what were to be among the first black churches: the St. Thomas Protestant Episcopal Church and Bethel African Methodist Episcopal Church, respectively (Frazier, 1974, p. 33). The latter would lead to the creation of the African Methodist Episcopal (AME) denomination in 1816 (Quarles, 1969, p. 100). The African Methodist Episcopal Zion denomination was established in 1820 and was also created, in part, because of segregation. It is important to observe that the first response of Allen and Jones was not to immediately establish a black church but to establish a mutual aid society.

Following the emancipation of the slaves, blacks continued to rely heavily on their religious institutions to provide services to their communities. A key concern of many organizations after the Civil War, particularly black churches, was to formally educate the newly freed slaves (Jones, 1984, pp. 59–60). Black churches established a large number of elementary schools, high schools, and colleges (Quarles, 1969, p. 102). Of twenty-three black institutions of higher education established by the American Baptist Home Missionary Society in 1908, fourteen were owned by blacks (Meier, 1963, pp. 132–133). Of 5,000 schools constructed for blacks by the white philanthropist Julius Rosenwald, the black community, primarily through the church, contributed 17 percent of the total cost (Frazier, 1974, p. 46). During this time, black churches of all denominations were the center of philanthropic activity in the black community. As Benjamin Quarles (1969, p. 102) writes: "The Negro church was a many-sided institution performing many functions besides worship. In towns which barred colored children from the public schools, the church hall became a makeshift classroom, with deacons and elders as teachers of the three R's. . . . The Negro church was a meeting place for reformist groups, particularly abolitionists."

It is important to note that support of traditionally black institutions of higher education by black churches continues today. For example, in 1987, the Asbury United Methodist Church in Washington, D.C., made its annual contribution of $5,000 to Morristown College in Morristown, Tennessee, as well as provided scholarships to fourteen college students. Likewise, Union Baptist Church in Atlanta makes an annual contribution of $10,000 to Morris Brown College and the Morehouse College Chapel, both located in Atlanta. Such support is not surprising given the fact that many of the black churches that make these contributions have ministers who are alumni of these schools.

When the civil rights movement began in earnest with the Montgomery bus boycott in the late 1950s (see Garrow, 1986), it came as no surprise to find that the black church was at the forefront. The black church was perhaps the only institution within the black community that was capable of compelling socioeconomically diverse segments of the black community to combine their respective talents, including their financial and volunteer resources, to challenge successfully widely held beliefs and laws about the fairness of the doctrine of separate but equal. The black church's participation in the civil rights movement was viewed as a natural step given its historical role in addressing the problems of black people through mutual aid societies and the abolition of slavery movement.

Today, the black church continues to provide for the needs of the black community. Black churches are involved in day care for children, food distribution programs, and housing, to name only a few of the activities sponsored by black churches. As detailed in the following sections, the black church continues to be a primary focal point through which blacks direct their charitable resources.

Degree of Religious Involvement

Before examining the giving behavior of blacks and whites to their own churches, it is useful to know the religious preference of both groups and the extent to which they are active church-goers. Factors such as religiosity and frequency of church service have been found to be important factors in determining who is likely to give. In a study by Yankelovich, Skelly, & White, Inc., a strong relationship between church attendance and giving to religious organizations was uncovered. The study also found that those who gave to religious organizations were likely to give to other types of charitable organizations (Hodgkinson and Weitzman, 1986, pp. 39–41).

Understanding the relationship between religious denomination and philanthropy is important in two respects. First, highly structured, hierarchical denominations that require member churches to pay costly dues may leave local congregations with only limited funds to pursue their own independent charitable initiatives within their community. Further, in some instances, funds raised by the local church can only be disbursed with the prior approval of a higher authority within the church's denomination. Second, the amount of emphasis that religious leaders place on giving within and across denominational lines may be an important predictor of the charitable behavior of some church congregants. While the religious designations of Protestant[2] and Catholic contained in the JCPS survey are too broad to allow for a thorough examination of the extent to which any particular black or white religious denomination is engaged in charitable activity, the categories are useful for making more limited comparisons.

The majority of both blacks and whites in the survey reported that they were Protestant, with blacks far more likely than whites to be Protestant, 89 percent and 58 percent, respectively. Whites were much more likely than blacks to be members of the Roman Catholic church, 29 percent and 6 percent, respectively. It should be noted here at the outset that the small number of black Catholics in the survey severely limits generalizations about their charitable behavior.

The frequency of church attendance by blacks and whites can be seen in Table 11.1. Whites are significantly more likely than blacks to have never attended church services, 13 percent compared to 5 percent, respectively. Among those who do go to

Table 11.1. Frequency of Church Attendance by Blacks and Whites in 1986.

	Blacks	Whites
More than once a week	12.6%	9.7%
Once a week	34.1	32.7
Once a month	15.6	11.6
A few times a year	17.9	15.5
Hardly ever	12.7	15.6
Never	4.5	13.2
Unreported	2.6	1.7
Respondents	918	916

Source: Data based on 1987 JCPS survey.

church, similar percentages of blacks and whites attend church with the same level of frequency. These findings lend support to the belief that much of the black community's historical attachment to the church remains intact, that is, that only a small percentage of the black community is unchurched. This is important because having had an introduction to church values may be a key indicator in understanding how individuals choose to engage in philanthropy.

Who Should Be Helping the Poor?

A long-standing belief has been that America's charitable beliefs have been greatly influenced by our religious heritage. As Brian O'Connell, president of INDEPENDENT SECTOR, notes, "A very large part of America's attractive voluntary spirit stems from our religious heritage. The lessons are as varied as the religions of hundreds of groups that came and still come to our shores. The common root of these varied testaments is an awareness that service beyond self is both an obligation and a joy" (1983, p. 1). To the extent that Americans have learned the value of charitable activity through religious teachings, they may be more inclined to believe that churches should be the primary source through which charity is dispensed.

The attitudes of respondents as to what group has the greatest responsibility for helping the poor are shown in Table

11.2. While the largest percentage of both blacks and whites felt that the federal government had the greatest responsibility for helping the poor, 39 percent and 24 percent, respectively, the church was the second most popular response by blacks (18 percent) and the fourth most popular response for whites (15 percent). These data indicate that for blacks the church continues to be perceived as one of the primary organizations that should bear chief responsibility for helping the poor.

What is also interesting to note is how few blacks (3 percent) or whites (5 percent) felt that private charities other than the church should have the greatest responsibility for helping the poor. This data indicates that both blacks and whites may prefer either to be taxed by the government to help the poor or to aid others through their church rather than doing so through private charities. If this is true, then a church can provide a vital role in legitimizing the requests it receives from organizations for its congregants. In any event, the present topic merits more extensive study.

Giving to the Church

One reason underlying this concern with giving is the tremendous influence that members of the clergy have in making

Table 11.2. Groups That Blacks and Whites Feel Have Responsibility for Helping the Poor.

	Blacks	Whites
Federal government	38.6%	23.9%
Churches	18.3	14.7
State or local government	13.7	17.6
Private charities	3.2	5.0
Relatives of poor people	5.3	6.1
Poor themselves	6.8	17.6
Someone else	0.6	0.4
Don't know	13.6	14.7
Respondents	643	695

Note: Respondents were given several examples of private charities, including the Red Cross, Salvation Army, United Negro College Fund, and March of Dimes.

Table 11.3. Contributions to Respondent's Own Church in 1987.

	Blacks	Whites
Less than $50	7.7%	4.5%
$50–$99	5.7	5.1
$100–$499	21.8	20.5
$500 or more	13.1	19.4
No contribution	33.8	35.5
Unreported	17.8	15.1
Respondents	643	695

appeals for money. Of all the various types of appeals for a charitable contribution, particularly for blacks, none is more effective than one that comes from a religious leader, for example, minister, priest, and so on. In 1985, 37 percent of blacks compared to 22 percent of whites reported that they were most responsive to appeals from the clergy, the largest percentage of any appeal mentioned (see Carson, forthcoming). Because of the tremendous influence of the clergy and the large sums of money that are raised by black churches, there is often a great deal of skepticism about what these churches do with the money that they receive.

Despite misconceptions to the contrary, similar percentages of blacks and whites were found to make charitable contributions to their own church. Table 11.3 indicates that nearly identical percentages of blacks and whites reported making similar levels of contributions. For example, 8 percent of blacks compared to 5 percent of whites reported making contributions of less than $50, whereas 13 percent of blacks and 19 percent of whites reported making contributions of more than $500.

When one examines the giving behavior of blacks and whites with the same level of household income to their own church (table not shown), the magnitude of the differences described above become even smaller and, in some instances, reverse direction. For example, 36 percent of blacks and 31 percent of whites with household incomes greater than $40,000 reported making contributions of $500 or more to their own church in 1987. Overall, these findings suggest that there is little difference in the giving behavior of blacks and whites in making contributions to their own church.

When one examines contributions to the church controlling for religious preference (see Table 11.4), two important findings emerge from the data. Perhaps the most striking finding is that the percentage of Protestants and Catholics, regardless of race, who reported that they did not make any contribution to their church in 1987 is fairly uniform, ranging from a low of 31 percent for black Protestants to a high of 38 percent for black Catholics. Equally interesting is the fact that black and white Protestants, respectively, gave nearly double the amount of their Catholic counterparts in the $500 or more category. This may suggest that Protestants are either more willing or more affluent than Catholics. Further research with more detailed data is required before any definitive conclusions can be reached on this point.

Knowledge of Church-Supported Activities

The central issue addressed in this section is how knowledgeable congregants are about the degree to which their church is involved in supporting individuals and organizations outside the church. Few issues are more sensitive within church congregations than how church contributions are distributed. Even be-

Table 11.4. **Contributions to Respondent's Own Church in 1987, by Religious Preference and Race.**

	Protestant		Catholic	
	Blacks	*Whites*	*Blacks*	*Whites*
Less than $50	8.1%	4.7%	1.8%	5.0%
$50–$99	5.9	4.3	8.2	7.4
$100–$499	22.9	19.4	23.4	27.4
$500 or more	13.7	23.4	5.9	14.9
No contribution	31.4	32.6	38.4	34.0
Unreported	18.0	15.8	22.4	11.3
Respondents	569	405	39	205

Table 11.5. Was Money Collected by the Church from Members Given to Other Individuals or Organizations?

	Blacks	Whites
Yes	34.4%	39.1%
No	15.2	14.5
Don't know	50.4	46.3
Respondents	318	363

fore the recent media reports examining charges of impropriety and mismanagement by several prominent evangelical television ministries, congregations had begun to question their religious leaders about how church contributions are allocated. Perhaps one reason for this concern on the part of many congregants is that they simply do not know how their church uses their contribution.

When asked if any of the money that respondents gave to their church in 1987 was given to other organizations or individuals, 39 percent of whites and 34 percent of blacks responded that they were aware of church-sponsored charitable activities (see Table 11.5). Far more surprising was the fact that 50 percent of blacks and 46 percent of whites reported that they did not know whether any of their church contributions were given to individuals or organizations outside their church. This lack of knowledge among blacks and whites about the charitable activities of their respective churches suggests that religious leaders need to be more active in making congregants aware of the church's activities. A greater understanding of the charitable activities of the church by congregants is not only desirable on equity grounds (they contribute the money), but it may also have the effect of encouraging greater contributions as congregants accept and support the charitable mission of the church.

Depending on both the church and the denomination, decisions about how charitable contributions raised by the church are distributed vary greatly. The most common arrangement is for decisions regarding the distribution of a church's collection for charitable causes to be made by the church leader

with the help of a small group of the church's most active and/or
oldest members and/or through standing committees consisting
of members of the congregation. In some instances, funds raised
by the local church can only be disbursed with the prior approval of a higher authority within the church's denomination.
However, other mechanisms are in place. For example, permanent programs to be implemented by Durham's St. Titus
Episcopal Church must first be approved by the state diocese.

Some black churches have begun to address this issue of
accountability directly. One strategy that is being used is for
churches to set aside a fixed percentage of their total budget to
provide charitable services. For example, the well-known
Ebenezer Baptist Church in Atlanta tithes 10 percent of its
budget for community service. The church requires that organizational charters ensure that each organization affiliated with
the church annually sponsors at least one community service
program that does not benefit the church.

Similarly, Chicago's Trinity United Church of Christ sets
aside 8 percent of its total budget from church offerings for
charitable giving. In one year, among other charitable donations, the church distributed $14,000 to its scholarship ministry,
$11,000 to the United Negro College Fund, $15,000 to the
Deacon Crisis and Benevolence Fund, $10,000 to a poorer
United Church of Christ church in Chicago, and $27,000 to the
United Church of Christ seminary. Although the church's total
budget was not disclosed, the church hopes to raise its level of
charitable giving to 10 percent of church offerings. These and
other strategies may prove successful in informing congregants
of the charitable activities of their churches. Trinity Church is
but one example of how black churches throughout the country
are involved in providing essential financial support to other
types of black organizations, without which, many would cease
to continue.

In contrast, some churches have what one might consider
to be very democratic processes for allocating funds. Each of
Detroit's Tabernacle Missionary Baptist Church's programs is
funded through a line-item budget, which is approved by the
church's congregation. Similarly, the Church of the Good Shep-

herd in Chicago encourages members of the congregation to make recommendations to the church's "cabinet" (group of active church members). The cabinet then considers each idea and makes a presentation to the congregation on the idea's merits. Finally, the congregation votes to decide whether to implement the idea.

While it is clear from interviews that members of the clergy had varying degrees of control over how the funds of their particular church are distributed, it would be a mistake to believe that the clergy, regardless of the process, does not have substantial influence in how such decisions are made. Many of the churches included in the interviews declined to reveal their total budget, and this continuing sensitivity is perhaps, in part, responsible for the questions that many have regarding what churches do with the money that they raise. In nearly every church interviewed, the clergy had autonomous control over discretionary funds that were to be used to provide assistance to individuals in an emergency situation.

Serving the Least of These

The data described above suggest that similar percentages of blacks and whites are ill-informed about whether or not their church uses their contributions to support individuals and organizations outside their own church. However, the key concern of this chapter is not only to examine the question of whether blacks and whites who attend church differ with regard to how much they know about how their own church allocates their contribution, but more important, to determine whether a larger percentage of black contributions than of white contributions are used to support individuals and organizations outside the church.

Table 11.6 examines how much of the contributions that blacks and whites (among those who knew that their church was engaged in such activity) gave to their churches was used to support individuals and organizations outside those churches. A greater percentage of blacks than whites reported that their church contribution had been used to support other charities.

Table 11.6. Portion of Money Donated by Blacks and Whites
to Their Churches in 1987 That Was Used for Other Charities.

	Blacks	Whites
Almost all	10.1%	4.7%
More than half	5.7	5.1
About half	13.3	9.6
Less than half	15.0	23.0
Some	21.0	33.1
Very little	8.2	13.8
Don't know	26.7	10.6
Respondents	113	137

For example, 10 percent of blacks compared to 5 percent of whites said that almost all of the money that they had donated to their respective church had been used to support other groups. At the other end of the scale, 14 percent of whites compared to 8 percent of blacks reported that very little of their church contribution had been used to support other charities. These data provide some evidence to substantiate the belief that blacks are somewhat more likely to attend churches that support other charities than are whites. The differences between the two groups become even more pronounced when one takes into account region of the country and metropolitan area.

There is anecdotal evidence from the case studies that some black churches use some of their charitable collections to support other black organizations. In certain instances, such contributions have become so routine that they are essential to the continued provision of services by the recipient organizations. In addition, many well-known black organizations are regular recipients of the financial contributions of black churches. For example, the Bethel AME Church in Chicago makes annual donations to the National Association for the Advancement of Colored People (NAACP), the United Negro College Fund (UNCF), the Chicago Urban League, Operation Push, and Chicago's Dusable Museum. Similarly, the Central Congregational Church in New Orleans annually contributes to the Urban League, the NAACP, the Amistad Research Center, and the United Way. Additional research is required to determine the actual extent to which church support is essential to the continued operation of specific black organizations.

There are at least two other issues to be considered in examining the extent to which blacks attend churches that are more likely to support other charities. One is that regional norms and influences may explain why the churches attended by blacks and whites use their contributions differently, and the other is that individuals who live in areas where social needs are more evident are more likely to belong to churches that financially support other charitable institutions.

Table 11.7 shows the portion of money respondents donated to their own church in 1987 that was given to other charities according to the region of the country in which they live.[3] Notwithstanding the small sample size of blacks who live in the West, which prevents reliable comparisons between blacks and whites in that region of the country, several interesting findings emerge from the data. For example, while nearly the same percentage of blacks and whites who live in the South reported that half or more of their church contribution was used to support other organizations (15 percent and 17 percent, respectively), blacks in the South were three times more likely than whites to have about half of their contribution used to support other groups. Blacks and whites who live in the East exhibit a similar pattern.

By far the most striking finding is that 19 percent of blacks compared to *none* of the whites who live in the Midwest reported that half or more of their church donation was used to support other groups. While it is clear that further research is warranted to explain the regional differences between blacks and whites, particularly in the Midwest, these data convincingly show that regional norms and influences do not account for the apparent inclination of blacks to attend churches that are more likely to use their church donation to support other groups.

Another reason that churches attended by blacks appear to be more likely to support other charities than churches attended by whites might be explained by examining the metropolitan area where respondents live. It is not unreasonable to

Table 11.7. Portion of Money Blacks and Whites Donated to Their
Churches in 1987 That Was Used for Other Charities, by Region.

	East		Midwest		South		West	
	Blacks	Whites	Blacks	Whites	Blacks	Whites	Blacks	Whites
Half or more	18.7%	12.6%	18.7%	0.0%	15.2%	16.5%	0.0%	10.7%
About half	18.2	6.5	6.6	10.7	12.3	3.9	23.5	17.4
Less than half/								
Some	32.3	41.7	48.8	75.0	32.7	39.6	44.4	64.2
Very little	10.9	19.5	0.0	9.0	10.4	22.9	0.0	4.6
Don't know	19.9	19.7	25.9	5.3	29.4	17.2	32.1	2.9
Respondents	30	26	22	39	56	40	5	32

believe that people living in the density of central cities are more
likely to encounter the social needs of others, for example, the
homeless, and feel a need to respond to those needs through
their own church. Similarly, people who live in rural areas may
have less exposure to the needs of individuals not already associated with their church and, as a consequence, may be less likely
to attend churches that provide financial support to charitable
organizations.

Table 11.8 shows, according to metropolitan area, the
portion of money blacks and whites donated to their churches
that was used to support other groups. One would expect that of
all metropolitan areas, congregants of both races who lived in
the central city would be more exposed to the needs of others
and would be more inclined to attend churches that sought to
alleviate those needs. Surprisingly, while 15 percent of blacks
who lived in central cities reported that half or more of their
church contribution was earmarked for other charities and 19
percent of blacks said that about half of it was, *none* of the whites
surveyed reported that half or more of their church contribution went to other groups, and only 2 percent reported that
about half of it did. Blacks in the suburbs were nearly four times
more likely than whites (28 percent and 7 percent, respectively)
to have half or more of their church contribution used to support charitable organizations.

Table 11.8. Portion of Money Blacks and Whites Donated to Their Churches in 1987 That Was Used for Other Charities, by Metropolitan Area.

	Central City		Suburb		Rural	
	Blacks	Whites	Blacks	Whites	Blacks	Whites
Half or more	14.9%	0.0%	27.5%	7.0%	4.4%	15.7%
About half	19.4	2.3	12.1	10.7	5.0	11.9
Less than half/Some	27.2	71.4	33.0	60.4	52.9	47.0
Very little	9.4	13.9	9.0	15.3	5.6	12.8
Don't know	29.0	12.4	18.4	6.6	32.1	12.5
Respondents	47	27	37	48	29	62

Interestingly, the one demographic area in which whites (16 percent) were more likely than blacks (4 percent) to have half or more of their church contribution used to support other organizations was the rural. This finding is difficult to explain given the assumption that individuals who live in sparsely populated rural areas would have a more personal knowledge of individuals and organizations in need of support and would attempt to respond to their needs through individual efforts rather than through their church.

The data presented in this section provide strong evidence that the churches attended by blacks in the central city and suburbs, where social problems are widely believed to be more severe than in rural areas, are more likely to provide financial support to individuals and other organizations than are the churches attended by whites.

Conclusion

This chapter has shown that blacks continue their tradition of using their churches as an important conduit for the distribution of money to individuals and organizations in need of financial support. While similar percentages of blacks and whites make the same level of contribution to their respective churches, blacks were found to be more active than whites in using church contributions to support individuals and organizations, particularly those blacks who live in central cities and suburbs. Despite the effectiveness of supporting black organizations through church contributions in the past, many of the conditions that precipitated the need for the church to assume this role — for example, legally sanctioned, overt racial discrimination — no longer exist.

As stated earlier, the evidence is growing that black participation in churches may be declining and that black churches may be increasingly unable to gather and channel the philanthropic resources of members of the black community, in part because of the exodus of upper- and middle-class blacks from the inner city. Therefore, the desirability of relying on church mechanisms to support black organizations warrants serious and extensive discussion. These factors suggest that now may be an appropriate time to begin to consider strategies for encouraging a more direct relationship between congregants as individual givers and the charitable organizations in need of support.

The ability of the black church to raise money on behalf of other charitable organizations during the last 200 years has provided a vital and much-needed nurturing process for the successful operation of many black charitable organizations. However, to the extent that these black organizations are overly dependent on contributions directed to them from black churches (a crucial aspect that has not been examined here), black charitable organizations may find themselves unable to continue to provide charitable services if church-sponsored support were to either shrink or be withdrawn in the future.

These concerns for the future prosperity of black charitable organizations make it important that strategies be developed, with the support and endorsement of religious leaders, to educate members of the black community about the need to provide direct support to charitable organizations outside the church while continuing their support of church-sponsored charitable activities. Such a gradual shift would also remove religious leaders from the often delicate position of deciding which of the growing number of charitable organizations are worthy of support. Given the esteem in which blacks hold their religious leaders, such a gradual change could not take place without the active and enthusiastic support of the clergy.

Notes

1. The importance of face-to-face interviews rather than telephone interviews for obtaining an accurate picture of the charitable behavior of poor blacks cannot be overemphasized. A total of 18 percent of blacks compared to 7 percent of whites reported in the 1988 JCPS survey that they did not have a telephone in their household. Another effort to promote accurate responses during the interview was to have interviewers of the same race as the respondent. Two-thirds of the interviewers that surveyed black respondents were black, and 96 percent of the interviewers that surveyed whites were white.
2. For the purposes of the survey, Protestant included the Baptist, Christian Church, Episcopal, Lutheran, Methodist, and Presbyterian faiths.
3. In the interest of space and clarity, Tables 11.7 and 11.8 have collapsed the categories contained in Table 11.6. The categories "almost all" and "more than half" have been combined into "half and more," and the categories "less than half" and "some" have been combined into a single category.

Bibliography

Branch, T. *Parting the Waters: America in the King Years 1954–63.* New York: Simon & Schuster, 1988.

Burgess, J. M. *Black Gospel/White Church.* New York: Seabury Press, 1982.

Carson, E. D. *The Charitable Appeals Fact Book: How Black and White Americans Respond to Fund-Raising Efforts.* Washington, D.C.: Joint Center for Political Studies, forthcoming.

Frazier, E. F. *The Negro Church in America.* New York: Schocken, 1974.

Garrow, D. J. *Bearing the Cross.* New York: Morrow, 1986.

Hodgkinson, V. A., and Weitzman, M. S. *The Charitable Behavior of*

Americans: A National Survey. Washington, D.C.: INDEPEN-
DENT SECTOR, 1986.

Hyer, M. "Detroit Cardinal Orders Closing of 31 Parishes." *Washington Post,* Jan. 10, 1989, p. A3.

Jones, L. N. "Serving the Least of These." *Foundation News,* 1984, *25,* 58–61.

Meier, A. *Negro Thought In America: 1880–1915.* Ann Arbor: University of Michigan Press, 1963.

Nored, R. E. "More Than a Tinkling Cymbal: The Philanthropic Activity of Black Parishioners." Unpublished paper, Joint Center for Political Studies, Washington, D.C., 1986.

O'Connell, B. *America's Voluntary Spirit: A Book of Readings.* Washington, D.C.: INDEPENDENT SECTOR, 1983.

Quarles, B. *The Negro in the Making of America.* New York: Collier Books, 1969.

Stehle, V. "Of $41.4 Billion Donated to Churches, Almost Half Goes to Charitable Work." *Chronicle of Philanthropy,* 1988, *1* (5), 1.

Stepp, L. S. "Black Church Losing Historic Role: Drug Use, Teen Pregnancies Seen as Consequences." *Washington Post,* Aug. 20, 1988, p. A1.

Part Three

The Future of Philanthropy in Religious Institutions

Despite the fact that television, science, higher education, technology, and the pressures of big government and the marketplace have all reinforced a prevailing secular ethos in American culture, religious institutions remain relatively strong. So does the voluntary sector in general. Government initiatives to provide welfare services have not been able to replace the work of volunteer agencies, nor have for-profit firms. Indeed, political officials and corporate heads have in the past decade turned increasingly to volunteer agencies for help in addressing such seemingly intractable problems as homelessness, AIDS, drug abuse, alcoholism, child abuse, and urban decay.

These developments do not threaten to erode the strength of the voluntary sector, but they do impose new burdens upon it and generate new expectations that may significantly alter its composition. Because of constitutional restrictions separating religious organizations from government and because of social norms preventing religious organizations from functioning as for-profit firms, there is some reason to fear that the role of religious organizations within the voluntary sector may be diminishing. The chapters in this final section address this possibility, asking by way of summary to the foregoing chapters what is distinctive after all about the contribution of religious organizations and whether they can survive the challenge of increasingly active and well-funded secular voluntary organizations.

The chapters in this section also address a wider range of

questions about the future of the voluntary spirit in American society as it relates to religion. Although voluntary associations are nearly as old as the United States itself and have been studied nearly as long, many questions that require research and investigation remain unanswered. Specifying some of these questions and suggesting fruitful directions for research is one of the goals of these chapters. But the voluntary sector is also a matter of continuing practical importance in our society. The passing of each day, almost literally, presents it with new challenges. We have also tried to survey some of these challenges and pose ideas for policymakers, religious leaders, and officials within the voluntary sector to think about in the months and years ahead.

Chapter 12

James R. Wood

Alternatives to Religion in the Promotion of Philanthropy

"Philanthropy" is "active effort to promote human welfare" (Mish and others, 1986, p. 882). Philanthropic activities include the numerous ways in which people give their time and money to help other people. Describing our society's independent sector, the source of philanthropic activity, Brian O'Connell (1988, p. 2) argues that "the uniqueness of the sector is its relative independence and freedom to contribute to innovation, advocacy, criticism, and where necessary, reform." Religious organizations have long been major actors in the field of philanthropy. However, in recent decades, even as our knowledge of the extent of religious philanthropy has increased, there has been concern that a decline in religious organizations would mean a significant drop in overall philanthropy. This chapter argues that many aspects of religion's role in philanthropy can be (and in some cases already are being) taken over by other organizations in the third sector and by business and government organizations.

First, I will characterize religious organizations' philanthropic activities. Then I will examine and discuss some of the ways in which other third sector, business, and government organizations facilitate similar activities.

Annual giving to religious organizations in the United States exceeds $40 billion—about 47 percent of all philanthropic giving. Much of this money, as well as much of the estimated $35 billion worth of volunteer time, was spent on philanthropic activities that reach far beyond narrowly defined "religious" activities (AAFRC Trust for Philanthropy, 1987, pp. 7, 63). A landmark report of INDEPENDENT SECTOR released in 1988 demonstrates the wide philanthropic impact of religious congregations. The study concluded that 87 percent of religious congregations in the United States are active in human services (such as family counseling, youth programs, and meal programs); 78 percent support international activities such as overseas relief and refugee-related programs); about 70 percent are involved in public/societal benefit activities (such as community development, civil rights, and social justice); about 68 percent are involved in health activities (including hospitals, nursing homes, crisis counseling); 42 percent are involved in arts and culture programs; 38 percent are involved in elementary and secondary education; and 27 percent are involved in improvement of environmental quality (Hodgkinson, Weitzman, and Kirsch, 1988).

Similar activities are supported at national and regional levels. In 1984, the Council on Foundations conducted a survey of national and regional religious organizations to determine "the nature and extent of religious funding for social and human services exclusive of funding for solely religious purposes" (Joseph, Reckard, and McDonald, 1985, p. xv). Combining data from that survey and other sources, the authors of the report concluded that annual philanthropic giving from religious organizations (including national, regional, and local) may reach $8.5 billion. The most frequently supported activities, ordered by the number of religious organizations supporting them, are food, nutrition; refugee aid, resettlement; day care, camps, recreation for youth; issue education, advocacy; justice, human rights; emergency assistance, disaster relief; clothing; temporary shelter; schools (preschool through high school); and adult education, tutoring (Joseph, Reckard, and McDonald, 1985, p. 21). Focusing for the moment just on the "services traditionally associated with religious compassion," the report concluded that the major denominational and ecumenical service agencies "reported such impressive work in feeding, clothing, sheltering, counseling, and rehabilitating the needy that if they were all to stop tomorrow, the fabric of society would be seriously weakened" (Joseph, Reckard, and McDonald, p. 23).

Religion's contributions to philanthropy include designing and carrying out philanthropic projects, motivating and recruiting for philanthropy, sponsoring philanthropic organizations, and shaping the character of American society. Under each of these headings I will illustrate ways in which nonreligious organizations serve as alternatives to religious organizations in facilitating philanthropic activities.

Designing and Carrying Out Philanthropic Projects — Both Alone and as Joint Ventures with Other Organizations

About one-third of the total wage bill in business and industry in the United States pays for fringe social benefits for employed workers. Some of these, for example, unemployment insurance, are mandated by government and many result from labor-management negotiations. In addition to health benefits, some businesses and industries provide children's day care and educational and recreational activities for employees. There is enormous potential for the expansion of such services (Morris, 1982).

Even in the area of looking for individuals who may need special attention — an area in which many religious organizations are particularly strong — some government and business organizations have immense capacity for such activities. Keller (1986, p. 186) gives an important illustration:

> In a three-way partnership with management and the nonprofit sector, organized labor founded Carrier Alert, a cooperative effort of the National Association of Letter Carriers (NALC) and the United States Postal Service (USPS). The program, which grew out of local NALC projects in many parts of the country and was launched nationally in 1982, has been credited with saving lives on a number of occasions. Letter carriers "monitor" their elderly, handicapped, and homebound patrons by noting

anything unusual that may signify illness or an
accident in the course of their daily rounds. Warning signals could be an accumulation of un-
collected mail, lights burning in midday, pets crying, or daily newspapers stacking up.

Patrons are "registered" through a local social service agency such as the Red Cross, Council
on Aging, or information and referral hot line. A
sticker is placed inside the patron's mailbox to
notify carriers to be on the alert. When evidence
points to a possible problem, the carrier contacts
his/her supervisor, who notifies the appropriate
social service agency. The agency checks on the
patron and contacts the family, police, or emergency services if something's wrong.

Union leaders estimate that this program is operating in a
hundred cities across the country. Moreover, a number of utility
companies across the country have adopted similar programs.

Another example includes voluntary associations. A British study of how voluntary organizations help to support caring
for relatives found that a number of organizations, including the
Lions Club, the Community Health Council, Age Concern, and
Arthritis Care, offered services to people who needed some
relief from the responsibilities of caring for an elderly or ill
family member. Typically these services provided someone to
relieve the carer several hours a week, usually during the afternoon. Sometimes the volunteer would prepare a meal as well
(Moore and Green, 1985, pp. 93–130).

The national and international structure of civic clubs
facilitates the rapid diffusion of knowledge about human needs
and ways to meet those needs through particular types of service
projects. A 1983 survey showed that Kiwanis clubs alone raised
$35 million and recruited 19 million volunteer hours for com-
munity service projects ("Who Are the Kiwanians?" 1983).

Motivating and Recruiting Individuals and Organizations to Be Involved in Philanthropy

In a 1986 study of a representative sample of Indiana residents, I found that 18 percent of them had recently been involved in some volunteer activity "assisting people who need help *or* trying to change [their] community's policies for helping people." When respondents described organizations that recruited them and/or served as the context of their helping behavior, churches were the organizations most often mentioned; in fact, churches were mentioned by 25 percent of the respondents who volunteered to help others. But a variety of other organizations were also mentioned. Those mentioned by at least 5 percent of the volunteers were youth organizations, hospitals or nursing homes, schools, government agencies, civic clubs, health-related organizations, and senior citizens' groups.

Though no single category of voluntary associations currently uses a vast social network for motivating and recruiting volunteers comparable to that used by religious organizations, such associations could certainly expand their philanthropic activities. Also, "umbrella groups" that coordinate the activities of hundreds of associations of various categories might provide communication chains, social networks, and other opportunity structures that would match those traditionally provided by religious organizations. The INDEPENDENT SECTOR's current program Daring Goals for a Caring Society may provide the prototype for such activities. That program seeks to enlist "all voluntary organizations, government at all levels, foundations, and the business community, as well as . . . men, women, and youth from all parts of the country and all segments of society" in a program that will "double charitable giving and increase volunteer activity 50 percent by 1991" (INDEPENDENT SECTOR, 1986).

The systematic involvement of businesses in recruiting and supporting volunteers is growing. The Honeywell Retiree Volunteer Project provides one example. That project links volunteers and agencies, utilizing 850 retired people who spend

a day or two a week in a total of 230 community agencies
("Retiree Volunteers," 1987). One survey in Canada found that
almost 70 percent of more than 900 employer respondents
supported their employees' voluntary work, many of them per-
mitting the employee to adjust the work schedule or take time
off from work (Hart, 1987). An overview of U.S. corporations
suggests that more than 500 have volunteer programs. Moreover,
a number of cities now have citywide corporate volunteer councils (CVCs) in which several corporations coordinate their volunteer programs. These programs include

> involving employees in assessment of community
> needs, providing a clearing house for matching
> employees' skills with volunteer openings in non-
> profit agencies, referring staff to volunteer place-
> ment councils, sponsorship of group projects such
> as telethons, walk-a-thons, community clean-up
> drives, loaning of staff and executives for short- and
> long-term assignments with educational institu-
> tions and community organizations, in-house
> training of disadvantaged youth by corporate em-
> ployees, and community involvement grants to or-
> ganizations in which employees already volunteer
> their time [Leonard, 1984, pp. 11–17].

A 1985 study of 736 representative U.S. cities showed that
72.6 percent of them use unpaid volunteers in city government.
Volunteers were used in a variety of jobs. While fire fighters were
most mentioned, a number of people-to-people jobs were also
mentioned, including recreation program staff, senior citizen
center assistants, library aides, hospital and nursing home atten-
dants, counselors, and language teachers (Duncombe, 1985).
    The Domestic Volunteer Service Act of 1973 establishes a
volunteerism policy for the federal government:

> Sec. 2. (a) Because of the long-standing importance
> of volunteerism throughout American history, it is
> the policy of the Congress to foster the tradition of

volunteerism through greater involvement on the
part of both young and older citizens.

(b) The purpose of ACTION, the Federal domestic volunteer agency, is to foster and expand
voluntary citizen service in communities throughout the Nation in activities designed to help the
poor, the disadvantaged, the vulnerable, and the
elderly. In carrying out this purpose, ACTION shall
utilize to the fullest extent the programs authorized
under this Act, coordinate with other Federal,
State, and local agencies and utilize the energy,
innovative spirit, experience, and skills of all Americans [Superintendent of Documents, 1988].

Of course, one could expect government programs such
as the Peace Corps and VISTA to appeal to altruistic motives.
But even the Internal Revenue Service recently carried out a
national advertising campaign for volunteers. The ad pictures a
very grateful elderly woman planting a kiss on the cheek of an
IRS volunteer. The text of the ad is as follows:

GIVE YOUR TIME TO THE IRS, AND YOU'LL GET SOMETHING IN RETURN

Volunteer your skills and experience to the IRS.
And everyone gets something in return. Taxpayers
with questions get the answers they need. And volunteers like yourself get the satisfaction of a job well
done. And sometimes a little bit more. For free IRS
training, call 1-800-424-1040. Volunteer now. And
you'll make someone's taxes less taxing later.

Apparently even strong missionary fervor is not limited
to religious organizations; Reeves (1988, pp. 156–158) describes
the Peace Corps and VISTA volunteers of the 1960s as "putting
the agency's social mission above their own self-interests" and
with "a secular missionary faith" pursued "the goal of rescuing
the poor from their misery."

Sponsoring Philanthropic Organizations and/or
Providing Facilities for Philanthropic Activity

One important philanthropic activity of religious organizations is the training and socialization of youth. Comparing religious organization involvement in just one aspect of this activity— serving as charter organizations for the Boy Scouts of America—with that of organizations of other sectors demonstrates both the tremendous importance of religious organizations and the fact that alternatives do exist. In 1987, the top fifty chartered organizations accounted for 128,426 Boy Scout units. Almost 51 percent of these organizations were religious organizations, but other third sector organizations (such as parent-teacher groups and civic clubs) accounted for just over 29 percent, and public schools for 11.3 percent. Moreover, government agencies (including fire departments, law enforcement agencies, and the armed services) were responsible for 6 percent of the units, and industry and business accounted for almost 3 percent.

Plinio and Scanlan (n.d.) show that corporations' noncash assistance to philanthropic causes is increasing. These gifts include products, property, personnel, facilities, and services. In 1982, noncash assistance was valued at $244.1 million, or 17 percent of total corporate cash and noncash giving. By 1984, the value of noncash assistance had risen to $388.7 million, or 23 percent of total corporate giving.

Shaping the Character of American Society

Few doubt the influence of the churches in the passage of the landmark Civil Rights Act of 1964 and 1965 (Spike, 1965). However, several labor unions were also part of that successful lobbying effort. And a number of third sector organizations, such as the NAACP, the ACLU, and several women's organizations, have been instrumental in ensuring the implementation of the 1964 and 1965 Civil Rights Act.

Occupational groups provide important alternatives to the church in promoting such issues as peace, disarmament, and human rights. Not only do many occupational and professional associations speak out on such issues, but there are increasing numbers of single-issue organizations composed of people who share a particular occupation and dealing with such issues. Here are just a few examples on the issue of disarmament: Architects/Designers/Planners for Social Responsibility, Artists for Nuclear Disarmament, Computer Professionals for Social Responsibility, Editors Organizing Committee and Writers' and Publishers' Alliance for Disarmament, Educators for Social Responsibility, Lawyers Alliance for Nuclear Arms Control, Librarians for Nuclear Arms Control, Life Insurance Committee for a Nuclear Weapons Freeze, Performing Artists for Nuclear Disarmament, Physicians for Social Responsibility, Psychologists for Social Responsibility, and Social Scientists Against Nuclear War. Occupationally rooted organizations concerned with human rights include Committee of Concerned Scientists, Lawyers Committee for Human Rights, and Physicians for Human Rights. Just the fifteen organizations named in these examples have, in the aggregate, more than 75,000 members. Yet these are only a few of thousands of occupationally rooted organizations that seek the goals of justice and peace so long sought by religious organizations.

Discussion

The advantages of philanthropic action through government include those that derive from universality of coverage, resource raising through taxes, and police power to enforce such policies as affirmative action. Eugene Lang, in a remarkable speech in which he describes his "I have a Dream" program, makes a strong plea for private involvement in providing educational opportunities for minorities and other potential high school dropouts. But he emphasizes that private initiative, even if it mushrooms, can hardly begin to solve the problem, and he applauds efforts of state governments to begin programs with similar goals. Moreover, even if it were possible to do far more than Lang imagines through private initiative, the coverage would still be uneven and the opportunity would depend on whether one happened to be in the right location. Government is ideally situated to deal with these problems of coverage.

Because of these advantages some argue that more of religious organizations' attention should be focused on influencing government philanthropic efforts (with religious organizations possibly designing and testing programs in pilot projects).

Though businesses do not have the powers of taxation and law enforcement, they do have vast communication networks and they are the environment in which millions of Americans spend most of their waking day. The recent successes of a major grocery chain in marketing flowers and of a major retailer becoming a formidable "bank" card competitor dramatically illustrate how strategic location and sophisticated communication networks position businesses to take on new functions. It is heartening that many businesses are including philanthropic activities among the new functions they are promoting with their resources.

These avenues of increasing nonreligious philanthropy are worth pursuing even if religion does not decline. The general thrust of religious organizations in mission fields has been to provide services that a government or society needed but had not provided, such as education, health, agricultural expertise. When societies were able to provide these services for themselves, then mission efforts (at least of mainline denominations) were redirected to new frontiers of service. A redistribution of philanthropic efforts among the various sectors of society has now become a trend within our own society. Moreover, one churchman has argued forcefully that many of the philanthropic activities of churches should not be carried out by the churches but by church people working through voluntary associations (Hutcheson, 1981).

There may be disadvantages for a society's achieving philanthropic goals through government and business. Weisbrod (1988) found, for example, that nursing homes operated by religious organizations were of higher quality on a number of dimensions than other nursing homes. With government organized philanthropy, there may also be efficiency problems, partly because of political pressures. Some also see a tendency for government to throw money at problems.

Business may have some advantages of efficiency. But philanthropic values might be especially precarious in business organizations where the basic values are economic. There are some strong arguments for business to encourage philanthropic activities out of its own enlightened self-interest; still, these programs would probably be the first to go during an economic crunch. Just as important, businesses and, to some extent, government agencies also are far more likely to encourage programs that pursue noncontroversial goals. For example, both the Honeywell Retiree Volunteer Project ("Retiree Volunteers," 1987) and the Domestic Volunteer Service Act of 1973 (Superintendent of Documents, 1988) specifically forbid political or legislative advocacy. Yet it may well be that the distinctive contribution to American society by those aspects of traditional religion most expected to decline—the liberal mainline denominations—has been their ability to draw large numbers of people and great amounts of resources into addressing controversial issues and championing unpopular causes.

Though the future of religious organizations' influence on philanthropy is not clear, it is clear that other third sector organizations, business, and government all have important infrastructures and considerable experience that could allow them to serve as alternatives to declining religious organizations. Potential, of course, is not actuality. Further research is needed to discern the conditions under which these organizations would in fact vastly increase their philanthropic activities.

Further research is especially needed to determine whether there is some residual of religion's impact that cannot be supplied by other organizations. Though, in principle, government, business, and a host of third sector organizations could greatly increase their "market" share of carrying out philanthropic projects, sponsoring philanthropic organizations, and shaping the character of American society, it is far from certain that these organizations can ever approach religion's ability to provide sustained, intense motivation for philanthropic activity. Government and business organizations may have to draw on values and motivations anchored elsewhere in society to sustain philanthropic efforts. If so, there may be nonreligious third sector organizations that, alone or in the aggregate, can foster those values and motivations. But religious motivation may be unique. If religious motivation is essential to philanthropy, we do not know whether either civil religion or diffuse faith not anchored in religious organizations can substitute for traditional religion. It is possible, for example, that religious organizations play an essential role in motivating people to serve humanity in these other organizations. Nonreligious organizations, especially those outside the third sector, may lack the institutionalized values, symbols, and rituals that sustain philanthropic efforts. (See Wood, 1981, and Wood and Davidson, 1988.)

If religion makes a distinctive contribution to philanthropy, that contribution is likely related to religion's means of activating people's selfless values as motivation to help others. Values may be defined as enduring beliefs that specific behaviors or goals are personally or socially preferable to opposite behaviors or goals (Rokeach, 1973). A value system is an enduring organization of values along a continuum of relative importance. Though we learn values as absolutes, experience of situations in which values compete cause us to integrate values into a hierarchically organized system, wherein each value is ordered in priority or importance relative to other values. According to Rokeach, the values that are internalized as a result of cultural, societal, and personal experience are psychological structures that are determinants not only of attitudes and ideologies but also of virtually all kinds of behavior that could be called social behavior.

Rokeach and his co-workers (Ball-Rokeach, Rokeach, and Grube, 1984) demonstrated both that when individuals are stimulated to think about inconsistencies in their values, they may reorder their values and that those values can be used to leverage individuals into action. For example, the researchers devised a television program that caused people to think about the inconsistency in placing high value on freedom but low value on equality. In a talk show format the program used data from a survey taken just after the assassination of Dr. Martin Luther King, Jr., to try to change the way people value equality. It was pointed out that most Americans rank freedom quite high (third of the eighteen values in the survey). Then the show's hostess said: "Not so with equality. Those who felt sad or angry about Dr. King's assassination ranked equality sixth on the average . . . those who reacted with "he brought it on himself" ranked equality thirteenth. This raises the question whether those who are against civil rights are really saying they care a great deal about their own freedom but don't really care that much about other people's freedom" (p. 384).

The result was that those who watched the program both shifted their value rankings so that equality ranked higher and contributed more (compared to a control group who did not watch the program) to antiracism mail solicitations arranged by the researchers.

In a similar but possibly more powerful way, religious rituals and sermons can raise our consciousness of our selfless values.

To induce a person to get involved in helping others, it may be necessary to raise his or her consciousness of the more selfless values in his or her value hierarchy. Worship and Bible study provide especially effective contexts for value consciousness raising. The important thing here is not just that the minister preaches the Bible and that she or he discusses community issues—it is the way in which preaching the Bible and discussing community issues interact with each other.

In a 1978 study of Indiana residents, I found that when respondents described organizations that recruited them into volunteer activities, churches were the organizations most often mentioned—more than twice as often as the next-most mentioned type of organization, youth organizations. In a later study, I was able to link a person's perception of the church's value appeal strategies with his or her volunteering. For example, in a sample of church members from forty Indiana and Illinois churches, more than 97 percent of those who volunteered in the community agreed (or strongly agreed) that "My church cultivated the faith that led to my volunteering." Almost 99 percent agreed that "My church helps me to see that volunteering to help others is an expression of my faith." More than 78 percent agreed that "I decided to volunteer because my pastor showed me how Jesus's teachings apply to today." And 54.4 percent agreed that "I decided to volunteer because my pastor persuaded me to follow the example of Jesus."

The fact that the experiment based on Rokeach's value scheme worked in a secular setting shows, of course, that a sacred setting is not necessary. Still, it seems plausible that the supernatural beliefs that underlie the dynamics just discussed would provide a distinctive and powerful contribution of the churches. Moreover, the churches are reaching millions of Americans every week with this type of value-leverage appeal. And, importantly, the churches are presenting these appeals in the context of an opportunity structure. More than 91 percent of those surveyed agreed that "My church gave me information about the need for volunteers." More than 97 percent agreed that "My church provided opportunities to volunteer." And 77 percent agreed that "Someone in the church asked me to volunteer."

Though recent decades saw a great deal of controversy over national policies of religious denominations and an arguable decline in their influence on local churches, thousands of local churches continue week after week to link faith-based value appeals to specific opportunities to help others. I see no reason to expect any appreciable diminution of this vital wellspring of philanthropy.

A strong alternative to churches would have to couple appeals to strongly held values with an effective structure for implementing those values concretely. Though the Daring Goals campaign mentioned earlier attempts to incorporate these elements, the fact that it draws heavily upon the churches lends credence to the possibility that they provide something distinctive. At least for the foreseeable future there appears to be no clear alternative that can rival the importance of religion in the promotion of philanthropy.

References

AAFRC Trust for Philanthropy. *Giving USA*. New York: AAFRC Trust for Philanthropy, 1987.

Ball-Rokeach, S. J., Rokeach, M., and Grube, J. W. *The Great American Values Test: Influencing Behavior and Belief Through Television*. New York: Free Press, 1984.

Duncombe, S. "Volunteers in City Government: Advantages, Disadvantages and Uses." *National Civic Review*, Sept. 1985.

Hart, K. D. "Emerging Patterns of Volunteerism." *Canadian Business Review*, Spring 1987.

Hodgkinson, V. A., Weitzman, M. S., and Kirsch, A. D. *From Belief to Commitment: The Activities and Finances of Religious Congregations in the United States*. Washington, D.C.: INDEPENDENT SECTOR, 1988.

Hutcheson, R. G., Jr. "Will the Real Christian Program Please Stand Up?" *Christian Century*, Oct. 7, 1981, pp. 994–997.

INDEPENDENT SECTOR. *Daring Goals for a Caring Society—A Blueprint for Substantial Growth in Giving and Volunteering in America*. Washington, D.C.: INDEPENDENT SECTOR, 1986.

Joseph, J. A., Reckard, E. C., and McDonald, J. A. *The Philanthropy of Organized Religion*. Washington, D.C.: Council on Foundations, 1985.

Keller, S. "Volunteering: Organized Labor's Best Kept Secret." In C. Vizza, K. Allen, and S. Keller, *A New Competitive Edge: Volunteering at the Workplace*. Arlington, Va.: Volunteer—The National Center, 1986.

Leonard, K. L. "Corporate Volunteers Cooperate in New York City." *Public Relations Quarterly*, 1984, *29*, 11–17.

Mish, F. C., and others (eds.). *Webster's Ninth New Collegiate Dictionary*. Springfield, Mass.: Merriam-Webster, 1986.

Moore, J., and Green, J. M. "The Contribution of Voluntary Organizations to the Support of Caring Relatives." *The Quarterly Journal of Social Affairs*, 1985, *1* (2), 33–130.

Morris, R. "Government and Voluntary Agency Relationships." *Social Service Review*, Sept. 1982, 1–15.

O'Connell, B. *America's Voluntary Sector*. New York: Foundation Center, 1988.

Plinio, A. J., and Scanlan, J. B., *Resource Raising: The Role of Non-Cash Assistance in Corporate Philanthropy*. Washington, D.C.: INDEPENDENT SECTOR, n.d.

Reeves, T. Z. *The Politics of the Peace Corps and Vista*. Tuscaloosa: University of Alabama Press, 1988.

"Retiree Volunteers" (Honeywell Retiree Volunteer Project, Minneapolis). *Personnel Administrator*, 1987, *32*, 26.

Rokeach, M. *The Nature of Human Values*. New York: Free Press, 1973.

Spike, R. W. *The Freedom Revolution and the Churches*. New York: Association Press, 1965.

Superintendent of Documents. *Compilation of the Domestic Volunteer Service Act of 1973: As Amended Through December 31, 1987*. Washington, D.C.: U.S. Government Printing Office, 1988.

Weisbrod, B. A. *The Nonprofit Economy*. Cambridge, Mass.: Harvard University Press, 1988.

"Who Are the Kiwanians?" *Kiwanis Magazine*, Oct. 1983.

Wood, J. R. *Leadership in Voluntary Organizations: The Controversy Over Social Action in Protestant Churches*. New Brunswick, N.J.: Rutgers University Press, 1981.

Wood, J. R., and Davidson, J. "Value and Interest Theories of Church Social Action" Paper presented at the meetings of the Religious Research Association, Chicago, Oct. 1988.

Chapter 13

Robert Wuthnow

Improving Our Understanding of Religion and Giving: Key Issues for Research

As a number of the foregoing chapters have indicated, research on the connections between religion and giving remains relatively underdeveloped. Many studies in the past explored small aspects of these connections, asking, for example, about how many evenings a week parishioners spent on religious activities and whether they were involved in any other charitable activities. But on the whole it has been only in recent years that scholars interested in the nonprofit sector have discovered the importance of religious giving and that students of religion have begun to think systematically about its role in relation to the voluntary sector more broadly. As a result, many important research questions remain unanswered.

What follows represents the major topic areas that, in my view, need to be given priority in research efforts on religion and the spirit of giving and volunteering in American society. Some of these issues have been raised specifically by the discussions in previous chapters; others have arisen more from examining the broader literature and from thinking about questions that have largely remained unasked. In mentioning each topic, I shall also suggest briefly why I think it is important and what some of the specific questions and approaches that might prove useful would be.

Research on the Motivational Links Between Religious Convictions and Philanthropic Behavior

The chapters in this volume provide some evidence on the ways in which religion may actually motivate philanthropy, for example, by reinforcing a sense of obligation to others from the same ethnic or religious roots, by putting moral pressure on individuals to contribute, or even by providing material incentives (such as the rewards promised by church raffles). But other than this scant evidence, we know little about the ways in which religious organizations actually evoke giving behavior from their constituencies.

Churches have often in the past (as Chapter Six on Catholic stewardship suggests) been accused of playing on the fears of their members to elicit contributions. In our society, television preachers have perhaps been the most visible target of such accusations. Whether people give primarily because they fear for their own souls or for the future of their way of life is, however, something about which little is known. Even the evidence from experimental studies dealing with guilt and fear as more general forms of motivation is far from clear. Certainly, there are theological arguments that play on guilt. But there are also theological arguments that point toward love, affirmation, and freedom as stronger motivating orientations.

One of the most suggestive findings in the foregoing chapters is that from the Chapter Eleven study of black and white giving, which shows that a large percentage of both blacks and whites claim to be uncertain as to their motives for giving. Some would perhaps argue that this is an undesirable state of affairs because people with uncertain motives are surely less likely to give reliably and generously than people with a clearer understanding of their motives. And yet an alternative interpretation is also plausible. It may be that we give more generously of ourselves when we are able to disguise our true motives. Too much calculation, or even too much self-examination, may run counter to our deepest understandings of altruism. We do, after all, have countless stories in our cultural repertoire that tell us compassion is simply an instinct, or perhaps an impulse.

In teaching courses on religion and on caring in other contexts, I have generally found students to be far more actively involved in formal and informal acts of caring than they are used to admitting in public. For example, when pressed to disclose their activities, many stated that they had done volunteer work in high school, some had cared for relatives and friends with chronic illnesses or handicaps, and a few had even been involved with missionary service of one kind or another. Once the discussion turned to these activities, stories of personal experiences poured out freely. Indeed, a kind of cathartic release sometimes seemed to underlie these discussions. Yet, many students admitted that they never talked about these activities with their friends, and some said that they felt embarrassed whenever the topic arose. It is perhaps not overstating the case to say that having a language with which to talk about giving is part of what keeps the voluntary spirit alive. In other words, giving depends not only on having some free time or having somebody ask you to give, but also on a way of talking about it that makes it a legitimate part of one's life. Certainly, the likelihood of others being drawn toward giving and volunteering will be diminished if those who are already involved feel too embarrassed about it to discuss their activities openly.

Religion enters into the picture in at least three possible ways. First, it may provide a language with which to talk about giving and volunteering. One of my students, for example, said he felt no embarrassment or uncertainty about his motives for doing volunteer work because he was a Christian and he always figured "God has given me so much, the least I can do is pay back a little by trying to help people who are in need." Even the way he said this suggested it was an argument he had heard articulated many times at his church. He had no need to make up a language of motives for himself because his religious community supplied him with one.

Second, religion may provide a context in which motives for giving and helping need not be discussed. It is simply taken for granted that people will help. I heard a sermon not long ago that illustrates this possibility. The minister recalled driving home late one Saturday evening with three of the deacons from his church. As they rounded a curve, they noticed a vehicle that had swerved off the road and came to rest in the ditch. In his words, "Without anyone saying a word, we simply pulled over and went down to see if anyone was hurt." What he was modeling by this statement was in part the view that truly religious people need not think about their motives or discuss them; they can simply act because they already know what to do.

The third possibility is that religious commitment actively discourages believers from talking about giving or the motivations for giving. Instead of just providing a context in which one automatically responds to a visible need (as in the previous example), religious commitment explicitly admonishes practitioners to be silent about their charitable deeds. Traditionally, religious teachings have warned believers against the sin of pride and have admonished them that it is better to pray in one's closet than to make a show of one's spirituality and better to give in such a secret manner that even one's left hand is unaware of what one's right hand is doing. Such teachings, it appears, have also become part of the secular norms of giving in our culture. We consider ourselves a compassionate people, but we also scorn "do-gooders" who make a public show of their activities and we feel at least mild disgust whenever we see pictures on the fashion page of well-dressed couples sipping cocktails at the latest charity ball.

In addition to the traditional admonitions against pride, religious teachings may also discourage talking about the motivations for giving by bringing the issue of motivation itself into doubt. The biblical tradition, like modern therapeutic discourse, teaches that motives are complex and deceptive. If we think we have done a kind deed out of the goodness of our heart, we also need to remember that our sense of goodness may be a masquerade for selfishness, or in more contemporary language, "false consciousness." When people in surveys say that they are unsure of their motives for giving, therefore, they may simply be expressing the view that motives are always too complex to understand clearly.

These are only possibilities. Religious communities may make it easier to articulate one's reasons for giving and caring, make it unnecessary to articulate any reasons, or discourage one from talking about one's activities and motives at all. What all these possibilities suggest, however, is that research needs to move beyond efforts to uncover some deep motivational impulse that is assumed to be hidden away in one's psyche (or even, as some now argue, in the genetic structure). Instead of taking the existence of motives for granted, research needs to pay attention to the ways in which talk about motives is constructed. Whether a religious tradition encourages or discourages discourse about motives may be as important as the kind of motives it is presumed to reinforce.

Research on the Role of Religious Narratives in Shaping Ideas About Giving and Helping

Although religious tradition contains many doctrines and teachings that encourage altruistic behavior, these doctrines and teachings are often expressed most vividly in stories, parables, testimonials, and other narratives. Thus the role of religious tradition goes well beyond that of merely encouraging a compassionate response to the needy: Its narratives shape our very definitions of what it means to be needy and what an appropriate response may be. Even for those who wish to be helpful, some situations will be more likely to elicit a caring response simply because those situations conform to a pattern recognizable to those familiar with religious narratives.

Anyone who has worked in fund-raising or who has solicited volunteers knows the power of narrative. Personal testimonials that describe how one decided to become involved with volunteer work and what one learned as a result of this activity are common fare in churches and synagogues—from testimonials by young people who have volunteered a weekend to paint the church to testimonials by missionaries telling how they decided to spend their lives working in a distant land. These testimonials call on the listener to identify with the speaker; they model the process of thinking about becoming a volunteer, show the internal struggles involved, and then bring the story to a climax intended to show that the decision was correct and rewarding.

These narratives often depict a certain kind of victim or needy person or opportunity as well. The parable of the Good Samaritan is not only a story about being compassionate. It is a story that defines a certain kind of need, someone lying directly across your path who is obviously in physical pain and in danger of dying. One learns that compassion is an appropriate response to this kind of victim. One is less likely to make large leaps of inference from the story to other kinds of victims or other kinds of helping behavior (for example, to the idea that one might be a Good Samaritan by going back to Jerusalem and organizing a political action committee to press for better police patrols along the road to Jericho).

The chief fund-raiser for a large international relief agency provided a vivid example of the shaping power of religious narratives in a recent interview. In describing his agency's efforts to provide relief for victims of drought in Africa, he indicated that contributions seemed to come more from church people than from others and speculated that the gospel message encouraged people to think about their responsibility to the needy. But then he went on to lament: "We would like to solicit contributions to dig wells to help the people become more self-sufficient; instead, we have to show those pictures of starving children with bloated bellies because that's what gets a response." Clearly the picture of a starving child paints a more graphic image, but it is also an image that suggests a familiar response: being "moved with compassion" in the same way the Samaritan was moved by seeing the injured man on the road, and responding by giving help to a specific individual, not by attempting to alleviate some broader economic condition.

Another episode that illustrates the importance of narratives in defining caring responses was recounted by the pastor of a local church. He told with some pride how his flock had pitched in when a prominent man in the church found out his wife was dying of cancer. Through the long period of illness and grieving, members of the congregation took in food, prayed, and provided emotional support. Nearly all of them could think of stories from their own experience of similar situations, and the pastor himself found it easy to encourage giving and caring from the pulpit. With some chagrin, though, he told of another member of his congregation who had experienced a major midlife crisis involving severe anxiety, anger, and questioning of her faith. Neither the pastor nor the congregation knew how to respond to this need. Some of them drew on biblical narratives suggesting that anger and anxiety were simply a symptom of inadequate belief. Others found themselves too embarrassed to respond because the presence of anger and anxiety in their midst contradicted the warm consensual sentiments they thought should prevail in a religious community. Still others defined the issue in psychotherapeutic terms that removed it from the domain of needs to which a religious community should respond at all.

These examples suggest a need for more research on the content of religious narratives themselves and on the relations between knowing these narratives and attitudes about victims, needs, and caring responses. A very useful place for such research to start would be sermons about love of neighbor. Analysis of Sunday school materials, children's Bible story books, and religious periodicals would also provide useful information.

Research on the Giving Patterns of Religious, Ethnic, and Racial Minorities

Chapters Seven and Eleven in this volume, which deal with giving among Jews and blacks, attest to a special need for more research on these and other minority groups. Although an increasing amount of attention has been paid to these groups, most of our knowledge about religious behavior in general continues to be based on studies of white Protestants and Catholics. Consequently, it is often difficult to know how generalizable these results are and, indeed, whether our basic theories of religious behavior need to be revised.

The comparisons provided by Chapter Seven on Jewish giving and Chapter Eleven on black giving point especially to the interesting variations in philanthropy that may be present among minority groups in the United States. Jews appear to give not only to Jewish philanthropies but also to non-Jewish organizations; in short, giving is rooted both in a distinctive ethnic identity and in assimilation into the broader culture. Among blacks, while the evidence is far from definitive, more distinctive patterns of giving seem to be present. These patterns, moreover, are heavily conditioned by region of the country and by differences between residents of urban, suburban, and rural areas. Still, the evidence suggests that giving behavior in both groups depends to an important extent on the existence of churches and synagogues that appeal to the special needs and interests of their constituencies.

Some valuable contributions to the research literature in this area can be made by studies that simply document in greater detail the extent of giving in various religious subgroups and that examine the correlates of this behavior. Much needed are studies of the Hispanic community, especially studies that make possible more detailed comparisons of the religious and philanthropic behavior of Puerto Ricans, Mexican-Americans, Cubans, and other Latino populations. Also needed are studies at the congregational and parish levels, not only among Hispanics but among blacks, Asian-Americans, and other ethnic groups.

In addition to studies of individual giving patterns in these communities, more research is needed on the organizations to which time and money are donated. As Chapter Eleven suggests, black churches in metropolitan areas and in some sections of the country may serve as major conduits to needy people in the community at large. Other churches, as the author suggests in passing, may be sufficiently hierarchical that much of the money donated is channeled directly to high-level agencies within the denomination itself. Even for the mainline white Protestant and Catholic churches, we know little about how much of each dollar contributed goes for organizational maintenance and how much is passed back to the community or to the needy in other communities.

Research on Religion's Contribution Within the Voluntary Sector to Public Discourse About Collective Values

Much of the research that has been done in recent years on religion and giving has focused on the provision of services: how much the labor power given voluntarily to churches amounts to, where the money given to local churches goes, whether individual church members become involved in community activities, and whether religious organizations contribute significantly to helping the needy. These are worthwhile activities, and they need to be nurtured through better understanding. Research can sometimes foster that understanding. But a focus on services should not overshadow the other role that religious voluntarism and giving play in our society.

A century and a half ago Alexis de Tocqueville observed that Americans were already noteworthy for their participation in voluntary associations and that churches seemed to foster this participation. He thought this participation was terribly important, not only because it got things done but also because it strengthened the American spirit. It gave people a chance to interact with one another and to discuss their common problems and aspirations. It stood in the way of passiveness and totalitarianism; it preserved democracy.

That vision is still common among many Americans. Volunteers with whom I have conducted interviews tell me that voluntarism is an intrinsic good. It symbolizes freedom and initiative. It stands in the way of crass materialism and the impersonality of large government bureaucracy. Even if the government or corporations or the helping professions could provide all our services, they argue, we would benefit from people voluntarily helping others.

A look at the mass media tells us that voluntary acts of caring do indeed contribute to our public understandings of our society. Mother Teresa of Calcutta is a topic of insatiable fascination. Local newspapers sing the praises of unsung heroes who quietly devote their spare time to helping the handicapped, tutoring the mentally retarded, and supporting the bereaved.

When politicians want to put a human face on their efforts, they visit soup kitchens and pose with the children of homeless families. And when political candidates wish to flatter the American people, they call on us to be kinder and gentler, to espouse social kindness, and to engage in acts of charity that enrich and ennoble us all.

In more substantive ways, the work of nonprofit organizations also contributes immensely to the articulation of public values. These organizations provide an open space, as Max Stackhouse suggests in Chapter Two, in which values can be discussed. They constitute a vehicle for public expression that is neither bound by the constraints of government nor restricted by the demands of the profit-oriented marketplace. In recent decades the public debates that have arisen over civil rights, war and peace, gender and sexuality, abortion, and morality all attest to the importance of the voluntary sector and to the prominence of religion within this sector.

There are, however, indications that all this may be changing. The role of government has steadily expanded over the past half-century. It constitutes a larger share of the labor force and of the economy, takes a larger share of the average family's income, extends its regulatory and legislative arms into more and more of public and private life, and increasingly defines the social needs to which voluntary organizations are asked to respond. At the same time, the marketplace has also expanded. Services such as health care and counseling that were once provided by volunteers or nonprofit organizations have increasingly been incorporated into the service sector of the market economy. Both developments threaten the overall size and significance of the voluntary sector. In addition, the composition of the voluntary sector itself appears to be changing. Special-interest groups that can compete for government funding appear to have grown while other organizations, such as churches, which are precluded from receiving these monies, have declined (at least relatively). Moreover, within the religious sphere, entrepreneurialism and commercialism appear to be on the ascendancy at the expense of neighborhood values and emphases on genuine compassion and a concern for social justice.

These developments point to a need for research, first, on the changing composition and functions of the nonprofit sector. Aggregate indicators are needed on the number and size of religious and nonsectarian voluntary organizations and on trends in these indicators. Second, more information needs to be obtained on the interaction among religious and secular nonprofit organizations at the local and national levels. Third, more attention needs to be paid to the public pronouncements of these various organizations to determine their contribution to collective values. Fourth, the ways in which government, media, and the for-profit sector impinge on the activities of religious organizations are matters of continuing scholarly and practical concern. Finally, comparative research on other advanced industrial societies could play a useful role in putting the American pattern in perspective and predicting what the consequences of the current changes in the voluntary sector may be.

Research on the Ways in Which Giving Reinforces Religious Faith

Although the focus of this volume has been primarily on religious commitment as a source of giving, this relationship is also reciprocal: The experience of giving may contribute significantly to strengthening individuals' faith. An example will illustrate this possibility.

> In 1954 I met a black Baptist preacher whose God was real, alive, and active. Man, he was a worker for God and his people. One time is still fresh in my mind. Usually they had fifty or more at the Friday night prayer meeting, but this night we had only seven. Most nights he started on time, but this night he didn't. He told us why—that he was asking God in his prayer study if there wasn't some way God

could help them pay off their church's mortgage.
"You know, God," he said, "many of our church
members are dying off; isn't there any way you could
show those who have worked so hard that they
haven't worked in vain?" "Well," God said to him,
"this coming Sunday your church mortgage will be
paid off." God didn't say how, just that it would be
paid off. I was sitting in the front row and looking
up into his six-foot-seven face, saying to myself, who
does he think he's kidding. I never told him this. For
I am still ashamed. I never gave this another
thought until the middle of the next week. And
right then I knew I had to find out what had happened. I knew one older member of his church—a
very hard worker whose sugar diabetes made her
lose most of one foot. When I asked her what had
happened at the church, she let out a scream and
jumped up hollering: "You never saw such a sight in
your life. People starting to come down the aisles
laying their gifts upon the altar. To the sum of $785!
All they needed was $700. The pastor was so over-
come that all he could say was 'my cup runneth
over,' and with tears flowing down his face he sat
down unable to give his sermon.

I received this account in a letter one day from a total stranger,
an elderly man who had read something of mine in the newspaper and wrote to share an example of how big and wonderful
his God was to him. He concluded: "This letter isn't written in its
best language, but writing from the heart is what I tried to do."

How typical are such experiences? I suspect many people
have felt deeply blessed by the outpourings of kindness and
generosity they have seen in their churches, among their friends,
and in their neighborhoods. Religious literature, sermons, and
testimonials are filled with accounts of such experiences. Often
the logic involved is easy for the skeptic to pick apart. But for the
faithful, these accounts demonstrate the possibility of God working in human hearts, the value of someone praying earnestly in

faith, and the reality of caring and helping within human communities.

Surprisingly, we know little about these kinds of experiences. Research has focused more on the mechanics of giving and on the motivations leading people to respond to appeals for money than on the place these experiences may have in individuals' spiritual journeys. We need to pay more attention to these accounts — as narratives — as stories told and retold in the folklore of local congregations. And we need to understand better how they nurture the spark of faith and hope on which the spirit of charity thrives.

Chapter 14

Virginia A. Hodgkinson

The Future of Individual Giving and Volunteering: The Inseparable Link Between Religious Community and Individual Generosity

> The individual in society at once feels very close to and very far from other human beings, but always there remains the strongest of desires, to be related to one's fellow man. Human beings have devised no more successful means of achieving this relatedness than religion.
>
> Ashley Montague,
> *Man: His First Million Years*

The strength of voluntary religious organizations in the United States is their ability to establish community. In a nation consumed by materialism and excessive individualism, community is, at best, difficult. Alexis de Tocqueville recognized this in *Democracy in America* ([1835] 1956), and Robert Bellah and his colleagues confirmed it in *Habits of the Heart* (1985). Divided by a century and a half in the analyses, the point on which both agreed was that community is both elusive and critically important, and it is fostered by religious association. The findings of *From Belief to Commitment* (Hodgkinson, Weitzman, and Kirsch, 1988, chap. 5) were not so much the importance of theology but of the power of the meeting ground, an emanation of the theological teachings of most major religious traditions. The purposes of this chapter are to explore the importance of such a meeting ground in motivating people to act on or, in other words, to be moved to behave in positive ways to improve the condition of their fellow human beings, as exemplified in voluntary contributions of time and money, and to suggest to practitioners some recommendations designed to use and to strengthen congregational communities and individual giving and volunteering to all charitable causes, whether sacred or secular.

The United States is unique in that it is a nation that espouses freedom of religion as part of its social contract — the U.S. Constitution, most particularly in the First Amendment to the Constitution. In spite of recent trends toward more selfish materialistic values that seem to pervade our current society, the authors of this volume demonstrate amply that religion is of major importance to Americans and that Americans are among the most religious people in the world. The great moral movements in the United States — universal public education, civil rights, women's suffrage, child labor laws, and the labor movement itself — have been led by religious believers. Such religious associations tell the story of immigrant congregations — whether Jewish, Polish, Italian, Irish, Hispanic, or African-American — helping their own people to assimilate into society through religious involvement. But these congregations also encourage and participate in the larger public discussions about poverty, health care, the care of the elderly, nuclear war, international peace, the global economy, adult literacy, homelessness, poverty, and the care of children and families.

One of the primary meeting grounds of this nation is not city hall but the local congregation. As Max Stackhouse argues in Chapter Two, religious associations have created "public space" or "free zones" for the renewal of moral and ethical traditions. Actions on issues relating to soup kitchens, shelters for the homeless, care of battered women and children, counseling for families under siege, child care, international efforts to curb hunger and provide disaster relief were not initiated by government but to a large extent by people in congregations who provided support to local efforts, to their regional and national denominational programs, and to other charitable organizations working in these areas.

If a new progressive movement ushers in the twenty-first century, its birthplace will not be in political parties or government but in the local congregations and adjutant religious organizations of America. Why should it start there and not in political movements? I suggest that religious organizations provide the opportunity for communal gatherings that permit the kind of discourse necessary to create the possibility of a new national consensus on values that can recognize and reconcile the diversity and pluralism of our current society. These organizations provide the opportunity for spiritual empowerment, as Schervish notes in Chapter Four, and create among people the possibility of psychological transformation of "an empathic bond to others."

At a time when public meeting space has declined, congregations also provide other organizations with facilities in which to meet and may therefore play a major role in creating and maintaining a sense of community beyond the congregation. As noted in *From Belief to Commitment,* over nine out of ten congregations reported making their facilities available to groups within the congregation, and six out of ten congregations reported that their facilities were available to other organizations in the community (Hodgkinson, Weitzman, and Kirsch, 1988).

Recently, Lyle E. Schaller predicted that 10 percent (35,000) of all Protestant congregations would need to move to a new site, and a substantial proportion of the rest would need major renovations because many congregations reported that more people used the congregational facilities during the week than on Sunday morning. In fact, he estimates that the number of people using the facilities during the week translated into person hours may be three times that of Sunday. According to Schaller (1988, p. 37), the typical congregational program could include "the weekday nursery school, the adult day-care program, aerobic dance classes, Mothers' Morning Out, Alcoholics Anonymous, a divorce recovery workshop, a men's prayer breakfast at 7:00 A.M. every Monday, a latchkey program, adult literacy classes three evenings a week, committee meetings, the weekly meeting of Compassionate Friends, the Tuesday luncheon for senior citizens, the women's Bible study group that meets every Thursday afternoon, tutoring classes after school, the regular Tuesday evening Bible study, and a variety of other events and activities."

Schaller (1988) also comments on the fact that people who use church facilities and who are members of congregations no longer walk a few blocks to the local church but rather go to services in other neighborhoods. These trends in addition to other research suggest that community formation in the future may be even more reliant on voluntary religious associations than they were in the past because families tend to move more often in our increasingly mobile society. Schaller's estimates seem to confirm findings from *Giving and Volunteering in the United States* (Hodgkinson and Weitzman, 1988): that length of residence in a community did not affect individual giving and volunteering behavior, but that membership in a religious organization had a notable effect.

A similar relationship was also found in volunteering. From 45 to 56 percent of members between eighteen and sixty-four years of age volunteered, and 38 percent of members sixty-five years of age or older volunteered. Among nonmembers, from 28 to 37 percent of adults between eighteen and sixty-four years of age volunteered, and 26 percent of those sixty-five years of age or older volunteered. Members were 50 percent more likely than nonmembers to volunteer.

Congregations and Communities

Although a direct causal relationship cannot be established, the characteristics of members of religious organizations and the activities of religious congregations suggest that what is learned in religious institutions seems to have an impact on giving and volunteering generally. Over 85 percent of all individuals who contribute time to religious congregations are volunteers. In an average month, volunteers to religious organizations contribute approximately 107 million hours per month, of which 56 million hours are devoted to religious ministry and education, and 51 million hours are devoted to other activities in education, human services and welfare, health, the public benefit, arts and culture, international causes, and environmental quality improvement. According to analyses of individual giving and volunteering, individuals who are members of religious organizations are half again as likely to be both contributors and volunteers.

The basic tenet of most major religious traditions is that all human beings are equal. This may be one reason why 78 percent of American congregations report supporting international relief and development. Recognition of human equality may also explain why congregations in the United States are the largest supporters of the homeless, the hungry, the children (day care), and the elderly. In most religious traditions, these groups are to be given special care. According to our survey on individual giving and volunteering, individuals who were members of religious groups were the most likely to make contributions to human services, youth groups, health organizations, and educational organizations. The biblical statement "Man cannot live by bread alone" suggests that people need bread, but once they have had that, they need spiritual fulfillment. Research in psychology and sociology has shown that moral understanding does not predict moral behavior (Hodgkinson, 1990) but that community, through religious association, may. I say, "may," only because psychologists and sociologists have not studied religious association adequately; in fact, Sigmund Freud, in psychology, and Auguste Comte, the founder of sociology, thought that their new areas of knowledge would liberate people from religious belief and provide them with the kind of rational knowledge needed to create better people and societies rationally and exclusive of belief systems. Their underlying hypothesis, never proven, was that such truths would change behavior.

To motivate means "to move to action." Along with reason, emotion is important in convincing individuals to act. Hume had it right when he talked about "moral sentiments," for it is not enough to conclude rationally that poverty for most people is a social and not a moral condition; one must be *emotionally* convinced that it is a social condition in order to move toward improving that condition. When one's reason and emotion are given reality in the company and consensus of others and bolstered by faith, action is possible. All sorts of studies provide evidence to this effect. Let me just mention the findings of a few that are very suggestive of the connection between the community of congregations and moral action.

In a Red Cross study, from 45 to 64 percent of staff and various volunteer personnel reported volunteering to a church or religious group. The percentage was highest for field service chairpeople (64 percent) and chapter volunteer leaders (61 percent). Other major areas of volunteering were service organizations, youth groups, hospitals, and health organizations (American Red Cross, 1988).

Local Heroes (Berkowitz, 1987) reports that one of the major similarities among leaders who established new voluntary movements or organizations in communities was that leaders involved in social causes were also more likely to be attached to religious organizations. Although Bill Berkowitz admits that a "direct connection between spiritual or religious background and community accomplishment is unproven," he does conclude that "the evidence is suggestive enough to make one wonder more about the linkage between spirituality, religious life, and community work" (p. 318).

According to Oliner and Oliner (1988), although rescuers of Jews during the Holocaust were as likely to report that they were members of religious organizations as nonrescuers (90 percent), rescuers were far more likely to interpret Christian values as a belief in the equality of all people. Although the differences between religious membership and observance did not differ significantly between rescuers and nonrescuers, bystanders were "significantly less religious in their early years," and their fathers were "significantly less religious than the fathers of rescuers." Furthermore, "rescuers did differ from others in the interpretation of religious teaching and religious commitment, which emphasized the common humanity of all people" (p. 156).

In a study of the varieties of religious presence in Hartford, Connecticut, sociologists Roozen, McKinney, and Carroll (1984) chose the local congregation as the most important unit of study because they believe this institution is fundamental to understanding major religious traditions. They argue that local congregations are important for several reasons: They are important economic and social institutions, particularly as they provide sustenance for members and help to give meaning to people's lives; they provide members with a "visible presence" in the community; and they provide an intermediate ground between the family and large bureaucratic structures, such as corporations and government. Furthermore, these scholars assert that they recognize the importance of congregations to "the larger religious tradition," its potential for community service and influence, and its valuable role in serving as a mediator "with respect to the larger society and its institutions and structures" (pp. 26–28).

"Community" in its ideal sense has been a fundamental myth and ideal in America. From John Winthrop's vision of a "City upon a Hill" in his sermon aboard the *Arbella* in 1630 through the experimental communities, such as Brook Farm and the Oneida community, in the nineteenth century to the communes of the 1960s and 1970s, Americans have experimented with visionary communities. Not many have survived, but they typified either new groups or old groups acting out their visions of the creation of ideal communities during periods of societal upheaval. Those new communities that did survive sprang primarily from religious movements, whether the evangelical movements of the first and second awakenings, the Church of Jesus Christ of Latter-day Saints (the Mormons), or the more modern Moral Majority (Fitzgerald, 1987). Anthropologists have found that religious organizations provide coherence in communities by bringing people together, motivating them, and encouraging them to interact collectively with a divine being (Montague, 1958, p. 167).

Many social and religious commentators report on the decline of religion and the increasing secularization of social institutions, as well as the increasing privatization of individuals within society. While there seems to be a trend in individuals shopping around for congregations rather than remaining in the religious denomination of their parents, Americans have changed denominations throughout their history. Furthermore, the decline in religious membership, though real, is not major when taken in context with trends in the past. Though church membership declined to 65 percent for adults in 1988 from a high point of 76 percent in 1947 (Gallup Organization, 1987), one finds that current church membership is still amazingly high even with some membership decline; and church attendance has remained steady over the past decade (Gallup Organization, 1987). While denominational loyalties are changing and religious membership and belief are becoming more privatized (Roof and McKinney, 1987), the congregation is still the most common social group where people find fellowship, seek and find common ground in their beliefs, and develop individual and communal behavior to serve other people and communities.

Finally, religious institutions foster philanthropy and voluntarism, both within their own communities and generally for other causes, including community and public service. As several of the authors of this volume have noted, a constant source of voluntarism to assist in solving community problems through a plethora of organizations—whether secular or religiously sponsored—has emerged from congregations. As Emerson Andrews (1953, p. 85) stated: "Religion is the mother of philanthropy." And more recently, as Michael O'Neill (1989, p. 20) has stated: "Religion is a large and important part of the nonprofit sector and has given birth to many other nonprofit institutions: health, education, social service, international assistance, advocacy, mutual assistance, and even some cultural and grantmaking institutions. Directly and indirectly religion has been the major formative influence on America's nonprofit sector."

In fact, part of the movement attributed to the secularization of voluntary organizations may be the increasing practice of religious groups to incorporate separately new organizations to meet social needs, as noted by Clydesdale, Wood, and

Wuthnow in this volume. The trend toward secularization, through creating separate new organizations, may actually indicate more of a legal, structural decision than lack of religious support. Each separate incorporation creates more "free space," to use Stackhouse's term, and allows for multidenominational and individual support for organizations that serve public needs. Organizations such as World Vision and Habitat for Humanity that provide assistance to the homeless and the hungry both at home and abroad probably get more support by being interdenominationally inspired rather than the organization of a single denomination or congregation. In fact, these separately organized but religiously inspired organizations provide the opportunity for consensus among many religious groups on issues of common concern. In their transmission of religious and moral traditions that lead to stability and cohesion in society, religious institutions teach about the traditions of giving and voluntary service. According to Moberg (1984, p. 156), "Religious duties of giving and the increasing consciousness of churches' social responsibilities have undoubtedly affected charitable giving to secular as well as religious welfare. The functions of the church as a social institution extend far beyond the limitations of its own direct activities."

The themes that emerge from this discussion suggest that practitioners in religious and secular organizations can enhance their effectiveness in understanding and building community by recognizing and engaging in more collaboration on issues of common concern.

Building Community

The congregation, today, is perhaps the major social institution that transmits spiritual, cultural, and social values to a majority of Americans. This is particularly true in a nation characterized by geographical mobility, by a decline in the function of the family in transmitting moral values due to the increasing incidence of families with single heads or two working parents, and by the lack of attention and perhaps inability of schools to teach ethical and moral traditions and values. While the weakening of both schools and families increases the burden on religious institutions to transmit moral values, there is increasing evidence from research that those people who are more religious (about 30 percent of the adult population) are more active in their communities; serve in leadership roles in schools, hospitals, other voluntary organizations, and their communities; vote more frequently; and are more generous with their time and money to both their churches and other organizations (Yankelovich, Skelly & White, Inc., 1986; Hodgkinson, Weitzman, and Kirsch, 1988).

Congregations help to build community cohesion, provide a pool of leadership for community service, contribute to the development of institutions to solve community problems, and improve the community's quality of life. In a report about how congregations play a role in community development (SEEDCO, 1988), it was found that congregations, including both clergy and lay people, play several important roles: They are conveners of people to discuss common values and to develop visions of building better communities; they provide the confidence and motivation to improve the community; as legitimators, they lend moral force to community programs by participating in them; as advocates, they help support implementation of community agendas and influence such agendas through the leadership of their lay members; they build partnerships through the clergy and lay members through their various associations with community groups, voluntary associations and institutions, neighborhood associations, advisory committees to government political associations, and business associations; they serve as sustainers, stewards, and trustees to community efforts; they also provide leaders and managers and serve as resource providers by donating to community projects.

Numerous examples abound of congregational and denominational leadership in providing partnerships or in creating new programs to foster development in many communities both at home and abroad. Among the more famous organizations is Habitat for Humanity, which provides housing and home ownership through volunteer work and contributions both in the United States and in Third World countries. A recent report (SEEDCO, 1988) published by the Council on Foundations provides several other examples of congregations participating in various ways in community development. These include the Holy Name Parish, which helped form the Holy Name Parish Corporation to undertake activities in community revitalization in Omaha, Nebraska; a coalition of congregations that formed a new organization, Eastside Community Investments, to provide affordable housing for low- and moderate-income residents in eastern Indianapolis; the partnership between labor unions, congregations and synagogues; the Episcopal and Catholic dioceses; and the Connecticut Citizen Action Group that established the Naugatuck Valley Project to offset unemployment caused by plant closings. More than fifty-three churches and synagogues participated in the founding and support of this project.

In another report, Peirce and Steinbach (1987) review the growth and success of community development organizations that were started in the 1960s with the idea that community residents could "define and control development in their own communities." The authors state that although this was a "radical" idea in the 1960s, after twenty-five years and the establishment of thousands of community development corporations, the idea is the "one element of the 'experiment' that is widely regarded as an unqualified success" (p. 12).

Peirce and Steinbach found that congregations, religious denominational organizations, coalitions of organizations, and separately established religious organizations, such as World Vision, were an important part of the development from the beginning:

> Regional and national religious councils, led by such organizations as the Catholic Church's Campaign for Human Development and the Presbyterian Self-Development of Peoples Fund, have committed millions of dollars of financial support for organizing and projects. Thousands of local congregations, including some affluent suburban churches and synagogues, have contributed staff

services, volunteers, meeting space, and equip-
ment, or prevailed upon their members to fill collection plates for community programs and
projects.

The greatest asset religious groups bring to
the CDC movement may be their almost universal
presence, penetrating every nook and cranny of
American communities. Congregations have become especially important community development building blocks in underclass neighborhoods, where traditional bastions of organizing—
the unions, ethnic associations, and political
clubs—have fled along with middle class residents
[Peirce and Steinbach, 1987, p. 64].

Here, a secular movement that was initiated to improve
low-income communities, owes much of its success to the "meeting ground," the "building block" of these communities—the
congregation.

Another more recent partnership, the National Association of Interfaith Voluntary Caregivers, originally supported by
a grant of the Robert Wood Johnson Foundation, was founded in
an effort to find more humane and cost-saving means to serve
the elderly and disabled in our society. In a few years, these
programs have been established in congregations and generated thousands of volunteers who provide services to the elderly,
the disabled, and the very ill; such as those with AIDS. Such
groups work in partnership with congregations, health agencies, and public agencies, but the source of volunteer and program commitment is congregations.

A few years ago, the Council on Foundations formed a
study group, the Religious Philanthropy Program, to help religious leaders and grantmakers explore common ground in
solving community problems. The separation of church and
state has led a majority of grantmaking organizations to exclude
support of religious organizations and their activities from their
missions. The development of this meeting ground led to the
establishment of the Forum on Religion and the Public Life,

with the following four purposes: "(1) to promote awareness of the historic role of religious philanthropy in American public life; (2) to serve as a link for grantmakers with a common concern for religion and public life; (3) to discuss the visions and concerns of these grantmakers with other members of the Council on Foundations, regional associations of grantmakers, and leaders in the wider world of corporate philanthropy; and (4) to encourage grantmakers to form partnerships in the interest of the common good and the improvement of public life." This forum was established in recognition of the fact that the largest source of giving is religious giving and that the chief focus of religions is not religious, but the welfare of the wider community.

One of the best ways to achieve community development, to improve service to the community, to serve those in need, and to improve the quality of life in the community is for all organizations, secular and religious, to recognize the contributions that congregations make in providing a moral vision and moral conscience for our society and in instilling, by practice and example, principles of voluntary service and philanthropy. Far more recognition needs to be given to these institutions and their importance in sustaining philanthropic institutions and democratic values. Therefore, my recommendations to practitioners are as follows:

1. Before reinventing the wheel, look to the network of congregations locally or denominational groups regionally or nationally who are probably already working on your issues. Religious organizations may be a source of volunteers, support, or potential partners. They provide a large pool of people associated with all kinds of community, governmental, and business organizations. Using their talents to identify networks already in existence or to help build new networks and to marshal new resources can provide strength and support for important projects and causes at the local level.

2. Involve leaders of religious organizations and congregations on advisory and program committees. Whether you

are involved with a local United Way, youth group, social service agency, environmental group, or a local grantmaker, securing participation from congregational clergy and lay people can lead to increased support and resources. Religious organizations are not afraid to advocate for community needs.

3. Encourage interdenominational participation in the solving of community problems. Coalitions of congregations and other voluntary organizations have proven their great effectiveness in attacking some of the most difficult problems of society. Congregations can be great advocates to advance moral issues, whether in attacking problems of hunger and homelessness or in advancing the dignity of all people. In partnership, they can provide the motivation for people for "principled behavior," as Stackhouse mentions.

Religious association is capable of inspiring social reform and experimenting with meeting human needs. The experiments of religious organizations in housing, community development, and international relief and development are but a few of the profound recent examples available in social reform. If we forget the spirit and the moral vision that congregations can bring to these problems, or forget the importance of religious organizations in creating the motivation for commitment and service, as Stackhouse warns, our society could lose its "inner coherence because the transcendent foundation is lost."

Acknowledging the separation of church and state as a fundamental freedom and a glory of our nation is very important. Just as significant, however, is the role of congregations in transmitting moral traditions and in renewing community through the voluntary service and contributions of their members. Separation of church and state does not mean that congregations have no role in society. They, in fact, serve the public good by providing a moral tradition. Not understanding that distinction and not recognizing the important role of religious institutions in providing and transmitting democratic freedoms, in providing their members with the opportunity to participate in solving community problems that extend to all humanity is to neglect one of the richest sources of human, financial, and moral support available for the success of most social and community projects. Falsely interpreting the meaning of the separation of church and state can only lead to further privatization of these important institutions that preserve moral traditions for all societal institutions—both religious and secular. Religious institutions also provide the space for discourse on moral issues where there is no consensus; see, for example, Wood's description in Chapter Eight of the process that a mainline religious institution has developed to discuss abortion.

Increasing Individual Giving and Volunteering

From Belief to Commitment (Hodgkinson, Weitzman, and Kirsch, 1988) clearly demonstrates that voluntary time and contributions given by members of congregations provide the major sustenance of each congregation. *Giving and Volunteering in the United States* (Hodgkinson and Weitzman, 1988), along with the results of an earlier national survey *The Charitable Behavior of Americans* (Yankelovich, Skelly, & White, Inc., 1986) demonstrates that charitable giving and individual generosity to all charities is determined by religious membership and involvement. In light of weakening traditions in families and schools, the one great institution that bears the brunt of transmitting moral and democratic traditions is the local congregation. It is a terrible responsibility, because if it fails, the whole system could fail without alternative traditions. What congregations teach about the shared responsibilities of individuals to community is very influential in determining the involvement of people in community and nation. Through various proposals about national service, Congress and the administration are also realizing that neglect of service to community could weaken the fragile social contract of our democracy.

What functions do congregations perform that hold our mobile nation together? They provide the spiritual and moral underpinnings that motivate individuals to support the community. But lest we wax too optimistic about congregations and their transmittal of moral and democratic traditions, I suggest that most congregations and their denominational organizations have failed to train their clergy, and thus their congregations, in the meaning of stewardship or charity as love of others and responsibility to community. After demonstrating that congregations are the primary meeting ground in the United States, I must assert that in most congregations, there has been no substantial increase in per capita giving and volunteering in America over the past thirty years; in some denominations, there has been a decline. The reason for this decline seems to be the declining emphasis on the part of denominations to transmit the tradition of charity and stewardship and a concomitant failure to train clergy in the importance of this tradition. In Chapter Thirteen of this volume, Robert Wuthnow refers to stewardship in the Christian tradition as narratives about human compassion and generosity, and in Chapter Seven on Jewish giving, Rimor and Tobin refer to *tzedakah*, or the tradition of helping others.

Stewardship relates to an emphasis on social justice as well as compassion and community in black churches, as Emmett Carson describes in Chapter Eleven. It encompasses spiritual life and renewal for the Evangelicals as well as the Mormons, as noted by Clydesdale in Chapter Nine and May in Chapter Ten. In each of these studies of various denominations and racial and ethnic religious traditions, generosity to all causes, including religious causes, is found in ritual observance and communal activity. Rimor and Tobin conclude that "philanthropic behavior is an expression of religious identity" and that increasing peoples' "religious participation increases their philanthropic behavior." These behaviors reinforce each other. Making better givers and increasing religious and communal behavior increases individual giving to other secular organizations.

If this lack of attention to the traditions of giving time, talent, and money is continued, it will not only mean less individual giving and volunteering to religious organizations but also a decline in giving and volunteering to secular, private, and charitable organizations and to publicly governed agencies and institutions. In other words, in spite of the real increases in individual income, education, and mobility over the past thirty years, the failure of parallel increased generosity and time to community must rest with the neglect of congregations to teach important moral traditions and to help activate and support individual efforts to improve the human condition. This failure on the part of religious organizations to recognize the importance of stewardship over the last few decades has affected denominational leadership and no longer is an important part of the education of religious leaders. What is preserved, fortunately, as demonstrated in *From Belief to Commitment* (Hodgkinson, Weitzman, and Kirsch, 1988), is the enthusiasm and commitment of lay people in spite of religious leadership.

In case you read my assertions as an indictment, let me summarize some trends that led me to these conclusions. In a recent study (Ronsvalle and Ronsvalle, 1988), John and Sylvia Ronsvalle of empty tomb, inc., report on trends in per capita individual contributions to thirty-three denominations representing 72 percent of church membership in the mid-1980s. They found that from 1968 to 1985, average disposable per capita income in the United States increased by $2,511, or 31 percent, in real dollars after taxes and inflation, but that per capita contributions to these denominations grew by an average of $49, or 2 percent of disposable income. While individual disposable income in real terms increased 31 percent over the study period, member giving increased only 20 percent. From 1968 to 1986, nearly three-quarters of the denominations studied showed a decline in per capita membership giving, and per member contributions declined by nearly 9 percent. Furthermore, benevolences declined in real terms by 23 percent over the same period.

There are more than a hundred denominations in the United States and many nondenominational and independent churches. Studies of per capita giving in constant dollars have shown real growth in the 1960s and 1980s, with almost no growth during the 1970s. From 1960 to 1987, per capita giving by individuals increased from $165 to $281 in constant 1982 dollars. However, as a percentage of total personal income, individual contributions were highest at 2.29 percent in 1963, dropped to a low point of 1.77 percent of total personal income in 1979, and grew in real terms to 2.14 percent in 1987, still lower than they were in 1963 but appreciably higher than they were in the 1970s (Hodgkinson and Weitzman, 1989).

For the more than thirty-four years that *Giving USA* (AAFRC Trust for Philanthropy) has been published, the proportion of total contributions given to religion has remained at approximately half of total giving, including foundations and corporations, and at least two-thirds of total individual giving. National surveys on giving in 1985 and 1988 confirm these estimates (Yankelovich, Skelly, & White, Inc., 1985; Hodgkinson and Weitzman, 1988). Furthermore, nearly half of the activities and contributions of congregations were devoted to the whole range of human service activities (Hodgkinson, Weitzman, and Kirsch, 1988).

Throughout the last four decades, the ratio between religious giving and other giving has remained remarkably steady. This suggests that the future of increased giving to most other charities depends on the ability of religious congregations to increase giving and volunteering generally. Two-thirds of all giving from other charities comes from contributors who also give to religious congregations (see Chapter Five). There can be no clearer indication that for the most part religious givers sustain giving to most other charities.

Even though we do not fully understand what motivates people to give generously, studies reveal that people who take religion seriously participate more in their communities and give and volunteer in higher proportions both to their congregations and to other charities. One of the secrets is probably community or the common purpose shared by others. Those three out of ten adults who report that spiritual goals are absolutely essential personal goals are on average nearly three times as generous as other adults. Those adults who have no religious connections are half as likely to give money or time to any charitable causes—sacred or secular—as those who do. Like it or not, there does not seem to be a secular moral tradition that has the influence to generate such generous behavior among large segments of the population. For whatever reasons, those members of religious congregations who internalize and find meaning in religious moral traditions are most likely to give.

The question then becomes how or why has religious giving not increased as a percentage of income over the past thirty years and thus all charitable giving remained at 2 percent of personal income. While some real increases in giving did occur during the 1980s, offsetting some real losses in growth during the inflationary years of the 1970s, when giving as a percent of personal income dropped below 2 percent, total giving as a percentage of personal income was at its highest point in the 1960s. The answer may lie in the decline of transmitting the meaning of stewardship to the current generation and the lack of clergy education in stewardship typified by the fact that courses in stewardship are no longer taught in theological schools. While presidents of theological seminaries will state that stewardship is included in various courses, what is not emphasized as important by the leadership or by the community can soon be a good tradition lost.

For particular religious denominations, the loss of understanding about stewardship, which involves the use of time, talent, and wealth of individuals to serve community, has resulted in dramatic declines in giving and volunteering and brought about a crisis. This is particularly true among American Catholics. When findings of one study (Yankelovich, Skelly, & White, Inc., 1986) showed that giving as a percentage of income for all causes by Catholics was lower than for other denominations, Andrew Greeley and Bishop William McManus (1987) conducted a study to explore those findings. They found that per capita giving by Catholics in the 1980s was half what it was in the 1970s. Although both studies gave several reasons for the decline, one of their major findings was the decline of community typified in the closing of Catholic schools and other organizations in the church. They also found that Catholics were no longer poor but middle class and that, for the most part, Catholic thinking was still immersed in the philosophy of helping poor, ethnic Catholic immigrants. The findings of Hodgkinson and Weitzman (1988) confirmed the low level of giving by Catholics as well as the even lower level of volunteering. While most religious denominations showed a higher proportion of volunteers than the national average of 45 percent, only 39 percent of Catholics reported volunteering. Catholics who volunteered gave 1.9 percent of their household income to charity compared to 1.0 percent for Catholics who did not volunteer. This is compared to an average household giving of 2.9 percent among Protestants who volunteered compared to 1.6 percent among Protestants who did not volunteer. Forty-seven percent of all Protestants reported volunteering compared to 39 percent of Catholics. According to Hodgkinson, Weitzman, and Kirsch (1988), typical Protestant congregations had 400 members, while typical Catholic congregations had more than 2,000 members. Without activities to involve a large proportion of lay people, Catholic giving and volunteering to all causes, sacred or secular, has resulted in a precipitous decline over the past decade.

Bishop McManus, in Chapter Six, attributes part of this decline to a lack of understanding of the real meaning of stewardship. He attributes some of the reluctance to give to the church's engaging professional fund-raisers two decades ago, fund-raisers whose primary goal was the dollar goal and not the spiritual reasons for giving. In Chapter Three, Peter Hall also attributes some of this loss to a lack of understanding or compassion that permeates religious traditions. Protestant leaders of theological seminaries report that stewardship is no longer taught in seminaries because lay members of congregations think that churches only want money. What this reveals is a loss of the meaning of stewardship even among religious leaders. The meaning of stewardship is defined in *Baker's Dictionary of Christian Ethics* as "a spiritual principle and Biblical teaching. . . . Properly understood, the principle includes all of life; all men's actions and attitudes; personality and personal influence; in money matters, the acquisition, handling, spending, saving, investing, giving, and final disposition; use of the land, resources, and tools; one's profession, job or place of service; education and the use of education; one's worship, the witness of his life, his personal testimony, his purpose and goals in life" (Moore, 1973, p. 649).

Stewardship involves people in relation to their world and age as well as community behavior. It involves their spiritual responsibility and behavior to all human beings regardless of race, sex, or nation. Stewardship also applies to the use of church resources for its own operations and contributions to others, its responsibility for the use of the land, natural resources, and the whole environment. In short, "stewardship prompts one to ask: What is God's purpose for me in my specific interpersonal relationships, my use of resources, my attitude toward and my use of this created universe" (Moore, 1973, p. 649).

The hope for increasing voluntary giving and volunteering lies in the recognition of the importance of the religious traditions of charitable giving and voluntary service for religious organizations, as well as to the larger community. A tradition untaught is a tradition unrenewed. The loss of such a tradition could profoundly affect community service generally.

A heartening result of the study of this decline in Catholic giving is leading to further study of this trend by the U.S. Conference of Catholic Bishops. Archbishop Murphy of Seattle chaired an ad hoc committee on stewardship, and Bishop McManus also served on that committee. After more than a year of study, they recommended and the U.S. Conference of Catholic Bishops voted affirmatively to issue a pastoral letter on stewardship in 1991. The reason the bishops focused on stewardship is that they found that with the decline of Catholic giving, they no longer had the financial resources to do the work the church was currently doing or to meet new needs. The good news about a pastoral letter on stewardship is that such an action will support further study on the neglected theology of stewardship, which will include its full meaning, including time, talent, wealth, the use of natural resources, and the ecology of the earth necessary to sustain and preserve all of life and creation.

There is some evidence that when Catholic lay members recognize the needs and can participate in meeting those needs that contributions can be measurably increased. Catholic congregations and dioceses that have recognized the needs have moved more aggressively to increase giving among Catholics with great success. Between 1987 and 1988, some fifty-one dioceses launched fund-raising campaigns and increased giving overall by nearly 6 percent. But many dioceses increased their giving from 10 to 23 percent in one year. Much of this effort has been achieved by involving lay people in the needs of the mission of the church and allowing them to become personally involved in providing leadership to provide needed resources to the church and its work.

Stewardship is very personal; without engaging individuals actively, stewardship or trusteeship can decline. Research shows that there is both an environment and a capacity to increase giving and volunteering in the United States. In one study (Hodgkinson and Weitzman, 1988), 75 percent of Americans responded that it is an individual's responsibility to give and volunteer to help others. But when asked how many hours a week they thought they should volunteer or what percentage of income they should try to give, half of the respondents said that they did not know or had no answer.

INDEPENDENT SECTOR launched its "Give Five" program to set a standard for giving and volunteering to address this issue. Acknowledging that tithing is still a special standard, this giving standard developed by a national task force composed of leaders from voluntary organizations, including religious organizations, corporations, and foundations, gives all Americans a reachable goal to strive for. It states that all of us should volunteer five hours a week and give 5 percent of our income to causes of our choice and to give something back to our community.

The adoption of such a standard is getting support from some religious and voluntary organizations nationwide. The results for organizations and communities could mean substantially increased giving and volunteering. For example, in 1988, if just the 25 percent of Americans who thought that they should give 5 percent or more of their income to charitable causes had met their goal (rather than the 9 percent who actually did), total individual giving would have been triple what it was. Thus, setting standards — and understanding stewardship — could motivate people to share and to participate at greater levels, thus leading to improved quality of life and participation in all communities.

The Lilly Endowment, Inc., one of the few major large foundations that has a program to support religious studies, has launched a program to support action projects and research studies designed to assist congregations in community involvement and service programs and to encourage and support scholars interested in looking at religious organizations and philanthropy. Robert Lynn, former vice president for religious studies at the endowment and member of the INDEPENDENT SECTOR Research Committee, is the director of a new program on faith and stewardship at the Bangor Seminary. After *The Charitable Behavior of Americans* (Yankelovich, Skelly, & White, Inc., 1986) was published by INDEPENDENT SECTOR, the Council of Jewish Federations cosponsored a new project on Jewish giving as part of the North American Jewish Data Bank at the Center for Jewish Studies, the Graduate Center of the City University of New York. Such new research activities among religious faiths in the United States, including the research agenda provided by Robert Wuthnow, may help us to better understand the tradition of philanthropic giving and help us to increase the practice of stewardship.

Stewardship in its full meaning includes the preservation of the earth. According to Hodgkinson, Weitzman, and Kirsch (1988), congregations are least likely to be involved in environmental issues. One of the four major reasons that individuals give for contributing to religious organizations is a feeling of obligation. The only other type of charity where obligation is stated as a major reason for giving is environmental organizations. This reason for giving to the environment is stated by both members and nonmembers of environmental institutions and particularly by young adults eighteen to twenty-four years of age. Recognizing the importance of the environment as part of the meaning of stewardship will even be more important in the decades ahead as nations attempt to cooperate on environmental issues globally. Not recognizing the importance of such issues could lead to some decline in church membership.

The U.S. Conference of Catholic Bishops has included

the ecology of the earth as part of its definition of stewardship. At the first conference in Indiana in 1987, the North American Conference on Christianity and Ecology (NACCE), a group of environmentalists and leaders from several Christian de-nominations met to discuss the theology of environmental is-sues. This conference has led NACCE to develop some consen-sus on the importance of preserving the environment as part of the religious tradition, and NACCE will conduct workshops and forums for denominations in the United States. It is also work-ing with the United Nations in building a "common cause and creed" with other religious traditions. Pat Stone of *Mother Earth News* wrote an article reporting on what this new conference had to say about the power of religious organizations in creating constructive social action on the environment:

> Can the eco-Christian impact have a significant impact on our planet's health? Potentially, yes. In the 18th century the American Revolution was preached from the pulpits. A hundred years later, the churches helped teach people to address slav-ery as a moral and religious issue instead of simply an economic one. And two decades ago, Martin Luther King, Jr., used religious arguments and aid to motivate the civil rights movement of the '60s.
>
> Such instances remind us all that the church, though slow to stir, *can* make a mighty impact when awakened into action [Stone, 1989, p. 79].

Understanding that giving and volunteering emerge from spiritual commitment and experience in community, which are most commonly found in religious congregations, leads to the following recommendations:

1. The education of clergy should include knowledge about stewardship and the importance of narrations about char-ity and the standards of giving, similar to the tithe in the Old Testament.
2. Education of our children should include teaching about

religious traditions and voluntary associations and their importance in preserving democratic traditions. Teaching these traditions does not mean advocating a particular religious group, but it does mean acknowledging that freedom of religion in this country has preserved democratic traditions and that many of the major accomplishments of this nation, including the establishment of higher education, the civil rights movement, and women's suffrage, emerged from religious movements.

3. Scholars, particularly in the social and behavioral sciences, ought not to reject summarily, but rather study the relationship between religious membership and human motivation in voting, community service, public service, and mental health. Examining the assumptions of their disciplinary founders through research could measurably increase our understanding of the contributions or impediments that religion represents in establishing, preserving, and renewing our moral traditions; in transmitting moral values; and in creating cooperative human efforts through advocacy and human service.

4. Practitioners ought to understand how and where their supporters come from. As the Red Cross found out and other types of charitable organizations will probably also discover if they study the demographic profiles of their givers and volunteers, most secular charities are beneficiaries of members of religious congregations who learned the meaning of community participation, serving human needs, and improving the quality of life. Recognizing this connection can improve and expand networks and partnerships to serve worthwhile efforts. It may also help increase giving and volunteering to all causes.

It is easy to speak to the converted. As I began this chapter with the observation of a distinguished anthropologist about the importance of religion to the development of human civilization, I end it with the observations of a renowned psychologist in what must have been a most surprising and disturbing acceptance speech as the newly elected president of the American

Psychological Association. In 1975, Donald T. Campbell argued that psychologists ought to show more respect for traditional belief systems in order to preserve the structures of advanced civilization. He argued that "psychology may be contributing to the undermining of the retention" of the very moral and religious traditions that are needed to preserve complex civilizations, and

> that behavioral scientists who are sophisticated in their own field lapse into an epistemic arrogance and literalism when dealing with religious claims for truth. Because such behavioral scientists no longer believe in what they assume to be the literal referents of religious words, they lose sight of the possibility that these words refer to truths for which there is no language, which must be metaphorically or figuratively expressed if it is to be communicated at all. They hold up for religious discourse the requirements for a direct realism, a literal verticality even though they may recognize that this is impossible for science itself (Campbell, 1975, p. 1120).

Finally, Campbell warned that modern psychologists foster narcissism and individual selfishness at a time when cooperation and altruistic behavior are needed to preserve social evolution through complex societies. He asserted that scientists should give far greater attention to the study of the development of such belief systems and further claimed "that there can be profound social system wisdom in the belief systems our social tradition has provided us with" (p. 1123). Such statements from a distinguished scientist give hope that the religious traditions that have inspired members of the human community for several centuries may continue to motivate individuals to love, to feel compassion, to engage in community, and to behave generously to others for centuries to come. Our understanding, support, and recognition of the importance of these traditions will help all charitable causes — sacred and secular — to increase voluntary service and generous giving. Most of us need to pay heed to and provide support for traditions that have strengthened this nation's democratic traditions and provided so many Americans with the moral tradition of generosity and commitment to humanitarian causes.

References

AAFRC Trust for Philanthropy. *Giving USA*. (Various editions.) New York: AAFRC Trust for Philanthropy.

American Red Cross. *Volunteer 2000 Study*. Vol. 1. Washington, D.C.: American Red Cross, 1988.

Andrews, E. *Attitudes Toward Giving*. New York: Bureau of Social Research, 1953.

Bellah, R., and others. *Habits of the Heart*. Berkeley: University of California Press, 1985.

Berkowitz, B. *Local Heroes*. Lexington, Mass.: Heath, 1987.

Campbell, D. T. "On the Conflicts Between Biological and Social Evolution and Between Psychology and Moral Tradition." *American Psychologist*, Dec. 1975, *30*, 1103–1126.

de Tocqueville, A. *Democracy in America*. New York: New American Library, 1956. (Originally published 1835.)

Fitzgerald, A. *Cities on a Hill*. New York: Simon and Schuster, 1987.

Forum on Religion and Public Life. Washington, D.C.: The Religious Philanthropy Program of the Council on Foundations, 1989.

Gallup Organization. *Religion in America*. Report 259. Princeton, N.J.: Gallup Organization, Apr. 1987.

Greeley, A., and McManus, W. *Catholic Contributions: Sociology and Policy*. Chicago: Thomas More Press, 1987.

Hodgkinson, V. A. *Dimensions of the Independent Sector: A Statistical Profile*. New York: Foundation Center, 1990.

Hodgkinson, V. A., and Weitzman, M. S. *Giving and Volunteering in the United States*. Findings from a National Survey conducted by the Gallup Organization. Washington, D.C.: INDEPENDENT SECTOR, 1988.

Hodgkinson, V. A., and Weitzman, M. S. *Dimensions of the Indepen-*

dent Sector: A Statistical Profile. Washington, D.C.: INDEPEN-
DENT SECTOR, 1989.

Hodgkinson, V. A., Weitzman, M. S., and Kirsch, A. D. *From Belief
to Commitment: The Activities and Finances of Religious Congregations in the United States.* Washington, D.C.: INDEPENDENT
SECTOR, 1988.

Moberg, D. O. *The Church as a Social Institution.* (2nd ed.) Grand
Rapids, Mich.: Baker Book House, 1984.

Montague, A. *Man: His First Million Years.* New York: New American Library, 1958.

Moore, M. D. "Stewardship." In C. F. Henry (ed.), *Baker's Dictionary
of Christian Ethics.* Grand Rapids, Mich.: Baker Book House,
1973.

Oliner, S. P., and Oliner, P. M. *The Altruistic Personality: Rescuers of
Jews in Nazi Europe.* New York: Free Press, 1988.

O'Neill, M. *The Third America: The Emergence of the Nonprofit Sector
in the United States.* San Francisco: Jossey-Bass, 1989.

Peirce, N. R., and Steinbach, C. F. *Corrective Capitalism: The Rise of
America's Community Development Corporations.* A Report to the
Ford Foundation. New York: The Ford Foundation, 1987.

Ronsvalle, J., and Ronsvalle, S. "The Comparison of the Growth
in Church Contributions with the United States Per Capita
Income." Paper presented at the INDEPENDENT SECTOR
Spring Research Forum, Chicago, 1989.

Roof, W. C., and McKinney, W. *American Mainline Religion.* New
Brunswick, N.J.: Rutgers University Press, 1987.

Roozen, D., McKinney, W., and Carroll, J. *Varieties of the Religious
Presence.* New York: Pilgrim Press, 1984.

Schaller, L. E. "The Coming Boom in Church Construction."
Clergy Journal, Feb. 1988, *16*, 36–37.

SEEDCO. *Religious Institutions as Actors in Community-Based Economic Development.* Prepared for the Lilly Endowment. Washington, D.C.: The Religious Philanthropy Program of the
Council on Foundations, 1988.

Stehle, V. "With Needs Growing, Catholic Dioceses Are Stepping
Up Fund-Raising Efforts." *Chronicle of Philanthropy,* Sept. 19,
1989.

Stone, P. "Christian Ecology: A Growing Force in the Environmental Movement." *Utne Reader*, Nov./Dec. 1989. Reprinted from *Mother Earth News*, Jan./Feb. 1989.

Wuthnow, R. *The Restructuring of American Religion*. Princeton, N.J.: Princeton University Press, 1988.

Yankelovich, Skelly, & White, Inc. *The Charitable Behavior of Americans*. Findings analyzed by V. A. Hodgkinson and M. S. Weitzman. Washington, D.C.: INDEPENDENT SECTOR, 1986.

Index